TRANSFORMATIVE ACTIVISM

A VALUES REVOLUTION IN EVERYDAY LIFE IN A TIME OF SOCIETAL COLLAPSE

TIM STEVENSON

APOCRYPHILE
PRESS

THE APOCRYPHILE PRESS
PO Box 255, Hannacroix, NY 12087

Please join our mailing list at
www.apocryphilepress.com/free
We'll keep you up to date on all our new releases,
and we'll also invite you to download a FREE BOOK.
Visit us today!

CONTENTS

Dedicated to activists everywhere
Who value life, all life, unconditionally.
Whoever you may be.
And however you may be.

And for Sherry
with Love and Gratitude.

*"The ultimate hidden truth of the world
is that it is something we make
and could just as easily
make differently."*
—David Graeber

INTRODUCTION
THE SIGNIFICANCE OF THE EVERYDAY

Everyday life is the present moment, arising and passing from one moment to the next. It is the breath of life we are currently inhaling and exhaling: the milk we're splashing on the morning's corn flakes; the kiss we exchange with our partner at the end of the day; the pleasure we're enjoying watching our child take their first steps; the sharing of last night's ball game during the break at work. This is where our lives actually exist, where reality is created and re-created. Beyond our illusions of what we think life is all about—largely informed by our mental constructs of that which we imagine life was like in the "past" and what it will be in the "future"—it is the present moment alone where life is actually happening, where life is real. How we live in this moment—the choices we make, the actions we take—is what our lives are all about.

We have reached the moment in our millennia-long struggle for peace, freedom, social justice, and equality when we can no longer postpone a revolution of everyday life. To do so is fatal to our liberating purpose. By not living the revolution in the present moment, we miss the opportunity to live the way of life we have long sought to realize, and that we require more than ever at this time of pending social collapse and possible human extinction.

In order for revolution to be truly liberating, therefore, it must be grounded in each passing moment of everyday life. Only when it is integral to the ebb and flow of daily existence is revolution the transformative event that activists for meaningful change have sought all along. Only then do our ideals come alive.

It goes without saying that it is not simply the present moment alone, in the abstract, which is critical to revolution. The substance of life actually lived within the moment—our *behavioral content*—is what ultimately lends revolution significance. The living moment does not exist in a vacuum. It consists of countless factors that together, as part of an interconnected, codependent universe, influence the reality of what is. Our choices, our acts are part of that mix. They are our contribution to what is.

In the end, what we do with all of this, and how we act, makes the difference in determining whether we are free human beings or not. This is most apparent in our relationships with other living beings, particularly with our fellow humans.

As with human life in general, revolution is a social affair, reflecting our essential proclivity for interaction with one another. Its purpose is to liberate us from interpersonal arrangements that are controlling and exploitive, abusive and harmful. That is why everyday life is so crucial to the world we live in: it is where the quality of human relationships commonly manifests, and therefore the question of revolution arises.

Specifically, the presence of moral spiritual qualities displayed through behaviors that prize life, honoring and respecting the sacred momentary spark of *aliveness* that each and every living being possesses, is what allows human liberation to exist, just as the absence of such is the cause of oppressive conditions and renders revolution necessary.

This is not to deny the significant power that social constructs exercise on our behaviors and the lives we live. But regardless of how mundane and insignificant our everyday lives may appear to be by comparison, the basis of revolution rests upon our love of life and the commensurate values we display toward all living beings. Through everyday acts of kindness and compassion, acceptance and forgiveness, generosity and altruism, selflessness and gratitude, modesty and humility, moral courage and personal integrity, we exhibit the necessary interpersonal infrastructure that allows for a moment of human liberation. These interactions with others—partner and family, friend and enemy, neighbor and stranger alike—are cumulatively central to realizing *transformative possibilities*.

To not appreciate the importance of the everyday is to doom our vision of revolutionary change to the dust bin of irrelevancy, and to continue to suffer the fragmented existence of Civilized people by living lives that we don't want while wanting lives that we don't live.

As the book's dedication suggests, we honor anyone who values life, and who in a whole variety of behaviors demonstrates this love. Some may do so in ways that are commonly understood as "activism." Others are less apparent, but take "invisible" approaches that stand up for and treasure life and are therefore no less valid.

To begin with, it is important that you know that I am a white male, with all the baggage and responsibility to life for being born to this specific race and gender that such social determinants carry. Notwithstanding whatever progress I've made over a lifetime of being a more liberated being, I remain a mixed bag, an imperfect human being whose flaws are both apologetically and unavoidably part of what I have to offer you at this moment in what follows.

Over the course of my 60+ years as a social justice, climate, and peace activist and community organizer, I have increasingly been educated as to what it means to be an agent of change by learning to accept life as it is. In one sense, *Transformative Activism* can be viewed as a report on my progress thus far.

Significant to this learning process has been my involvement as a draft resister and anti-war organizer during the Vietnam conflict; a welfare rights organizer with largely single African-American mothers caring for young children; a member of a progressive, community-based newspaper collective, as well as a predominantly white, male/female activist commune. I opposed the support that the US government provided Central American dictators who were violently suppressing liberation struggles in their countries, including participation in the campaign to close the School of the Americas that trained the armed forces and police of these countries in counterinsurgency warfare and torture techniques. I have been an organizer of a successful anti-box store initiative (Home Depot left town, and the Select Board passed a box store ordinance); a facilitator of the Iraq Committee of our region's Peace and Justice Committee to protest going to war with Iraq; an activist in the effort to shut down Vermont Yankee, the nuclear power plant in our area; and for the past 17 years, a community organizer with Post Oil Solutions, a climate crisis group I helped found that is dedicated "to developing sustainable, resilient, and socially just communities leading to a self-sufficient post petroleum society."

Needless to say, the demands of this activism have involved a multitude of tasks necessary to building and sustaining this work, including countless meetings, marches, vigils, sit-ins, acts of civil disobedience, arrests, press releases, published articles, talks, and grant writing, as well as a book (*Resilience and Resistance: Building Sustainable Communities for a Post Oil Age,* Green Writers Press, 2015), and now this second one.

As individually important as these projects were for their own sake, they also served as the context for my evolution as an activist who sought basic change. For instance, securing winter coats that their children were entitled to from a welfare department that was denying them their rights was important to these mothers in and by itself. But as I increasingly realized, how they did so—how they empowered themselves to successfully prevail in their righteous quest—was equally important, for ultimately their participation and leadership spoke to the larger issue of their liberation.

In that vein, I want to conclude my introductory remarks by briefly discussing what at an earlier time was my subtitle for this book: *"An Exercise in Buddhist Anarchy,"* They represent the two major intellectual and spiritual influences of both my book and practice, especially around the fundamental issues of power and liberating change. These are non-violent anarchism and socially-engaged Buddhism. But because I'm not trying to sell or proselytize a particular ideology, this is the only time that I will refer to something I call "Buddhist anarchy."

The second of these is celebrated for its principles of non-authoritarian, non-hierarchical social organization, both by its proponents as well as those extoling freedom of choice, participatory democracy, nonviolence, voluntary association, and mutual aid. Because of my instinctive resistance and frequent acting out against a variety of authority figures in my life (mostly the male figures, and especially my father, high school principal, and the police in general) I was what you might call an anarchist in the rough. It wasn't until I had done some considerable growing up and began to accept my humanity that I became hip to the aforementioned values, which are basic to a more mature anarchist practice. It was then that anarchism began to inform my activism and made me increasingly appreciative of a democracy that is actually lived and practiced.

For even when my anti-authority sentiments were expressed in ways that were at times inchoate and inconsistent with anarchism's life-honoring values, I instinctively recognized the truth of Edward Abbey's statement that "anarchy is democracy taken seriously." Its values in practice are an exercise in walking the talk, the meat on the bones of a document such as the Declaration of Independence which, despite limiting its rights and freedoms to rich white males only, is a superb statement when it is applied to everyone.

The virtue of anarchism is perhaps best suggested by a statement of Rudolph Rocker's as to why he is an anarchist: "not because I believe anarchism is the final goal, but because there is no such thing as a final goal." Revolution as an open-ended, life-long process, one which is accessible to new experiences, awakened knowledge, and expanding consciousness, has long been the *implicit* meaning of anarchism, lending it its transformative flavor. As Rocker suggests, anarchism is not an end in itself, but rather a life-long process.

Though seemingly quite different, the second major influence on the growth of my activist practice began when I serendipitously attended a 10-day retreat at the Barre Insight Meditation Center in Barre, Massachusetts some 40 years ago. It was here I first discovered the values wisdom of Buddhism, the liberating potential of meditation, and the synchronicity of this spiritual approach with anarchism. Over time, with the practice of daily meditation, occasional retreats, and much reading, I came to understand and appreciate what became the core of my practice: accepting life for what it is, rather than being at war with what it isn't and should be.

The congruency of anarchism with Buddhism is particularly evident for me in the latter's emphasis upon the impermanence of life, hence, the importance of the living moment. The idea that existence is one of incessant change strikes me as anarchistic, compatible with anarchism's emphasis upon the absence of an established or governing authority, and a tolerance of instability and disorder, as a consequence.

Coming to understand existence as transient and insubstantial, here one moment, gone the next, helped me to accept a radically new perspective on what it meant to be an agent of change. The "future" was always down the road, a pipedream of what *should* be, and the "past" was dead and gone, unnecessary baggage that was best just let go of. Everyday life was really all that counted. The lesson I learned was that it matters greatly what I and every other human being is doing with our lives right now.

Finally, Buddhism (re)introduced and reaffirmed the importance of *heart (i.e., spiritual) values,* implicit to an anarchism whose commitment to such principles as individual freedom, participatory democracy, and mutual aid can only work in a world of compassion, forgiveness, kindness, and generosity.

Over time, I came to appreciate the importance of an activist practice that cultivated the lovingkindness, acceptance , and equanimity that are characteristic of the wholesome behaviors and moral well-being that allow one to be an agent of liberating change. Through this growth, an awareness of the inherent goodness of our species awakens.

Having together been instrumental in helping me to evolve an activist practice that plumbs the heart of revolution, anarchy and Buddhism provide the grounding of *Transformative Activism.*

Founded upon the understanding that it is one thing to finally comprehend that revolution is only transformative when rooted in a practice of moral values, and quite another to then translate this awareness into a consistent everyday practice, *Transformative*

Activism dedicates itself to largely addressing the latter concern. Apart from the blessed few for whom acting on our innate goodness seems to come naturally, most of us must work at achieving such a state. This is a serious challenge, one that we must go about with commitment and discipline if we are to supplant the political conditioning of power relationships and Self-serving behavior with an increasingly spontaneous practice of selfless moral constancy.

This is the issue that I will address throughout this book: the question of how we can forge an everyday practice of spiritual values. We begin with "The Theory of Stuck Ego and the Origin of the Political Universe," which provides the theoretical context from which a transformative practice evolves. Next, we discuss the basic qualities of this practice in Part II, "The Way of Liberation, "and then proceed to "The Practice of the Practice," which is about the daily discipline necessary to cultivating and maturing the skills of a revolutionary activist. Finally, in Part IV, "Being Free in the World as it is," we provide an extensive discussion of how this translates in the everyday social world. I conclude with an epilogue that argues that, despite our dire circumstances, these same conditions also provide an unprecedented opportunity to realize a transformed world of human liberation.

Throughout this book, I put forth that we cannot be agents of liberation without a practice of the values that exhibit and sustain commensurate behavior. The absence of this condition in Civilized human society allows oppression in all of its forms to exist and, therefore, necessitates a revolution of everyday life, one that goes to the very heart of our situation. Only then will peace, freedom, and social justice transcend the theoretical and abstract to become actionable in our lives.

The incomparable anarchist/feminist/Buddhist Rebecca Solnit addresses this situation in her splendid book, *A Paradise Built in Hell.* Observing that disasters often bring forth the potential good that inherently resides in each of us, she goes on to ask the question that has long beleaguered humankind: how do we maintain this degree of moral presence—this essential goodness —in the absence of life-threatening catastrophes? How do we *"stay awake in softer times because we are ordinarily sleepers, unaware of each other and of our true circumstances and selves? Disaster shocks us out of slumber, but only* skillful effort *keeps us awake"* [my emphasis].

"Only skillful effort keeps us awake": this is the challenge that *Transformative Activism* addresses, and that we as activists—and people in general—must meet if we are to make real the transformation of human existence that our inherent moral nature intends us to live. Nothing short of a practice of committed effort will do if we are to nurture and evolve a liberated existence.

It is my hope that *Transformative Activism* will serve as a useful contribution for you as you walk your own path in the process of developing a wholesome, righteous practice, helping to inspire the *how* of revolution—a values practice—that allows for the *what*—peace, freedom, and social justice—to emerge in your lives.

PART ONE
THE THEORY OF STUCK EGO AND THE ORIGIN OF THE POLITICAL UNIVERSE

CHAPTER ONE

THE PERSONAL IS THE POLITICAL

T HE BIRTH OF THE CIVILIZED HUMAN BEING
In order to fully appreciate the challenge involved in forging a consistent practice of values, we must start by framing the task involved within a theoretical context of Civilized human development. In this way, we can better understand what most of us are up against. Our challenge: to successfully live as a liberated human being with the phenomenon of *ego*—and especially its obstructing expression, *stuck ego*—as personified in everyday life as "I," and its projection on the social world as political power.

We enter life as part of an interdependent universe. Our existence is completely reliant upon the air we breathe, the water we drink, and the food we eat, not to mention the countless living souls, humans and otherwise, whose lives provide us with life. Not only is this interconnection the nature of the universe, we couldn't exist for a moment apart from the sustenance and support we realize from being a part of this web of life.

And yet, we are unaware of this elementary fact of our existence at this moment in our lives. In other words, we lack a consciousness of *interbeing*, of our oneness with the rest of life, to use the felicitous expression of the Vietnamese Buddhist monk, peace activist, and prolific author, Thich Nhat Hanh. To the contrary, we are seemingly on our own at birth. As long as this continues to be our sense of our existence, this absence of awareness imparts the essential condition of the human infant as it enters life: a commanding sense of powerlessness.

Perhaps no one has portrayed so vividly this experience of human birth as Shunryu Suzuki in his *Zen Mind, Beginner's Mind*. Poetically rendered, Suzuki compares the birth of a human baby to individual drops of water in a waterfall:

Before we were born, we had no feeling; we were one with the universe... After we are separated by birth from this oneness, as the water falling from the waterfall is separated by the wind and rocks, then we have feeling. You attach to the feeling... When you do not realize that you are one with the river, or one with the universe, you have fear. Whether it is separated into drops or not, water is water. Our life and death is the same thing. When we realize this fact we have no fear of death anymore, and we have no actual difficulty in our life.

When the water returns to its original oneness with the river, it no longer has any individual feeling to it; it resumes its own nature, and finds composure. How very glad the water must be to come back to the original river! If this is so, what feeling will we have when we die? I think that we are like the water in the dipper. We will have composure then, perfect composure. It may be too perfect for us, just now, because we are so much attached to our own feeling, to our individual existence. For us, just now, we have some fear of death."

This singular sense of separation from the rest of life, characteristic of our species, results in abject terror which arises from the state of powerlessness that such a feeling produces. This is —understandably—intolerable for us. We cannot live as viable living beings unless we are able to successfully stop this fear by coming to terms with our powerless condition.

The feeling of powerlessness would not be a problem if our state of consciousness wasn't developmentally unprepared to recognize the fact of our interconnection. This is possible if we experience a spiritually healthy maturation that is grounded in a clear view of reality.

Some human beings resolve this dilemma immediately, especially if they are fortunate enough to be born to a social environment populated with those adult beings who are profoundly aware of our essential connection to the rest of nature and go about living their lives with that wisdom. This serves as a model of interbeing existence, supporting, encouraging, and teaching the new members (e.g., expressing gratitude for the food and water that Earth, or Mother, provides all of us). From the beginning, this awakens in the nascent human what we instinctively know but have "forgotten" in the process of being born. We (re)learn our inherent interconnection with life from the people we are born to, parents and community alike, so that our pre-birth condition of wholeness is restored. Our separation from the universe, and its attendant fear, is momentary. Early in life, we bond with nature and treat all of its members with reverence and respect. As we embrace our instinctive awareness of our connected/dependent status, we are able to live successfully (and powerfully) with our powerlessness.

Those of us born to Civilization, however, where the purpose of existence is not to become one with the rest of nature, but rather to control Mother instead, are trained and habituated to serve a contrary function. Because we do not arrive at a social environment that prizes our inherent interconnection to other beings (though the exigencies of our survival make it unavoidable nonetheless), we are conditioned to value a kind of radical individualism in which we view ourselves as essentially separate and apart from, even superior to, the rest of nature. The latter is valued, not for its own sake, but as a means to enhance Civilized-directed ends. Nature becomes something to control, exploit and commodify. Rather than join with life as a kindred soul, we cut ourselves off from life.

The only way Civilized beings can realize a oneness with life is through a developmental process in which we have experiences that encourage and support the expression of our heart values. This is essentially what it means to *grow* up, at least in a spiritual and moral sense, and become a complete adult, responsible for our behavior in the world. We have to *mature* into a consciousness of interbeing.

This is highly problematic for many, if not most of us, because our agenda of becoming Civilized beings does not encourage a sense of interbeing or coming together with the rest of life. Rather, it requires us to exert power over our circumstances, to control the natural world, from which we are encouraged to separate, and to view it as *"other."* To accomplish this, we are socialized into radical individualism. What emerges is *ego*, the Civilized being's answer to our intolerable state of powerlessness.

THE EMERGENCE OF "I"

Ironically, what comes to the rescue at this moment of existential peril is the very same liability, the "individual feeling" that Suzuki writes about, when our experience at birth is that of an isolate, a living being detached from the universe. Being split off and separated from our oneness with life, we are highly vulnerable to becoming *"attached to our own feeling, to our individual existence."* This prevents us from realizing a life of "perfect composure." Short of being born to a social environment in which human beings are grounded in the natural world from the beginning of life, hence living an existence of interconnection and interbeing, we are faced with having to function in this mysterious, threatening place we have arrived in on our own, abjectly powerless. This represents an unbearable threat to our psychic existence.

As an unsolicited gift of the adapting organism, a false but critical sense of independent *Self* emerges from this original *feeling of individual existence*. Unreal and artificial, to be sure, in that it is not a natural part of our innate heart essence, ego is nevertheless a vital creation at this time in our lives. We desperately require something to help us cope with the debilitating fear and insecurity we suffer when engulfed at birth by the sense of pending annihilation because of the abject powerlessness we cannot tolerate.

We escape this destiny when we attach ourselves to Suzuki's "individual existence"; this pre-ego state evolves into the first rudimentary expressions of what we come to identify as "I," serving as ego's personal representation of us in the world. Ego is the original act in the creation of a Self, an artificial entity that while separate from the rest of life, nevertheless provides us with a power surrogate we desperately need; it is the genesis of the radical individuality that comes to characterize Civilized people .

In lieu of a social environment in harmony with the rest of nature, ego is Civilization's response to the powerlessness we suffer when we are not yet able to accept our individual powerlessness and collective interconnectedness. Ego overcompensates for this state through its creation of the god-like "I." The original state of Suzuki's "feeling" now becomes exaggerated and inflates into a Self. We have transmuted this "feeling" into a sense of an independent "I."

In this way, ego becomes a necessary life jacket to keep us afloat in a sea of insufferable powerlessness until a time when we can successfully live with this inescapable condition. At its best, ego serves as the developmental bridge between the helpless being we are at the beginning of life to the responsible, liberated adult we are intended to grow into.

Through ego, we create an illusion of power—of being able to control our life's circumstances. This is the hallmark of a Civilized being. However unreal it may be, ego's artifice is nevertheless useful, even essential, during this early stage of our development when we are not yet able to accept ourselves for who we are.

Born out of existential necessity, ego seemingly resolves our dilemma by transforming our isolated being into a narcissistic "I": an exalted position at the center of a pre-Copernican universe that the rest of life revolves around. The flip side of being an unconnected isolate is a Self-centered ego that endeavors to control life by attempting to exert power over it. We turn our liability on its head and convert our perceived weakness into an exaggerated and illusory strength.

As we mature, ego evolves as well. Depending on our growth experiences, and the extent of our spiritual and moral development, "I" increasingly becomes us, the person we are. When the need for power and control exert significant influence in our lives, "I" dominates our maturing selves.

Central to the space it occupies in our growth is ego's facility for personalizing reality, reducing it to binary value judgments. We find the origin of this behavior in Civilization's dichotomization of life and death into positive and negative values, a phenomenon I will expand upon in the next section. Through this divisive function, "I" exercises significant influence in determining the quality of our relationships and interactions with other living beings.

In the real world, life is just passing through without any value other than what "I" attaches to it. With ego's intervention, what is otherwise neutral becomes charged with personal meaning. To personalize our experiences in life is the very nature of ego and the means by which it attempts to exert control over life. The interpretations, opinions, commentaries, and verdicts that we then impose on reality shape the moment into what "I" determines is desirable and what is not, and elicits corresponding behavior. Rather than simply accepting what is, living with it as the passing phenomenon that it is, ego enmeshes us in its value judgments instead, which then acquire a life of their own, beyond their moment.

For example, we encounter someone who doesn't smile during their interaction with us. Rather than simply seeing someone who is not smiling, we interpret them as sad, or angry, or depressed, and so forth. The judgment we make of them not only distorts our present encounter, but also serves to cloud and shape a future interaction even before it has begun. No longer seen for who they are, we judge them as that sad, angry, or depressed person we had earlier interpreted them as being. Such is the power of personalizing reality.

As these judgments increasingly fragment and dominate our lives, they acquire an exaggerated influence as they are expropriated by ego as our personal possessions. By attaching us to them, "I" provides these value judgments with a weight and importance that they don't otherwise have, especially as they increasingly become who we are through the habituated behaviors we develop and exhibit in the world.

The power and influence of personalizing our lives serve as the building blocks of a developing identity and "personal(ity)" that allows us to face the world with at least an appearance of control—*of being someone!*—about which we are incessantly anxious and insecure. In this way, we flavor the moments that follow with personal content that has nothing do with what is actually taking place.

This emerging personhood provides a sense of solidity to the insubstantial, ephemeral beings we are, informing us as to who we are, a personal identity which we project out onto the world that let others know who we are as well. Personal identity is essential to manifesting the power we believe we need to get through life in this world. The resulting character structure, acquired through the egocentric-inspired choices we make, over and over again, and especially in our relationship with others, grows into a way of life. Rather than simply being the people we really are, many of us hang on to this more rigid and circumscribed version of "us" instead.

Life as it is becomes distorted. Based on our emerging personality, "I" acts out the scripts that ego manufactures for us. We retain the artificial Self's interpretations of what is "real" and what is not. This developing personality perpetuates the illusion of a separate, distinct entity. It allows "I" to appear to be real.

This development of a Self involves acquiring a behavioral repertoire that, together with what we bring to this lifetime as our *karma* and genetic inheritance, is forged in the furnace of our everyday experiences to get what we need to exist as viable living beings. Throughout this process, we find that we must adapt to the arbitrary expectations, capricious desires, anxious needs, and natural vagaries of our species. In ego's efforts to defend and protect our powerless selves, we learn valuable lessons about what works for us and what doesn't. We come to understand what is expected of us on the basis of our ranking on society's hierarchical ladder, learning what we can and cannot get away with.

In the course of these experiential lessons, we develop a personality: the public face of "I" that we present to the world. With the development of "I," we discover ways through which we can exert influence on the world. In addition to the real, spontaneous, heart-felt being we are at times, this personality osmotically absorbs how we need to behave, especially as it conforms to the political role we're expected to play.

We become wedded to a growing sense of a Self-identity,

especially as the personality seems to get relatively predictable results within the confines of the dominant culture. When we act in certain ways, we believe we can usually count on receiving generally foreseeable responses in return. Even though this isn't always true, such is the power of habit that we will continue to repeat the behavior even in the face of its continuing failure to elicit the desired result, and not venture forward with something new and untried.

We become this construct—a distorted and partly suppressed variation of the real us. This coalesces around and creates yet another *real* us, the person we are at that moment; this mixture of the "real" and the "not-real-but-real" is us at any given moment.

When we are more or less "I," we remain attached to our make-believe Self. Thus, our conduct with others is significantly shaped by the illusions and fantasies that our political role dictates. Unreality is our primary narcotic in political society, the facility for not seeing life for what it is at any given moment in order to "see" it the way we need to as dictated by ego. This original addiction to unreality keeps us in our place and provides the illusion of control over our circumstances, gracing us with a sense of order and continuity, however false. In so doing, this illusion helps to assuage our insecurities about life, especially its inherent uncertainties and unknowns.

This property of predictability—of knowing with false certainty—goes to the heart of why so many of us become and remain stuck in ego, even when it means continuing to be one-down, increasingly dysfunctional, and unhappy with life. We like to know what to expect. A formulaic life is difficult to move on from, especially if we have known nothing else or if we have been "brought up" in a heart-absent existence.

By its very nature, freedom is a state outside of ego's realm of the "known." This frightens the Civilized human being with our need to be certain about what the next moment will bring.

Comfort with knowing the consequence of behaviors that we have executed countless times in the past creates a powerful brake to venturing away from the campfire of our everyday habits and routines. The illusion of normality and stability is most enticing, especially when we believe we have no power to affect our lives otherwise, and we are too insecure to let go of the power we think we have through the illusion of Self. The repetition and reproduction of "I"-centered behaviors, lifetime after lifetime, generation after generation, renders us that much more dependent upon ego to the extent that it is the most natural thing in the world.

With ego, we are full of our Selves. We don't listen or talk with our hearts. We are consumed with words that are largely Self-promoting, signifying nothing. This is why we get into all the trouble we do with each other, why our interactions are freighted with misunderstandings and defensive reactions. Our conversations are often little more than monologues. Rather than sharing exchanges between interconnected beings in which we are open and vulnerable, we talk past each other, playing our role. Filled as we are with the agendas of "I," we don't see the other for the fellow living being they essentially are. Instead, we see who and what conforms to ego's expectations. This is why our relationships are as problematic as they are, so often incapable of actually connecting with each other, heart to heart. When we typically present ego-directed "I" as *us*, performing behaviors that are intended to project the illusory Self while trying to stay in control of the situation, it's no wonder that our relationships are artificial, lacking transparency and intimacy.

All of this role playing and make believe comes at a significant cost to the person we actually are. When we live in this more constrained, self-inhibited fashion, we cannot afford to be anything but a qualified expression of our life force.

Most importantly, we suppress the unconditional expression of our heart values—the same ones, ironically, that we tell ourselves render us "Civilized," distinguishing us from the rest of nature. Most of us learn to curb these behaviors and exhibit them in politically correct and socially safe ways, where the veneer of values—rather than their spirit and substance—is what we display. Wholehearted expression must be curbed, for it would involve being real at the expense of ego and its illusion of power, not to mention the larger political world. Of course, this elementary act of denial by the Civilized being makes all the difference in the nature of the lives we live and the kind of society we help to create.

THE SIGNIFICANCE OF OUR IMMINENT DEATH

While ego is useful in helping us make our way through the political world, we also pay a substantial price in the process, as the foregoing suggests. Crucially, despite its assistance at the beginning of life to assist us in coping with the existential dread of non-existence, ego also acts as a significant, even fatal brake on our growth as a fully realized human being. While necessary —at least in the Civilized world that fails to nurture its young in interconnection with the rest of the natural world—ego obstructs the development we need in order to become spiritually mature enough to live without it.

To live without ego is to accept our inescapable powerlessness in a world where the power to control life is viewed as the supreme value. This is what Civilization is all about. The control of life (or at least the attempt to do so) is also the cause of the oppressive existence we suffer.

Hence, the task of the liberation activist is to engage in a practice grounded in a consciousness which accepts that peace, freedom, and social justice can only be realized when we cease employing power over life.

To do so, however, we must reconcile ourselves to that which originally necessitated ego as our power agent, caused us to embrace ourselves as "I," and convinced us that we are an independent Self, separate and apart from the rest of life. I am referring, of course, to the primal crisis of our kind, imminent death, and the fact that we are powerless to avoid this fate.

During our early moments of life, separated from life and unable to realize our interconnection, we fear non-existence, hence Suzuki's assertion: "When you do not realize that you are one with the river, or one with the universe, you have fear." In the moment of being divorced from and unconnected to life, "we have some fear of death."

This is the organism's natural response to feeling alone and powerless. At this stage of our development, we lack the wisdom to understand that, as Khalil Gibran phrased it, "life and death are one, even as the river and sea are one," or as Sarah Kerr observed, "Death isn't the opposite of life, it's the opposite of birth. Life holds them both." Those are statements from a consciousness that knows the truth of interconnection. Absent this state, however, we view death as the polar opposite of life, and fear it accordingly.

Only when we come to fully accept death as part of life, and hence are no longer trying to escape, deny, or repudiate it, are we able to fully live our lives in the present moment: to have agency, to be a real person of heart.

Unique to our kind, at least as far as we know, human beings are conscious of our always impending death. Because at least the Civilized version of us lacks the integrity of wholeness and a sense of oneness with all other sentient beings, we do not accept death as part of life; we do not see the "two" as one. Rather, we dichotomize existence into discrete entities, "life" and "death," lending inappropriate heft and significance to the latter, while marginalizing or ignoring altogether the first, especially in its moment-by-moment essence. This gives rise to our species-specific anxiety about our inevitable demise and the unfortunate diminution of life, an inability or unwillingness to accept life for what it is—and thus live our brief moments as fully realized beings. This primal terror controls so much of how we live our lives, no matter how subterranean it may be. We only experience "perfect composure," like Suzuki's drop of water, when we return to the universe of the "original river" which we have never left, except in our heads. This is what it means to come home to our original state of interbeing.

Unfortunately, most of us in the Civilized world do not experience unimpeded growth, in which we successfully accomplish the path of human development, an expanded spiritual consciousness that recognizes our natural interbeing, and move on to adulthood. Rather, we increasingly become enmeshed with ego and its illusion of control. We grasp and cling to ego through a way of life that we feel will guarantee us security and safety, predictability and certainty—through material possessions, wealth, and social position, and ultimately the political power with which to realize these chimeras of earthly immortality. Together, they manufacture the illusion that we are in control, ego's imaginary antidote to our fear of death. Civilization, with its promise of eternal progress, serves as the signature project of ego, providing the illusion that we do live forever.

―――――――――

Death is especially problematic for us when ego becomes our power surrogate because "I" ups the ante by making death personal. When separated from life into a distinct entity, we don't recognize death as a neutral phenomenon; it becomes charged with subjective value that ego attaches to it. Life is valued as "positive," a condition to be held on to, even at the expense of the very life we are presently living, whereas death is rejected as "negative," something to be avoided at all costs. So potent, so personal is this dichotomy, that for many of us the subject of life and death is not even something that we can talk about.

By its very presence, ego exacerbates our dread of death and our distorted efforts to hang on to life by interpreting death—not incorrectly—as its own personal demise. Death is the end of "I," as "I" only exists during our mortal incarnation, and ego equates us, the Civilized being, with existence. From its isolated, egocentric perspective, the death of "I" is synonymous with the cessation of life itself.

This interpretation on ego's part underscores the power of the death-denial mission of Civilization and why it is very difficult for so many of us to let go of and move beyond "I" as part of a normal maturational process. Ego is hanging on for dear life!

Because it represents the end of "I," death is not just another moment of a larger process. Having identified "I" as *us*, and who we are as a living being, we cling to what ego defines as "life" and our identify as "I," rather than simply living life as it presents itself. The prospect of our demise is understandably unbearable. Death is feared; life becomes a daily project of denying death's inevitability through our continual efforts to achieve control over life, laboring to fashion a well-ordered Civilized existence that wards off the unthinkable. This way of life has aptly been termed by many as a "culture of death."

THE RISE OF STUCK EGO

It is not that we lack the wherewithal to become adults; we possess the potential to complete our developmental task of becoming a responsible human being. We are capable of accepting life as it is and acting on that basis in a wholesome way. It's more that in some basic way, we refuse to *grow up*. Essentially, we are too afraid to give up being "I," to live our lives as that which we are born to be and potentially are whenever we choose to be: spiritually realized, values-oriented human beings.

Yes, this is a choice we make, though as is the case with many "choices," we may not be aware of it as such. This choice is rooted at the crossroads we arrive at in our evolution as human beings, and the challenge that many of us have yet to successfully resolve when we get there. Above all others, it is the issue that has defined our continuing unwillingness to be truly civilized humans who live a moral existence and conduct a spiritual practice in our everyday lives.

When our spiritual development proceeds as intended, we arrive at a point where we *know* that we don't require "I" to live our lives for us. That is, perhaps with the heartfelt, gut-expressive laughter of sudden recognition, we catch a glimpse of ourselves in the rearview mirror. We suddenly awaken to the realization that not only do we not need to be in control, but we finally see that we never have been. With this expanded consciousness, we are less attached to "I" and more heart-wholesome in our behavior choices. We now live fearlessly in this selfless state of *ego independence* (or human liberation) without having to deny or defend ourselves against either life or death, but can embrace both as part of the journey of discovery we're on.

But when we cannot live without the illusion of domination and control, we become stuck. We approach the point in our development where being an adult is the next logical step—at least as the concept "adult" is commonly understood in terms of age, gender, physical and sexual development, and certain rites of passage as prescribed by the larger society. Developmentally, we have arrived at the officially sanctioned stations of Civilized adulthood: work, marriage, children, the right to drink, drive and vote, etc.

Yet, we choose, however unconsciously, not to take that final step of assuming full responsibility for ourselves as an inherently good person. We have accomplished all the socially acceptable benchmarks, but we don't make the most important decision: that of being a spiritually realized grown up. We balk at living without our ersatz power, without ego, as a free human being; we sacrifice growth and a life of heart—a leap into the void of the unknown as life really is—for a lifetime of Self-control.

Why is this? Beyond the not insignificant fact that we are habituated to ego, reluctant to give up the familiarity and routine it provides, the illusions of security and certainty it seems to offer, how does ego retain its hold on us, circumventing a developmental process that should conclude with our liberation? Why do we remain dependent on ego?

I will suggest a number of reasons for this in the remainder of this chapter. But the nature of ego itself is significant to answering this question—it is the very same power surrogate whose function is to provide us with the personal command we feel we require to live in this world. The problem is that rather than serve this function, ego actually disempowers us. Ironically, the very effort of trying to force life to bend to our will only makes matters worse. Rather than relieving, even mitigating, the chronic anxiety and fear that informs daily life for so many of us, the effort to impose control over our circumstances further contributes to our pervasive unease.

How could it be otherwise in a world with countless other egos trying to exact the same domination and control, playing the same power game as we are? The Self-centered approach of trying to be one-up in a world of "I" cannot help but result in the kind of conflict, hostility and insecurity that is such a standard feature of life in our political world. When social existence is characteristically adversarial, it invariably revolves around a defensive, push-back behavioral repertoire that ignores the moral and ethical values necessary for the peaceful existence we desire. Rather than leading to the "good life," ego stimulates hatred, greed, and violence. We return again to delusions, despite that they always and inevitably disappoint as they crash on the rocks of reality, as if what isn't real will finally work for us.

In so doing, ego eviscerates the very power we could potentially realize if we were able to simply accept our inescapable situation in life—both our powerlessness and interconnection—and live with the compassion and kindness, cooperation and mutual aid that a consciousness of this kind naturally inspires.

Imposing ourselves upon life, rather than allowing it to just come to us, only further amplifies our ego-tendency to see ourselves as separate from and above the rest of life. While this approach of radical individuality is hyped by our society as being a supreme virtue and viewed as the pinnacle of power in the political world, such a path only militates against the kind of empowering behaviors that arise from an acceptance of our interconnectedness and interdependency.

Ego does not bring out the best in us, a condition that is required in order to be truly empowered and to create a world of peace, freedom, and social justice. Though often muted and performed with a smile, the resulting social climate is nevertheless unkind and ungenerous; even in its milder expressions it is flavored with an undercurrent of mean-spiritedness and indecency.

———

However significant ego itself is, and our dependency upon it basic to our condition of *stuckness*, it alone is not responsible for our condition. Our social environment, which has evolved over time largely because of the presence of ego, also plays an important role in terms of the stuck people we become by reinforcing in a variety of ways the apparent reality of "I."

Dependency is a feature of our everyday existence. It is not that this state exists only at those times in our lives (both the beginning and the end) when we are particularly reliant upon others to take care of us in very basic ways. Dependency is present throughout our social lives, in our marriages and families, schools and workplaces, highways and public places where we are dependent on others to be reasonably responsive to our presence in order for our contacts and interactions to be, well, reasonable. We require others to be sensitive to our presence in order to encounter each other in a sane fashion on the highways of life. At least a modicum of caring and respect is needed as a condition of our emotional and physical wellbeing. In short, we are dependent upon others as a consequence of living in the interdependent world we do.

The problem is that this quality of mutuality is not a regular feature of life in a political world. By its very nature, the latter doesn't prioritize the kind of behavior required of people to live peacefully with each other in an interdependent society. Our society is characterized by transactional relationships, where people use one another for their own gain and are shaped and defined by the use of this power, as opposed to relationships where good will and respect are expressed for their own sake, without calculation or ulterior motive. Consequently, we live an oxymoron where, in spite of our seemingly sincere rhetoric, we essentially live a contradiction in terms of our actual everyday behaviors.

That is why we consistently return and become further wedded to ego and the illusion of power that we find in "I," our only available ally. Short of a sufficient growth of consciousness, that is our only choice. Ego is a compromise of necessity, a state that we may not be comfortable or happy with, especially with behaviors it elicits and are at the expense of heart, but one that we may feel we have no choice in making.

Though we are largely unaware of our inherent interdependent position with the rest of life, we nevertheless depend on our environment for our very lives—as demonstrated most vividly during our first years of life, when we are so raw and vulnerable that we require the care of others in essential ways to simply stay alive physically and emotionally. We need adult humans to feed us and wipe our bottoms, to talk to and value us, to touch and hold us as if we matter. We need them to contact our hearts. In an ideal world, this would be the culture we would grow up in.

To some extent, we do receive this nurturance from our social environment—some of us more than others, and many of us not nearly enough, for we don't live in that perfect world. Instead, we live in the political world where our dependency revolves around ego-bound adults who, however unconscious and unintentional, facilitate a maturation process that often doesn't promote our wellbeing and is at our expense. Rather than encouraging our empowerment and spiritual growth, the absence of being loved for our own sake and respected as an individual instance of life fosters a growing dependence on ego instead, and furthers its nascent attempts to exert control over its environment.

All too often, we are under the domination of people who lack the necessary maturity to provide the kind of care and guidance required for spiritual growth. Being members themselves of a species who have accumulated centuries of the trauma that comes with living in a political world, our caregivers can very likely be among the walking wounded; often overwhelmed with their own lives, and hence unintentionally careless, insensitive, and unaware, or perhaps abusive and exploitive in an effort to Selfishly attend to their own egocentric needs. But what could we reasonably expect in a society that doesn't encourage its members to become real grownups, capable of taking responsibility for themselves, and thus possessing the necessary maturity to nurture children to do the same?

Another primal example is evident in Civilization's authoritarian way of child-rearing, where children are cared for through what is considered a *naturally* one-down relationship to adults. This arrangement exists in most families and later in the school, both of which serve as the primary instruments of our acculturation and assimilation into the political world as well as the roles we're expected to assume in the hierarchical scheme of things. Under this regime, children take orders from and obey the commands of adults, however capricious and arbitrary, simply because the latter are adults, and *ipso facto*, superior people. Failure to obey results in punishment of one kind or another, which is assumed by adults to be their divine right, no matter how cruel. As adults, we Self-authorize ourselves to teach the offending child what it means to disobey through acts that are intended to be physically painful, or emotionally humiliating, or both. As is invariably the case with violence sanctioned due to our assumption of superior authority, the right to punish frequently degenerates into general abuse—emotional, physical and sexual alike—where the evil of the relationship becomes painfully transparent.

The adult community is aware of the more extreme acts and consequences of our punishing behavior with children and has created laws and agencies to protect them from such. What we have yet failed to appreciate, however, is the power dynamic itself and its contribution to shaping us as people that readily conform to the authoritarian demands of political society and, hence, necessitate the need for a transformative revolution of everyday life.

The compromises involved in submitting to a power relationship are especially problematic when it is a primal behavior learned during our most formative and vulnerable moments of life. This is a time when we are helpless and our well-being is dependent on the "big" people in our lives. For while genetics and past lives are significant to the people we become, our early history is no less important in bending, folding, spindling, and mutilating us to live a lifetime of submission to political power. It becomes reflexive, a routine that we unconsciously follow beyond family, one that is reinforced by the schools, workplaces, marriages, and other social arrangements of the political world that we become ensnared in. We are much less the heart-informed people we are born to be when the growth process is dominated by one-up/one-down relationships.

We have a chance to avoid this fate, however, if we're fortunate to grow up with adults in our lives who teach us what we need to know to be a free human being, a values-based citizen. With such circumstances we have a reasonable chance to be a positive presence in our everyday lives, able to help nurture a sane world for ourselves and others to live in. As a child, we can be accepted and valued for the instance of life that we are, encouraged to be the imaginative and creative beings we potentially can be, appreciated for the intuitive and passionate expressions of our hearts, and supported in our efforts to live an ethical existence. This context is important in our developmental process to arrive at a post-ego stage of growth. With such nurturing caregivers, wise mentors, and invaluable guides along the way, we are helped with the essential business of growing up and remaining true to our moral compass. We successfully traverse this developmental stage of human growth and become an adult who is no longer dependent upon ego to get by.

It should be noted that the moment when our heart begins to emerge as an active player in our lives is not necessarily age-dependent. People who in other respects are considered to be "children" can nevertheless be mature even at a very early age, precociously (by the standards of adults) exhibiting a responsibility for themselves and their actions "beyond their years." These children behave as true adults, perhaps because the conditions they were dependent on for their upbringing failed them, forcing them to learn how to take care of themselves in ways that accelerated their developmental process. Or, at the other end of the spectrum, they were exceptionally supported and encouraged to be the real person they are. Conscience plays an increasingly active role in the behavior of these children, as evidenced by their expressions of moral integrity.

Beyond the people we eventually become, and the challenge of *growing up* in order to reach our moral and spiritual potential, there is also the matter that we are the next generation of adults who impart to our children the sins and virtues of our own care-givers. We are cared for as children by those adults who are much like ourselves: powerless beings struggling to make their way through this world as best they can, not yet having come to terms with (and made peace with) the person of heart they are. In many respects, we are often in the hands of adults who—while physically older—are really children caring for children. As so often is the case in much of the Civilized world, this arrangement of adults and children is little more than the blind leading the blind. Thus, the eternal cycle continues unbroken.

As agents of transformative change, we must remind ourselves about the powerful influence that the political environment has on all of us. We cannot escape it; with the exception of the truly blessed, the best that we can do is learn to live with our situation as a free human being, behaving toward one another and evolving in ways that reflect our everyday values of human decency. We are not "bad" people; growing up is a challenging proposition, with no guarantees that we will find the nurturance, acceptance, and love that are essential to becoming a fully realized adult who is responsible for ourselves and, therefore, with other human beings.

As we know, citizens of moral integrity are not the kind of people a society dedicated to hierarchical social arrangements and authoritarian relationships are interested in encouraging. Quite the contrary: people who are responsible to themselves, therefore responsive to their heart values, are a serious threat to such arrangements.

———

Our developmental path toward full personhood and liberation is further complicated by the fact that despite the appearance of structure and order that we try to impose on our world, life is unpredictable and not necessarily responsive to our needs. This is a perfectly natural condition in the real world where incessant change reigns supreme despite our efforts to otherwise contain the chaos.

There is, of course, no reason to expect life to be receptive to our needs and responsive in the manner we would like. Significant to growth and maturity is the ability to accept that the universe is essentially indifferent to us, and most particularly "I" and its egocentric demands. This is a fact of life which "I," by its very nature, is not programmed to accept. Existence is beyond our power to control; it is inherently neutral and doesn't have a personal stake in the outcome of any particular scenario. The good news is that, as an impartial force, existence is not necessarily working against us, either, despite how we may feel at times: in the real world, there is no one to curse or blame for our lives!

———

But as I stated earlier, compromise is made at a huge cost. As with any addiction we continue to be enmeshed in over time, stuck ego becomes more pronounced the longer we ignore our inherent values. "I" does not concern itself with moral or ethical anxieties; the more our values are ignored or neglected, the easier it becomes for our innate goodness to become eclipsed and corrupted from disuse. Ego focuses exclusively on exercising sufficient power to get what it needs. This may even include a simulacrum display of heart values when they are seen as useful to realizing whatever ego's true objective is. A cynical *modus operandi* is very basic to ego, functioning as it does as an unprincipled agent in an unprincipled world of other egos where anything that serves "I's" purpose is employed. Given the context of the political power that we operate in, "I" cannot afford to consult our moral compass.

From the seemingly innocuous bull sessions and "little white lies" we routinely engage in as a matter of daily discourse—the manipulation, bribery, deceit and dishonesty we can employ—to the more serious threats and intimidation we resort to when the smile techniques don't work; to the outright theft and violence we may employ out of desperation, "I" is capable of using a variety of unwholesome behaviors that mute and deaden the shame the heart naturally experiences with each occurrence of ego's unprincipled effort to get what it wants.

By submitting to ego's quest for control, we plunge a knife into our own hearts. This is what it means to marginalize or ignore altogether the importance of acting on our values. We compromise our true self, the person of heart, when we act out of the False Self that we allow ourselves to be. Our integrity as a human being suffers in that moment. We become less than the *humane* person we are.

But compromise doesn't end here; to the contrary, it is only the beginning.

We also betray our heart's values when we give in to the power of another being and become dependent on them to meet our needs, and then when we submit to being one-down to them in return for meeting those needs. We may, understandably, conclude that this surrender is absolutely necessary in light of the circumstances we face and the choices we believe we have and don't have. This is certainly true when we are children and the power equation is so weighted against us. In most instances, submission to the domination and control of another is not even viewed as a conscious choice; it is just something we *naturally* do to get by.

Despite the fact that we seemingly have no choice, we commit an act of violence against ourselves whenever we compromise with our heart. Submitting to ego or to another's attempts to control us is always a blow to our moral integrity. Along the continuum of our moral development this is no small matter, contributing as it does to conditioning us to be stuck in ego.

This is one of life's cruelest ironies. We violate our hearts at those times in our lives when we refuse to accept our powerlessness and live with this inherent condition as a free human being. But we are harmed by the *quid pro quo* of submission and obedience—of being a False Self—demanded of us in return for meeting our needs. This is so terribly unfair, but it is also the way life is.

Repeated instances of this one-up and one-down dyad speak volumes to the phenomenon of stuck ego. This is why so many of us never realize our inherent potential of becoming grown-up human beings.

But being real as a person of heart is dangerous in the political world; it risks rejection, ostracism, punishment, even death. Most of all, it invariably courts the very condition we most want to avoid: the displeasure of those we feel dependent upon for taking care of us in ways we deem essential to the maintenance of our lives. When viewed from this perspective, selling out is nothing less than a necessary choice we make when we believe that there is no other choice. Going along with the demands of your boss, even when you know it's wrong, or accepting the unreasonable edicts of your father in order to avoid punishment, are common examples of this behavior in the everyday world. This submission is what most of us have felt compelled to make at one time or another to get what we felt we needed at the moment. The power of an adult, a man, a Caucasian, a parent, an employer, a teacher, a cop, an authority, a bully, or just someone who is bigger and stronger, is persuasive in a society that values the exercise of power-over.

Additionally significant here, though seldom understood as such, is that this dependency is also offensive not only to our heart, but also to our sense of "I." It is an insult to our Self-esteem, for ego loses here as well. Though ultimately responsible for the world of political relationships that we live in, "I" is clearly not in charge in instances when we are one-down to another dominant Self. It is as if the snake of our creation has now turned on and bitten itself. Dependency on anything is anathema to "I," given the ego's sense of radical individualism and its need to be in charge. Ego will naturally revolt from this arrangement and may engage in the hit-and-run guerrilla warfare common in families with children and women in efforts to reassert their Selves in the face of male authority. It may also adopt a similar strategy of passive-aggressive resistance behaviors as its way to maintain a semblance of Self-respect by way of trying to recoup its losses. However, we should not mistake this for anything other than the defensive posture of one who is, in essence, one-down.

Attachment to ego is further intensified through its attempts to defend and protect itself, one of its key functions. This characteristic is seemingly contrary to its appearance in the aggressive pose it typically assumes. Living in the political world of incessant strife and conflict, unprincipled and unwholesome conduct, we must constantly be on our guard. It is within this context that the defensive nature of "I" makes complete sense. Security and protection are primary concerns of ego.

This is due not only to ego's role of protecting us from the powerless reality we're not ready to accept about ourselves, but is further heightened by the fact that ego is defensive for its own sake. Because of its fictitious nature, "I" must constantly be on guard to protect itself from being exposed and called out as the fraud it is. Any suggestions—imagined or otherwise—that "I" is not the real thing (or worse yet, is unnecessary) cannot be tolerated. That kind of insight is the death of "I." Ego's Self-interest to protect itself from non-existence further solidifies our state of stuckness. While defending us, "I" is also busy guarding its Self to avoid being unmasked in the same hostile world.

The phenomenon of stuck ego is the product of several factors, most of which relate to our own development as a human being. But as suggested in the preceding paragraph, there are also dynamics at work relating to the needs of ego alone. Quite simply, it is a requirement of ego to continue to be needed. This is found in the insatiable hunger for Self-esteem that it exhibits. A bottomless, narcissistic need that necessitates constant reaffirmation, Self-esteem is so vital to the health and well-being of ego that, as evidenced by the amount of attention it is given in child development, it has come to be viewed by political society as an invaluable attribute for a successful Civilized human.

To no small extent, this is the basis of ego's continuing presence in our lives. Ego must maintain a sense of its importance to continue to exist and will do anything it can to convince us of its indispensability. Ego calls upon its powerful, albeit illusory allies—predictability, safety, and security—to aid in this purpose. These enticements are not easy for us to walk away from when we are unprepared to live with life as it is.

This is less of an issue early in our lives, when ego is important to both our survival and evolution. However, our dependency becomes increasingly problematic as the moment of adulthood approaches, and our physical and psychosexual maturation reaches the point where we are known as adults. A tension comes to exist between the call of our natural evolution and our pronounced habit of ego, which complicates the transition to responsible adulthood. This is especially true for people living in non-supportive social environments, where being a responsible human being, however it may be lip-serviced, is not part of our everyday routine and relationships. Most of us have not known any other way of life. Along with remaining attached to its service as our power surrogate, this historical factor allows for ego to endure beyond its developmental stage and remain significant throughout our lives as *stuck ego*.

The moral development of the human being is a rich process, subject to the variability of many factors peculiar to any one individual, and doesn't follow in a neat linear direction or schematic fashion. It can evolve out of pain and suffering that we learn to live with in ways that allow it to be a stimulus for spiritual growth. It can also arise as the consequence of blessed circumstances, especially in having the right person or people available to us at a crucial juncture of our lives. For some, it may be a sudden awakening: something that sparked in us seemingly out of nowhere, while for others it's a progression involving years that is contingent upon internal and external influences, including intentional effort.

But because all too many Civilized beings are unwilling to live without "I" we become stuck in ego.

This is all too apparent in the political culture we have created over the years. Rather than realizing our potential for a liberated existence, we have lived a way of life for millennia that is known primarily for violence and oppression that has now come full circle with the unraveling of the climate, the growth of despotic, fascist-like governments, the intransigent problem of white supremacy, the growth of an enormous plutocracy, the concomitant impoverishment of many, and so forth.

Stuck ego—and the power relationships it reproduces—is defined by power arrangements whose origin is located in the original expression "I," which is valued over being real. This is the source of that unique and unholy invention of Civilized beings: the political universe.

To move on from the tyranny of ego, we must come to appreciate how the reign of a delusional Self compromises our capacity to be true to ourselves. Because ego becomes second nature to us, we find it challenging to be mindful about ourselves and our world, to live in the present moment. This is critical to the power of stuck ego. Without being *awake* in the present, we readily conform to the expectations and interpretations of reality by powerful others. We are incapable of taking responsibility for seeing life as it is and acting on the choices we have as a consequence. Easily distracted by the incessant demands of "I," and the static it produces in our environment, our everyday existence typically passes by without notice; we are largely unconscious of what is happening in our lives in the living moment.

Hence, our interactions and relationships with others can easily deteriorate into a spectrum of behaviors that are careless, sloppy, thoughtless, indifferent, dishonest, selfish, unkind, greedy, cruel, indecent, violent, and inhumane. Our attachments to authority, social conformity, and the needs of "I" are particularly strong at times when our fear of being real prevails, tapping into our potential for the true horror that human existence can be when we turn our hearts away from ourselves and each other. All too often, the routine nature these behaviors can assume allows them to appear to be unexceptional, when in a more sober state we would recognize them as *evil*.

While acknowledging the limitations and liabilities of ego, as we have been doing throughout this chapter, it is important as we increasingly discuss the path of liberation that we remind ourselves of what we stated at the beginning. Bereft as we are of a salutary social environment to nurture us into an awareness and acceptance of our inherent state of interbeing, ego is vital to our growth as moral beings. This is one of the great ironies of our evolution toward liberation. As important as it is to follow our developmental arc to grow and mature and eventually transform into a fully responsible adult, it is equally imperative to not lose an appreciation of, and, yes, gratitude for who we have been all along, and the important role that ego has played. This will be significant when we arrive at the point in our lives, which transformative activists do, of wanting to disabuse ourselves of ego and to disown its destructive tendencies, something I will discuss later on.

Suffice it at this point to remind ourselves that apart from an exceptional few amongst us, we could not realize our necessary growth without the paradoxical but vital presence of the adversative "I." Ego is the necessary bridge we require to get us from here to there, providing us with what we need at a particular moment in our lives when we are not yet prepared to be real, to do for ourselves what needs to be done in order to get on in this world. Its role of providing vital assistance, while also being destructive of the real us, is a perfect representation of the mixed bag that we are and will likely always be. At the same time that we must become unstuck and become the adults we were intended to be, we also need to recognize and appreciate "I" for the necessary presence it has been in our liberating process. That recognition and appreciation is significant to becoming unstuck adults.

CHAPTER TWO

THE CRITIQUE OF
POLITICAL REVOLUTION

THE STUCK EGO/POLITICAL DIALECTIC

Although the idea that politics originates in ego is true, such an assertion is not completely accurate. More precisely, politics—that perversion of human decency and corrupter of morality through the exercise of power over life —achieves its most complete expression in stuck ego. This is that stage of arrested development where, despite our maturational progress, we persist in our ultimately futile efforts to control life, often in lethal, life-destructive ways. This is the moment that politics become a way of life.

Hence, the incestuous relationship between stuck ego and the political world it creates becomes the distinguishing feature of Civilized human existence. The latter could not exist without the former. Because of its thrust to dominate and control, the stuck ego-political dyad is the relational basis for the violence, injustice, subjugation, and oppression that we, as a people, routinely visit upon each other and other living beings in our pursuit of Civilization's grand vision of exacting dominion over life. It is responsible for the absence of morality in public and private behavior, which in turn has made possible the resiliency of patriarchy, the endurance of white supremacy, the naturalness of ruling class authority, the popularity of authoritarian governments and the real possibility of the collapse of Civilization itself, all of which are quintessential expressions of the dialectic in action.

Contrary to conventional wisdom, these calamities defy political solutions. We can no longer get away with the usual quick fix of electing a new President, passing a piece of reform legislation, or inventing a new technology. What is required transcends employing variations of the same old methodology we have turned to in the past. Rather than trying to *fix* our situation by exerting power over our circumstances, we must go to the heart of the matter by understanding that it is the very hierarchical relationships themselves that got us into the unprecedented mess we face today that require basic change. Rather than repeating the errors of the past, we must go beyond political relationships to ones founded upon spiritual values.

Needless to say, this represents a serious challenge for activists of human liberation. Unless we have grown to the point where we are aware of ego and its deadly influence on our behavior, and are therefore able to act in ways without suffering its negative impact on our actions, our efforts to produce change will be frustrated by the very same political force that inspired this need to begin with. As long as we are unable to conduct ourselves in the world without ego's influence, we are ensnared within a classic instance of catch-22. Transformative revolution is stymied from realizing itself when it attempts to do so within the confines of the political world.

The "naturalness" of political culture, institutions, and power relationships resides within each of us through the presence of ego. Its prominence in our daily lives allows political power to be seemingly instinctual. We appear to have been born to ego and its emerging political sensibility—which in a sense we have, when we understand it as the natural accommodation made for the terrified new human being, absent as it is of a consciousness to its state of interbeing.

For the Civilized activist, the consequence of ego's existence is that it is only natural that we would follow its compulsive need to be one-up and, therefore, believe that we can only change what we find intolerable by eliminating it through the application of political power. Then, and only then, will we actualize what we have considered to be the prerequisite of revolutionary change: the ability to impose our will on our social context, and in particular, on the oppressive other.

This perspective is significantly reinforced by the pervasive political environment we are intimately part of through the variety of political roles we are acculturated to throughout our lives. We could hardly grow up in this world without being conditioned to believe that politics is the way the world runs. This is the way things get done and why having power is the supreme value of Civilization. We may wish it to be otherwise, even actively oppose one or more of its most egregious expressions, and regret the compromises with our values that politics involve.

But it is difficult to avoid the conclusion that, in the end, if we are both serious and realistic about being an agent of change, we have to accept that securing dominant control must be our priority. Notwithstanding our sincerity and dedication to our noble cause, we are at the same time political animals. Born to ego and raised in a political world, it could hardly be otherwise.

This baggage we will most likely carry with us throughout our lives, at least to one extent or another, and this despite how effective we may become as a values-based activist. The bottom line is that to realize liberation entails learning how to live with our personal baggage of "I" without at the same time acting out of it.

To do this, however, we will have to cease denying the fact that all relationships that involve the control of others—including those which are embedded within moral values, and "Peace" and "Justice" slogans—negate our liberating aims. Typically, while regretting some of our acts, we nevertheless have sought refuge in old bromides—what we do is a *necessary evil*, for example, or an omelet cannot be made without first breaking some eggs—to justify our behavior. We've defended acts that we objected to when performed by our enemies by pointing to the flagrant conduct of oppressors, insisting that there are times when one has to fight fire with fire. In the same breath, we further justify our practice of power relationships and the oppressive conduct it involves by insisting upon the right-eousness of our cause. Somehow, fighting the good fight against a designated enemy confers authority for us to do whatever we choose because our mission is to stop the unacceptable behavior of the oppressive Other. Being on the side of the angels, our conduct is above reproach.

We will also have to cease practicing the standard rationale of politics: that the end justifies the means. That is how force—physical, psychological, economic, social and sexual—is sanctioned to whatever extent is considered necessary to secure and retain the desired power relationship. People and other living beings are always hurt or killed when the needs of the "Revolution" (as defined by the revolutionary authority) take precedence over all other concerns; collateral damage is acceptable because it is in the service of the larger purpose of establishing the power of the revolutionary regime. Lying, deception, betrayal, duplicity, corruption, and other such immoral acts are winked at, and crimes of state and those against humanity are deemed legal by those in power.

The political approach to change uses the ends and means

argument to also justify the argument that, to realize the world we seek, the right conditions must first be put in place, including the elimination of those enemies who would oppose and undermine us. This belief holds that peace, freedom, and social justice can only prevail when we have the power to ensure we are able to exert our rule over our circumstances. Our purpose will most likely be resisted in the beginning of our struggle, especially by the perceived enemies of the revolution, thus requiring a period of pre-revolutionary decontamination of what we consider to be pernicious influence. Only in this way will our ideals be armed with the power which we believe they require to take root and grow into our version of a liberated way of life.

What all of these politically reasonable justifications over-look, however, is that how we proceed determines where we end up. We define what we achieve by the very way we go about trying to attain it; process and result are one and the same in the real world of the present moment. If we want human libera-tion in the "future," then we need to act as liberated human beings in the present. We cannot wait to live a transformative existence until some forever receding "future" appears with conditions that are judged as favorable. An actual transforma-tion of social relations is not fixed, but is constantly unfolding according to what the living moment is, and the values appro-priate to responding to it at that time.

Otherwise, what we postpone to the legendary *mañana* will never occur. This is fatal from the perspective of a revolution of everyday life, where practice is rooted not in efforts to secure political power, but in the expression of those moral values that are the living manifestations of peace, freedom, and social justice.

This failure to recognize the essential importance of how we live our daily existence is why the victory for the forces of change eventually rings hollow. After the celebrations die down, we come to realize that all that has really taken place is a musical chairs variation of power relationships. Only when the "future" exists in the values that we are consistently exhibiting in the prefiguring behaviors of the present—when the revolution is taking place during the revolution—does the desired liberation take place.

As political activists, however, we tend to dismiss the moral concerns of the living moment as quixotic, counter-revolutionary, or worst of all, pejoratively *idealistic*. Human decency is represented as a luxury we can only afford after the revolution is in power to enforce it. Human nature is correctly viewed as problematic. But the assumption that we then resolve this problem by controlling people, rather than valuing life and its infinite expressions through an everyday practice of love, one that cultivates our inherent goodness and its potential for responsible behavior and self-regulation, is ultimately counter-revolutionary. Ironically, it is just such regulation that both creates and exacerbates behavior that society concludes needs to be controlled with laws, police, prisons and the like. Democratic transformation and social morality do not arise when the values that uphold and legitimize both are not lived as a matter of everyday course.

Even when it succeeds by coming to power and attaining dominance and control over the social landscape, revolution fails at the same time to attain human liberation, as such examples as the United States, Russia, and China, amongst others, ably demonstrate. Revolution suffers this fate whenever we attempt to resolve political problems with political solutions. It is the kiss of death to impose on people what we consider to be a better way of life. All that it accomplishes is a replication of the very same power relationship that originally inspired us to rise up against the oppressor. Though our intentions may be virtuous, the outcome is essentially the same. In the end, it is only when we go about living our intentions with life-valuing morality that revolution's ideals live! Only then is the revolution revolutionary.

THE INSTITUTIONAL EXPRESSION

As social beings in an interconnected universe, it is no surprise that relationships are the heartbeat of everyday life. So central is their role in the lives of most of us that it is no exaggeration to state that our relations with spouse and partner, friends and neighbors, work and school mates, casual acquaintances and strangers in passing are the major factor as to whether we're happy people or not. Our interactions largely define the quality of our lives.

This fact acquires added significance when we consider that our social context is governed by power arrangements. Not only are we communal through our interconnected world, but we are so within a hierarchical, authoritarian construction as well. Such considerations as gender, race, age, and social position play a decisive role in these relationships, however subtle and unconscious they may be at times. Their presence is so ubiquitous and our behavior so habituated to their prescribed roles that we are often unaware of the influence they exert on our lives.

And yet in our efforts to produce liberating change, activists largely ignore this relational essence that shapes quotidian life. The moment-to-moment, interpersonal nature of our existence has not been our focus. Rather, we have neglected it in favor of combating the more abstract considerations of the systems and institutions of oppression. While these unquestionably reinforce and give societal expression to our primal everyday relationships, they are nevertheless one step removed from that which actually takes place between people in the living moment of everyday life.

The institutional and systemic both reflect and compound the essence of our relationships, but it is the latter, through the ways we choose to interact and respond to others in our present moment, which then provides these larger-than-life entities their substance and power. Regardless of our circumstances, the question for a revolutionary practice is: do we behave as a liberated people by acting with our inherent heart values, or do we deny and suppress them, relating to others as less than the people we really are?

Ultimately, only that behavior which is occurring right now provides institutions with their oppressive power. They would otherwise lack the authority that we bestow on them through our daily actions. The absence of our necessary participation would prevent these despotic bodies from existing in the first place. Only through us, and the way we behave in the everyday normal, is the "system" created and constantly reproduced from one moment to the next. Through our everyday behaviors and relationships, we originate this insidious positive feedback loop of power with the systemic, institutional expressions of our predicament.

Because we haven't recognized this, activists have viewed the question of human liberation from the wrong end of the telescope. Doing so significantly contributes to why we remain wedded to the age-old paradigm of trying to build a countervailing force of greater political power, in order to vanquish the institutional expressions of oppression, and to replace them with "liberating" institutions of our own. This has blinded us to the importance of our everyday relationships, as well as appreciating that only through consistent interactions of life-affirming values can we determine whether our efforts are truly transformative, or just another changing of the guard.

It is when we plumb the depths of our situation that we come around to asking ourselves one of the most important questions of an activism that aspires to be revolutionary: where did these institutions of oppression originate from? How did they come to be the dominant societal forces they are? Only when we answer these questions can we begin to address oppression in a realistic manner. Did they just drop out of the sky one day? Probably not. Or, more plausibly, did some overwhelming evil force invade human society at some point in our past and impose its life-negating rule on an "innocent" populace? This is a credible possibility that has been advanced by some.

But while there is no question that a more physically powerful and ruthless force can overwhelm and subjugate a much weaker human entity, this scenario could only continue for centuries of generations through the participation of both oppressor and oppressed. While such a consideration is anathema for many activists to entertain, there is no such thing as an "innocent victim"—i.e., one completely without responsibility, agency, or choice. This may be our condition initially in the moment of conquest; but as long as we remain morally awake, human beings who value life (and especially our own!), we are still potentially liberated beings who are capable of making choices about how we live our lives. Our momentary situation does not have to become institutionalized, congealed into a permanent arrangement of one-up and one-down, generation after generation, where the oppressive arrangement becomes a part of a society's lifeblood. There are individuals whose lives attest to this possibility, and certainly the history of African American people in our own society provide ringing testimony to that fact!

Unfortunately, the Civilized species as a whole consists of unliberated souls, unwilling to be free. Oppressive institutions are the inevitable consequence of our reluctance to choose freedom. Over the course of time, everyday relationships consisting of these people metastasize into systems of oppression. The latter are the consequence of countless acts and deeds, some intentional, others mindless, often in seemingly insignificant, often unconscious, quickly forgotten expressions of unkindness, insensitivity, cruelty, disrespect, betrayal, dishonesty, greed, prejudice, mean-spiritedness, hatred, ignorance, and a host of other unwholesome behaviors whose cumulative effect is to diminish the life of another living being.

Over time, these individual deeds deprived of heart value accumulate into a prominent feature of our existence to the point where their monolithic presence allows them to appear as natural, the way life is. Through our projections of our conduct out on to the world and our obeisance to their larger-than-life appearance and Self-induced fatalism, they acquire an apparent independent existence, existing beyond human agency. Short of joining a revolutionary movement dedicated to their overthrow, the smashing of their existence, and permanently ridding the world of their malevolent presence, we believe that there is nothing we can do about them.

From this Self-perpetuating, self-defeating perspective, we fail to appreciate the current moment and the beings of consequence we actually are, not only in terms of creating and reproducing the world as it is, but potentially life as it could be. This is huge.

When as activists we don't connect the everyday with the heart of our practice, we cut off at the knees our source of power and the possibility of being an agent of revolutionary change. We stumble around in the dark, engaged in behaviors that are invariably counterrevolutionary.

This should not be interpreted to mean that it is wrong to want to rid our lives of those institutions whose oppressive function is responsible for so much of the pain and suffering that humans and other living beings experience in this world. Patriarchy, capitalism, and racism, to name the three most prominent, operate at a systemic level through government laws and enforcement, cultural norms and social conventions, not to mention the mindless habits of millennia that so often shape how the body politic behaves. This context plays an important role in our lives, to be sure: being born a woman or a person of color are not trivial factors for women or people of color in a patriarchal, racist society, dominated by institutional policies and laws, assumptions and attitudes, convictions and judgments that are both intentionally and subconsciously codified into weapons of domination and control by white males.

This is understandably why, rather than pursuing a transformation of everyday life, and ultimately of ourselves, as the way to freedom, activists have typically attempted to accomplish this goal by either reforming or overthrowing these institutions of oppression.

But to go down this road is to condemn ourselves to a practice that does not begin where we need to start. At best, we end up dealing with the symptoms of the problem, not the heart of the matter. We need to begin at home, instead, with our everyday lives in order to get to the root of our situation. When we do this—when we become and are ourselves the revolution we seek—the institutions and systems of oppression will lose their effect in our lives, bereft as they now will be of the power we have been giving away to them all along.

ZERO SUM CULTURE

Constantly present in our relationships with one another in political society, competition is a toxic brew that infects nearly all our interactions. Endemic to relationships based upon power is the unquestioned assumption that people are by nature competitive: "getting ahead" of the other guy is what life is all about. In the United States, we even celebrate this attribute as one that renders us as an exceptional people.

By sanctifying competition as the way life unavoidably is, however, we also legitimize its outstanding consequence, the one-up/one-down relationship that is the assassin of good will, loving kindness, basic civility, and the expression of other heart values toward our fellow beings.

So much of everyday life is embedded in competition, whether children trying to be the favorite of their parents, employees elbowing each other aside to curry the favor of the boss, or homeowners going into debt to keep up with and surpass their "perfect" neighbors. Our GNP-driven economy would not be the monolith it is without our competitive drive to have the latest, the fastest, the sexiest: the best. Our fascination with sports is a national addiction—not simply for the sheer beauty of superbly trained athletes performing at a peak level— but, much more fundamentally, for the competition of who wins and who loses. Our competitive ways are engrained in our conversations and exchanges with one another, from the zingers, "gotchas," and other put-downs we use to one-up one another, to our incessant gossiping, back-stabbing and the direct and indirect judgments that drown almost every comment we have about the other. These behaviors help to create an atmosphere of competition that blankets our daily social inter- course, reinforcing the premise that there are naturally winners and losers in a Civilized society.

Competition is the natural corollary of an ego-driven person- ality where beating out the other guy—being #1, if only for the moment—is a pervasive feature of political relationships. It could hardly be otherwise where control of life is the *raison d'être* of our Civilized existence. This is the zero-sum game that in one way or another we all play.

The rules of the game are quite simple. There are always winners and losers, but it is subtler than that. A zero-sum model reproduces the ancient one-up/one-down dyad that has governed Civilization from the beginning. So while I win, it is equally (if not more so) significant that *you lose!* Winning is deprived of its true significance in political interactions if there is no one that has been beaten, and whose losing has not been registered as such. Only through the invidious comparison between the winner and loser is the power of the political dichotomy established.

There is no third way, no concern for the wellbeing of all, as there would be in a values-grounded reality. Such a third way would be the province of a society that truly lives an egalitarian existence based on peace, freedom, and social justice, where people are not disunited, pitted against each other. As its proponents tell us, competition separates the wheat from the chaff. It's the survival of the fittest, from which "superior" people emerge, and the rest are eliminated for the good of Civilization.

Basic to creating the subjective underpinning for a political society, the zero-sum model is an experiential loop repeatedly playing in our homes, schools, workplaces, highways and other public spaces, and especially in our heads, to reinforce the seemingly intrinsic power of its disempowering message. Dividing us into winners and losers establishes our value within the power hierarchy. Much as love and other life-affirmative values serve as the spiritual soil for human liberation, so does the zero sum game serve as the psychological and social infrastructure for a power-driven society.

The touted naturalness of zero-sum is suspect even with a casual examination. For one thing, the game is not played on a level playing field, and this despite the protestations of its admirers that we all have the same opportunity in life. But as we know, even before an interaction begins, men are over women, whites over blacks, rich over poor, and so on. The game is rigged. With few exceptions, the outcome of the encounter is already decided by historically predetermined arrangements that provide some people with substantial advantages because of their gender, race, and class, and others with a decided disadvantage.

Additionally, the urge to win and then stay on top is so compelling for many that success is paramount before other considerations, including moral and ethical ones. This pressing need often involves less than wholesome behavior. Cheating and cutting corners are amongst the most common breaches of wholesome conduct, though it is not unusual for more insufferable acts to be committed in order to win.

Finally, there is a legitimate question as to whether the winner really wins, as is suggested by the title of Ernest Hemingway's 1933 collection of short stories, *Winner Take Nothing*. Today's success is no guarantee of a similar outcome tomorrow; the winner is always looking over their shoulder to see who might be coming up on them from behind. Winning does not render one immune from the dog-eat-dog competition that is merciless and unrelenting (especially in the company of other winners) in a zero-sum society, which suggests that winning is not all that it is advertised to be.

For activists, it invariably results in outcomes that make necessary yet another round of revolution in the name of revolution in the not too distant future. We must come to see that, when promoting peace and justice, we don't do ourselves any favors by weaponizing our purpose within the armor of a competitive political practice. The latter, by definition, is founded on the acquisition and exercise of power-over. A few winners and many losers do not a liberated world make, either for them or us. Inevitably, this situation involves imposing our will on others and forcing them to yield to us. The wheel of oppression takes another turn, another revolution appears necessary on the not-too distant horizon.

There is also the matter of the many "losers," not a small consideration in a society predicated upon a hierarchical model. The loser is a *Loser*, with diminished value in a society that only prizes winners. The loser is viewed as fair game for scorn, ridicule, abusive behavior, and ultimately banishment from society's inner ring of those of us valued as acceptable.

Zero-sum doesn't imply the pain and suffering the loser

experiences in a power relationship. Though sanctioned by law and custom and generally viewed as "the way life is," politics doesn't bring out the best in human beings. Invariably, it trumps what we know as our "better instincts."

Rather than a momentary incident that comes and goes, we feel losing in an ego-predicated world as blows to the heart because of the damage it does to our Self-image of "I." As long as we are ego-bound, we remain stuck in this assessment long after the moment has passed. Losing is personalized in a political world.

There is no "losing" and "winning," however, from the vantage point of an everyday values revolution, when we can be involved with others in an activity without the participation of "I." We "play the game" without ego, and focus more on the values with which we participate, as well as the pleasure we derive when engaging in the activity for its own sake. This is challenging, for sure, but the opportunity to avoid the winner and loser dichotomy of the zero-sum scenario is greatly enhanced when our involvement is offered in a selfless way. Achievement is celebrated by and for both "sides," not at the expense of another. There are no contending sides, no separation of people into opponents; therefore, the ancient duality of Us vs. Them does not exist. Our involvement with others is cooperative and collaborative, where the purpose is to accomplish a mutual goal and celebrate our joint victory together. More likely, we are pulling for and enjoying each other rather than trying to be individually victorious.

A society minus winners and losers is a prerequisite for one that is without oppression and injustice. It allows for the practice of values such as compassion, generosity, gratitude, selflessness, modesty, and humility, and the inherent enjoyment that this practice gives rise to.

THE REVOLUTIONARY STATE: "POWER TO THE PEOPLE"

When activists are preoccupied with the acquisition and exercise of political power, it should not surprise us that the pinnacle of success is defined as our coming to power through the realization of the Revolutionary State. This is the culmination of a project that, despite its call for people's freedom, is based not so much in the liberation of human beings but in their control. At one and the same time, the zero-sum game that political revolution engages in realizes both its supreme success and its ultimate failure. At this moment, when it arrives at the zenith of political power, the revolution becomes the antithesis of the ideals it was founded upon because of the inherently authoritarian nature of the state in its one-up/one-down, hierarchical relationship with the citizens it supposedly serves. This is so whether its methods are unabashedly despotic or couched in the appearances of a representative democracy. The state (and those behind the curtain who operate the levers of power) is really in charge.

For politically oriented activists, liberation is not recognized as actually existing as long as people are allowed to live our lives in a manner of our choosing. Freedom, as George Orwell would have it, is un-freedom. The freedom to be the people we are is typically interpreted as a threat to those who view this state as requiring external controls and especially by those of us who wish to be in control or to be controlled. We deny the true nature of freedom, its beauty and brilliance, when we follow the promptings of the unfettered galaxy of values that cluster around our heart's instinctual love for life. These values do not manifest in any spontaneous, unqualified fashion in a context that is mediated and circumscribed, limited to that which is deemed safe—hence legitimate—by the arbiters of political correctness. By its nature, the heart fully expresses itself only when given free rein.

Distinctive of ego-directed beings, however, is that we don't trust ourselves to live our lives as we will—because we are then out of control, not subject to some superior authority telling us what to do and how to live our lives, whether that power resides within or outside of ourselves. The absence of control leaves too much to chance. Because it ventures into the unknown and unpredictable, it is risky and dangerous. Besides, people are inherently imperfect, and very capable of evil, as we all know. We need to be controlled.

Therefore, we must be led and (re-)educated in order to learn how to be free. If peace, freedom, and social justice are to prevail, we must rely upon the State to regulate and enforce peace, freedom, and social justice (at least as we, the Self-appointed spokesmen [sic] for and guardians of the revolution, define these ideals), while at the same time using our Revolutionary armed forces, police, prisons and other means of general populace control to suppress all who would oppose our noble mission.

Yes, we know that the state with all its brutal apparatus has been the instrument of oppression in the past, but because the Revolutionary State will be motivated with the best of intentions, we have convinced ourselves that ours will serve as a force of liberation.

As history shows, the Revolutionary State, like the oppressive predecessor whose rule it supplanted, is the instrument of a ruling class whose privileged interests it serves. Whatever its "democratic" trappings, the agents of the State, whether elected from different wings of the ruling class or otherwise imposed on the people, are authoritarian. As the slavery of African citizens and their descendants, and the genocide of Native Americans that are so central to our own country's historical narrative demonstrate, along with the domination of men over women, and of the rich over the workers who created the wealth of the country, the Revolutionary State is an oxymoron. It is not a means through which the liberation of people has been or can be secured because this condition only exists when people express their inherent spiritual values through their unmediated behaviors. Power to the people is real only when it stands alone, independent from the intercession of either ego, or its agent in the political world, the State, to help make it appear to be so.

PART TWO
THE WAY OF
LIBERATION

CHAPTER THREE

BEING REAL IS ACCEPTING LIFE AS IT IS

"A false sense of security is the only kind there is."
—unknown Irish poet

PRELUDE: FREEDOM AND FREEDOM-FROM

As with revolution, so has there been a serious misunderstanding about what freedom is all about. We have mistakenly interpreted the purpose of revolutionary activism to be one of changing the world, rather than simply accepting it as it is and learning to live with it as a free human being. This in turn has led us to interpret freedom as a condition where we are free-from something that oppresses us, rather than just being free, regardless of our circumstances.

Instead of working to eliminate those oppressive conditions that we see as rendering us unfree, liberation is nothing more than being the people we inherently are. In this way, liberation is life-affirmative because freedom is unconditional, a matter of being real, a wholehearted instance of life we were born to be.

It is not the opposite of oppression, domination, and control, where, as the activist syllogism would have it, the elimination of these undesirable conditions is synonymous with freedom. This is not freedom: it is freedom-from. By posing freedom and oppression as polar opposites we defy the unitary whole of existence where, as with birth and death, love and hatred, and other dualities that an ego perspective divides life into, they are but different expressions of one.

Freedom-from is how freedom is commonly understood by Civilized society where, for example, we celebrate our vaunted economic progress as freeing us from physical labor and material want, revere our Bill of Rights and Constitution for freeing humankind from tyranny, and credit the Enlightenment with freeing the Civilized race from the darkness of ignorance and superstition.

Freedom, on the other hand, is simply being, not contingent upon any external circumstances to exist. Though just as subject to the momentary conditions of life as anything else is, we are not dependent on any specific condition outside of ourselves to be realized. Just as it is with any other human being, we are the sole agent of our freedom. That is why as revolutionaries we cannot free anyone else but ourselves.

While part of the larger order of the impermanent, interdependent universe, freedom is also its own state of being, complete unto itself, both subject to and independent of the larger mix. While the circumstances and conditions of our lives must always be taken into consideration, human beings only have to be true to the instance of life that we are, regardless of circumstances, in order to be free.

In short, freedom arises when we accept life for what is. Without it having to be something else—something better than we judge our present life to be—we are liberated. No longer burdened with the struggles of our kind to make life into something it is not, forcing it to embody our vision of what we in our Civilized fever dream believe it should be, we are free to simply be ourselves. When we come home to ourselves, revolution achieves its transformative potential. Acceptance allows us to live a life of peace, freedom, and social justice.

———

Another important dimension to acceptance that must be exercised in order for freedom to be possible is acting on the opportunity that choice opens up for us, provided by our acceptance of life. In order to be free, we must choose to be free. It will not happen otherwise.

The beauty of acceptance is that once we accept life and are no longer constricted by ego's obsession with power and control, our vision of reality expands. It becomes more inclusive of what is. By accepting life, we are provided with choices about life that we were unaware of before because, in effect, they didn't exist for us in the closed world of ego and the political world it confines us to. Acceptance opens us to many possibilities which by their very existence enrich choice and—need I say it?—are the heartbeat of freedom.

Through acceptance and the choice it provides us, we stand before the gateway to the unconditioned and unconditional life that is freedom. We are opened to and in the presence of our intrinsically heartfelt selves, the several dimensions of which I will explore in the sections that follow. This is the origin of the liberated instance of life we always have potentially been, and in fact now are. Unblinded, faced with freedom's reality and possibility, we now have the responsibility of choosing to be free.

Ego remains a choice, of course, and a compelling one at that, given our lifelong history as "I." There is nothing automatic here. We still have to choose and to act on that choice. The business of taking those fateful steps is what it means to spiritually become an adult human being.

SURRENDERING TO LIFE AS IT IS: IMPERMANENCE AND INTERBEING

A spiritual crisis is at the heart of the likely societal collapse that is already exhibiting an incipient presence in our lives. This is the result of our collective failure to cultivate the moral values that cherish life because of our Self-aggrandizing tendency toward trying to establish Civilization's dominion over life, a pursuit that only diminishes, exploits, and destroys life.

In contrast to the hierarchical, power relationships that our politicized world creates, (e.g., the archetype, Civilization over nature), valuing life is the necessary precondition to realizing an existence that is truly civilized, one that is capable of a life of peace, freedom and social justice for all of its citizens, where we cherish and respect all sentient beings through our moment to moment expressions of such inherent heart values as kindness and generosity, gratitude and compassion, selflessness and unconditional love. Because we haven't truly valued life, we have suffered a millennial breakdown of morality whose endgame is perfectly apparent today in the perfect storm of the apocalyptic climate crisis, emerging fascism, intractable white supremacy, bottomless greed of a heartless oligarchy, and the impoverishment of a growing underclass that together portend societal collapse.

At this critical juncture, we need a transformative morality, one that squarely addresses the spiritual root of our existential emergency. We need, that is, to accept life as it is and cease our efforts of trying to exact control over it. If a love for life is the basis of a truly civilized and democratic existence, then the acceptance of life as it is provides the foundational morality for such a society.

To accept life, we must first honor and live in accordance with its laws of impermanence—here one moment, gone the next—as well as our state of interbeing where we are one with all other living beings. Incessant change is the heartbeat of life, the one constant of our otherwise mutable universe; and we are inextricably connected to and dependent upon each other from birth to death as a condition of our existence.

The problem is not that we have failed to successfully evade living by these laws. Rather, it's that we madly persist in trying to do so, and hence preclude enjoying a liberated existence which is minus the unnecessary pain and suffering we routinely inflict upon ourselves and others, because we will not accept what unavoidably is. We have not escaped, try as we might, and continue to be subject to both laws as a living being on this planet. But because we have yet to surrender to the fact that there is no escaping their universality, we create the conflict that powers our oppressive, political world.

We're not in control. Death is certain and we are totally dependent on the rest of life for our life. These are truths that we may know in our heads, but they haven't percolated throughout our being, informing how we then go about living our lives. As long as ego and its mania to be in control continue to dictate what and how we behave in everyday life, the pathway to freedom remains blocked.

Rather than being oppressed, however, as some might fear, submitting to the laws of the universe is what liberation is all about. There is so much more we can be and do when we cease trying to be someone we're not, or allow ourselves to be goaded by Civilization's conviction that we're just not good enough and driven by its whiplash with *progress, forever progress:* after all, "making progress" is how we know we're Civilized. Out of touch with our hearts, we're not able to see the truth of our lives, and then to act on it as the free human being we always potentially are.

This is the origin of oppression. We're not at home with ourselves. This is a desperate position for almost any living being to be in, but most especially human beings.

The organism's gift to us is ego, that provides the holding pattern of "I." Along with our share of bumps and scrapes along the way, "I" allows at least some of us to get through to the time when, developmentally, we're ready to live as liberated souls, accepting the cold fact that we're not in control, and that the best we can do is ride with life as it is, acting upon the awareness that we can make choices about how we live our lives that allows them to be good enough. But understandably, in all but exceptional instances, most of us sell out to "I" and become lifelong stuck in ego because of its illusion of power and control.

But the latter is so paltry, so chimerical when compared to the power we enjoy when we accept life for what it is, and no longer live under the reign of ego. Rather than settling for its phony power and freedom, we uncover something much more valuable to our well-being when we recognize that we're not alone, that in fact there is a solidarity and compassion, and generosity that emerges when we recognize the momentary spark of life that we all share. This heartfelt feeling of commonality does wonders for how we approach and conduct our relationships with others, from the most intimate and personal to stranger and adversary alike, not to mention the nonhuman representatives who open our eyes and help bring us down to earth. It's like a seismic shift when we think about it, but no big deal at all while we're actually experiencing it.

Additionally, with death now employed as an advisor, we no longer are consumed with death, especially in its coded forms of security and certainty, money and status, past and future. We are not bogged down with the extraneous and irrelevant. Rather, we increasingly have time only for what our guardian of now, our heart tells us is real in the moment of now.

In doing so, we discover that there is also the virtue of living our lives as if our lives depended upon it. Not only does this remove the miasma of political existence that fogs over daily life, but it also lends integrity and authenticity that only being present in the present can provide. It is not that we no longer experience the pain and suffering that naturally accompanies our brief moment of being a living being—injury and illness, failure and defeat, aging and death—because in many ways, life is essentially the same. It's only that, when we live in the present, being alert to and acting on what is available to us in a given moment acquires the flavor of being good enough. We come upon possibilities that can only be seen when we are totally mindful in the living moment. Living in the present is whole and complete; we simply don't have time for anything else.

ACCEPTING OURSELVES

Nothing is more liberating than accepting ourselves for the people we are. It is precisely our inability or unwillingness to do so that lends such decisive influence to ego in our lives. When we accept ourselves—and especially for the good people we are —we cut off the source of our personal contribution to our Self-enslavement, without which neither "I," nor the political universe it creates, can dominate and control us as they do.

Self-acceptance is liberation in all dimensions of our existence, from the intellectual and emotional to the physical and spiritual. Energy is released that had previously been repressed. We come awake and alive in ways that we had not been before, open to possibilities and dimensions of ourselves that had been previously circumscribed and repressed. We witness the most visible sign of this growth in our daily practice. Increasingly, we interact with the world not as someone who is guarded, defended, and closed off, but with the awareness of ourselves as the whole person we actually are. We display behaviors that are transparently values-infused.

Accepting ourselves involves multiple aspects, not the least of which are our heart-centered values. Accepting the being we really are liberates us from the false Self of "I," set in our ways, locked in place, rigid and doctrinaire. Rather, we are relaxed and open, transparent and vulnerable. Not having to be in control, we are less judgmental. We loosen our grip, unclench our minds, unlock our spirit; we are softer and gentler, more flexible, adaptable to change and receptive to other points of view. We're not as attached to ideas of should and shouldn't as we once were. Not stuck upon either/or, black and white approaches, acceptance helps us to recognize the value of third ways.

Hence, we're not easily thrown off balance when a new normal replaces the old. We are more likely to roll with the punches and pick ourselves up off the floor than to whine and complain when things go wrong. For these reasons and more, acceptance cultivates ego-busting lessons that nurture a little more modesty and humility in our everyday dealings with the world. If not completely ready to adopt an attitude of not-knowing (because we really don't!), we at least are willing to hang out in the realm of the not-so-certain.

This is intimately allied with letting go of much that we have been attached to, including that which we would never have considered releasing at an earlier time. This lightening-up is the process of removing the layers of "I" that we have accumulated during our lifetime.

Our activism becomes less driven by a need to change others than it is with exploring and being curious about who they are. We are more apt to listen, rather than proselytize or debate. As we cultivate our values and allow ourselves to be living representatives of walking the talk, we find that, while no guarantee of anything, their universality at least invites the best from others. Which is all we can ever do, anyway, toward "changing" people, or more accurately, supporting and encouraging them to be who they are.

Acceptance should not be misunderstood as the absence of

conflict, but we are able to at least mitigate some of conflict's more injurious expressions when we come to adopt a "live and let live" attitude. We keep our cool when we accept ourselves as people of values because we have less to protect and defend. We don't personalize our encounters with adversarial others, but instead allow things to pass as they naturally will when "I" doesn't interfere. We are less attached to or identified with a particular outcome. As a result, we are better able to at least contribute a peaceful presence towards a conflict when one arises. At the same time, we don't get bogged down in the extraneous and unessential—the "small potatoes" that so much of life's altercations consist of. We walk around situations that invite unnecessary confrontation, hostility, and conflict, and avoid personal entanglements, the stickiness of ego encounters. This is greatly aided by the fact that self-acceptance lessens our "I" tendency to be defensive when our sense of (False) Self is threatened: we act with the confidence of *knowing* who we are.

Self-acceptance not only includes the rational and logical, the narrow framework which any sensible Civilized person usually confines their interpretations of reality to, but also opens us to that which we have largely suppressed: the intuitive, the instinctive, the imaginative, the insightful, and the spontaneous, all of which we have been taught to keep in tight check. Acceptance opens us to our inner domain, the home of our anarchistic being: the beating heart.

This is the realm of our subjective dimension, not the personal that is "I," but our generally unexplored subterranean depths. Beyond ego's explanations for how things are, independent of "I," these innate qualities are essential to the fully mindful state required of any moment that is fully accepting. Closely related to our heart values, they often serve as agents of the heart in their facilitation of both our awareness and acknowledgement of its "messages." This inner dimension is second to none for being true to ourselves.

By eschewing the scripts we have relied on in the past to navigate life, we let go of our constant search for the security and certainty that they were supposed to provide us with. Forgoing the illusion of control, the freedom to simply be entails the risk that comes with accepting life as it is. Acceptance involves stepping out into the unknown and learning to live with our doubts, fears and insecurities, acknowledging what they have to say about ourselves without allowing them to be the final word on who we really are.

As this suggests, being real also involves accepting life as a bit untidy, as something that can't be neatly encapsulated within a bureaucratic memo or a stereotypic behavior. Life is too contradictory and paradoxical, inconsistent and ambiguous, and totally illogical and absurd at times to conform to something that is always the predictable same.

By being this way, however, life is also very, very funny— hilariously so once we (re)discover our sense of humor, tripping over ourselves in those inconvenient, unreasonable moments that are always popping up when we have fallen on our face because we expected life to be other than it is. Humor is both the saving grace and reward that comes with living life as it is.

Another unanticipated benefit: life becomes uncluttered when we come to accept it for the empty space it really is beyond the personal accumulation of "I." When we are able to empty out and clean house, we are less burdened with our ideas, concepts, and dogma (not to mention their material incarnations) as they evaporate into spaciousness. This is one of the great joys of acceptance, where we no longer feel weighed down by the load of Self-baggage we schlep along with us. Being free of accumulated litter— mental and emotional as well as physical —we are so much better able to see the trees from the forest: to find what is useful to living life now, and what is not.

Most of all, empty space helps us discover what is really important in life. We finally realize that the priceless joy of acceptance is an unconditioned, unconditional love of life. Acceptance is the basis of love. It is the necessary ingredient which unlocks the potential of love in each and every one of us. We are agents of love when we can accept life for what it is.

ACCEPTING OUR INHERENT GOODNESS

Perhaps the most difficult part of accepting ourselves is being open to the fact that we are essentially good people doing the best we can to make it through this world. This is so despite the evidence to the contrary at times, and notwithstanding the opinions of others and ourselves, some of which are well-founded! All too many of us, perhaps most of us, don't accept that we're inherently good, and by extension that our fellow human beings are as well. This quality contributes significantly to why we as a people accede so readily to the control of an external authority. We don't trust ourselves to do *right* for ourselves. Seeing life through a negative lens, we are then readily disposed to act in Self-fulfilling ways.

Certainly, there are times when we embody our potential for moral integrity and rise to the occasion, in moments of crisis or emergency when the best in us takes command of our behaviors. But we see these as the exceptions (which, unfortunately, they are!) and not as dramatic examples of behavior that, in their more low-key, mundane ways, are not uncommon throughout our quotidian lives. That is why we make so much of these moments, treating them as heroic, exceptional acts. We just don't see ourselves in this fashion otherwise.

This blindness is exploited by ego, as it takes advantage of our original inability to recognize our interconnectedness which, had we been able to do so, would have spared us the need for ego in the first place. Ego can hardly allow us to see this truth about ourselves without putting itself out of business.

The inability to see ourselves for who we really are conveniently legitimizes our inconsistency in acting upon this capacity. At the same time, it gives license to behave in the less than salutary ways that we resort to, believing that this is the way we have to operate if we want to get by in a political world. Which, of course, only further solidifies ego's importance to us.

Fully accepting ourselves as good people awakens us to a moral responsibility to be that person not only in an emergency but during those "softer times," in the everyday flow of things. Building on our incipient though underused presence, such acceptance awakens our conscience to full-time function.

This touches on the heart of the matter, the difficulty many of us have with being true to our inherent heart values—the "good side of human nature," as we might express it, with day-to-day consistency. As this expression suggests, it's not that we aren't aware of these values; it is a rare one amongst us who doesn't at least pay lip service to their reality as attributes we possess as Civilized beings, even when we qualify this by noting that it is *unrealistic* to expect us to behave with moral constancy given the kind of world we live in.

It is noteworthy how the fact of moral values is not denied. Regardless of actual practice, and the various rationales for its laxity, almost all people instinctively know what we're talking about when we mention such behaviors as kindness, compassion, or generosity. That we irregularly and inconsistently act on these values should not be interpreted to mean that we aren't sincere when we claim to respect, even honor, such behaviors that exhibit selflessness and cooperation, fairness and forgiveness, courage and integrity, along with other moral virtues. They often are enshrined in our religious and government documents, and honored in the public statements we make about ourselves. They seem to touch us in some elemental way, suggesting their natural presence in us and a synchronicity with life.

Most significant is that these same values, while not totally absent by any means, are nevertheless muted and certainly irregular expressions, uneven players in the human drama of everyday life. In a very characteristically Civilized manner, we ignore and deny, compromise and contradict them, most often in "small" ways that anyone hardly notices or just dismisses as harmless peccadillos that human beings commit all the time.

But it is this dearth of morality in our daily routines, the unmindful, half-asleep interactions and behaviors that create the gulf between who we inherently are and the people we actually are in our day-to-day lives that accounts for the state of the world and the need for a revolution of everyday life. Countless "small" behaviors all add up to create an immoral culture, one that is capable of unfathomable, profoundly shocking evil.

We have created a world of hate, greed, violence, oppression, war and injustice, not because we are inveterately bad people, but because we will not accept, and hence act, in a reliable, constant fashion, like the good people we innately and potentially are. At the same time, we blind ourselves to this fact by sincerely insisting we are the Civilized people we claim to be. This failure to accept our life-affirming heart values through commensurate, consistent behavior produces evil in the world, whether that be as active agents or by abetting on the sidelines with our moral stillness. When people are not themselves and are acting out from that false place of a Self-perpetuating ego, mired as it is in political relationships, bad things happen. Sometimes very bad.

Accepting ourselves, especially as the good people we are, is the lynchpin to the transformative revolution we seek. If we are to realize such a state of being, we can't depend upon a devastating hurricane or terrorist bombing to wake us up to our full potential. We need to realize that now, through a discipline and commitment to a values practice which allows such behavior to grow into a spontaneous response to the moment-to-moment occurrences of everyday life. While not a complete solution to the problems of the world, especially given the fact of human imperfection, a people acting on the awareness of our essential goodness would go a long way toward greatly reducing the various evils that beset us today.

A revolution of self-acceptance addresses the quality of everyday life that allows us to go through life asleep at the wheel. In contrast to crisis, when we often exhibit an active mindfulness, daily existence requires so little of us most of the time. Often we are just going through the motions, able to do what needs to be done in a half-hearted fashion. Many of our lives are characteristically repetitive and routine. They're frankly so boring that many of us require the stimulants of drugs and alcohol, popular culture and consumerism, social media and pornography to provide whatever sense of *aliveness* we can find in life.

Consciously or not, we come to accept that we can get away with playing less than our best game. In an environment that dulls and enervates us, we tend to be lazy, careless, indifferent and uncaring as we go through the routines of the everyday. Most lives are absent of verve and vitality, creativity and imagination, excitement and joy, requiring only a fraction of our capacities to manage the deadening details of our lives.

This is not fertile ground for a practice of spiritual values. To the contrary, it is the very nature of a political society that it discourages spiritually moral behavior. This is in contrast to the more politically useful moral behavior it does promote to keep people in line and to be following the habitual norm from one day to the next, rather than rising and asserting ourselves. Outside of our compliance with the imposed rules of the game, very little is expected of or even wanted from us in this spiritually deadening environment. Political society operates on power —the power to control life, not to empower us to be the best people we can be. The latter is anathema to stuck ego and the repressive society it produces. As a condition of living in this society, we deny and suppress the expression of anything other than a muted facsimile of our values-selves.

Only when a life-threatening crisis jolts us out of our somnambulist state do we *wake up!* and come alive to who we are. We are in such a situation right now in the midst of accelerating climate change and environmental destruction, the mother of all crises, as well as the continuing pandemic, the growing fascist threat to our democracy, and the seemingly unresolvable issue of white supremacy. To recognize this situation and respond accordingly would, perhaps, be a silver lining in our circumstances.

But to do this, we need to awaken now to the good people we are born to be. We can't afford to wait until the apocalypse is here, full-blown. It will be too late then to engage in everyday versions of the behavior we have exhibited at other times in the past when faced with a short-term, life-threatening emergency. Our present circumstances are unprecedented. We can't afford the luxury of waiting until they're upon us to respond with our best. We need to be acting now, as best we can, as if the apocalypse is already here. Because it is.

FORGIVING OURSELVES

"Compassionate towards yourself,
You reconcile all beings in the world."
—Lao-Tzu

"To accept reality is to forgive reality for being what it is."
—Richard Rohr

Being open to our hearts is vital to providing the spiritual strength that we require in order to accept ego. There will be times when we will not be successful behaving without "I." In fact, we should make room for this possibility throughout our lives. There is no conclusion to this process; at best, there is only growth, which is good enough. We will fall short at times, continuing in the ancient patterns of identifying with ego, behaving as "I," acting out in unskillful, unwholesome ways. It will seem at times that our very human nature destines us to be mindless, to behaving in ways that we know at some level are wrong or commit a deed we never thought we were capable of doing.

Especially as activists who are making deliberate and conscientious efforts to remove our behavior from ego's influence, falling short of our standard can be disheartening. We need to live with and accept ourselves in those moments as much as we do when our behavior is more skillful, more wholesome.

We do so in a way that ensures we don't get stuck in the shame and embarrassment we're nevertheless fully and rightfully experiencing. Name the deed and the feelings around it for what they are, without judgment; apologize to whomever we need to apologize (including ourselves); and move on, hopefully knowing something about ourselves we didn't know before. This is how to be a perfectly imperfect human being. This is how we also live with "I," when we use a mistake to learn and grow through acceptance and humility. In this way, triumphs can come dressed as defeats.

The common problem that arises and thwarts our efforts is that it is not uncommon for us to personally identify with our efforts. "I" sneaks in the back door of our attempts to reduce and minimize its influence in our behaviors by personally attaching us to this goal. Hence, what is in reality nothing more than a neutral mistake or failure, one that will pass if not latched on to, becomes something more as the property of ego. When this happens, we take our "failure" personally. This is when we can be hard on ourselves. We are down for falling prey to "I"'s temptations to behave in a Self-oriented way.

But by hitting ourselves over the head for doing so, we add to the original error of acting out of ego by doing so once again. That is, we blame ourselves for *personally* failing. By identifying ourselves with our dedication to forging a skillful practice and making personal our virtuous endeavors, we become subjectively invested in this conduct. It invariably leads to ego-prompted expectations of success where what we do is not for its own sake but for a reward or pay-off beyond the simple act itself. Behavior that is free of ego's influence is not sufficient by itself; it has to be successful as well.

In this way, we not only avoid accepting responsibility for our error (blaming is a behavior where we don't assume responsibility for ourselves), but by attaching ourselves to the incident, we also allow our error to become baggage that we carry around with us long after the original event. When this occurs, we only reinforce, rather than diminish, the power of "I."

This, of course, is our challenge. How can we calmly and dispassionately accept ego—accept ourselves—when at the same time we are imperfect beings, susceptible to ego not only in terms of making mistakes, but also by punishing ourselves for having done so? How can we untangle ourselves from the knot of "I?"

By blaming ourselves as *bad people,* we allow ourselves to be convinced that we are not worthy of forgiveness. Thus we fail to shine its gentle light on ego and to see "I" compassionately for the protective, defensive response that it is. In this way, ego keeps us in our place, evading the liberating embrace that comes when we take responsibility for ourselves. We miss an opportunity for growth and maturity, a moment of selfless self-love.

We can only accept ego by forgiving ourselves when we fall prey to its ensnaring designs. Without extending to ourselves this gift of self-compassion and humility, we cannot move on.

We remain stuck. Being able to forgive ourselves is necessary if we are to avoid falling into a morass of Self-denunciation, hating who we are: that essential feature of stuck ego.

In order to be truly accepting, we have to live with ourselves at those times when we fall on our face, act like a jerk (or worse), and find ourselves behaving in ways that are contrary to the values we have committed ourselves to live by. Feeling that we are unworthy of forgiveness emanates from personalizing our behavior, making it a statement of who we are. It's ego in action!

Judging ourselves unworthy of forgiveness is a Self-preserving maneuver of ego to maintain its control over us. It is not in ego's Self-interest to encourage insight and mindfulness, ownership and responsibility, not to mention the growth and development of a maturing human being that results from being able to move on with our lives unburdened with guilt and shame. Rather, its true interest lies in keeping us down with a sense that we are essentially bad people. Self-forgiveness removes the guilt that characterizes Civilized beings and acts as an essential internal mechanism of Self-control in a political society.

Forgiveness is a threat to the continuation of a political way of life. It is the merciful way that imperfect human beings can live with themselves without feeling one-down to themselves. Forgiveness is how we accept our unskillful and unwholesome behavior in a restorative rather than punitive fashion. It may be the behavior, before all others, that liberates us from our Self-imposed bondage. In that moment of forgiving ourselves for being less than the *good* person we want to be, we are the good person we want to be; we are the values-inspired person we fell short of being at an earlier time. In this way forgiveness is liberating.

What all of this points to is that transformative change cannot be realized until we resolve not only the one-up/one-down paradigm that has bedeviled our relationships with one another throughout history, but also, and more importantly, the power dynamic that allows the political world to operate in the authoritarian way it does in which we are one-down to ourselves. This is so regardless of the particular power role we may occupy, for whether we are one-up or one-down, we are all trying to compensate for this devastating psychology that, to one degree or another, has defined us since birth. By cultivating the self-actualizing art of forgiving ourselves, we are then able to live with ourselves as a free human being.

This wholesome practice is the golden road to our heart values. It is in this moment that we expose ourselves to our inherent compassion and kindness, ethical integrity and moral courage. We lay bare who we really are in all of its naked glory. We do so because in forgiving ourselves—in realizing this state of openness and vulnerability—we also contact two of the most important values of the heart—humility and modesty. This is acceptance unadorned. Forgiving ourselves as a momentary instance of life is the love that is required to unlock our heart values and make them available to our practice in the world.

For activists especially, being able to forgive ourselves has the added benefit of being able to forgive others. This is an essential behavior in a practice dedicated to promoting wholesome relationships. Like most matters in life, forgiveness begins at home, with ourselves; what we extend to others is only real to the extent that we are able to provide the same gift to ourselves. This is the road to reconciliation, which is the prelude to a truly peaceful society.

Our facility for forgiveness allows us to avoid the error mentioned already—the self-defeating approach of treating ego

as an enemy. Unfortunately, making an enemy out of our oppo-
nent is so representative of a political activist practice.

Ultimately, forgiving ourselves involves accepting responsibility for ego. Rather than warring, we make friends with it,
expressing our gratitude to "I" for being there for us when we
weren't yet prepared to be there for ourselves. We thank ego for
taking care of us in ways which were helpful—even necessary—
to get us to the developmental stage we are at today. Despite
that ego has also been counterproductive and often self-
defeating to becoming a responsible being—and that yes, it has
blocked as much as it has advanced liberation—forgiving
ourselves for having been (and for still being) ego is essential to
coming to live with ego, not as the enemy, but as another
passing phenomena, much like us.

In a more general fashion, forgiving ourselves means
coming to terms with the compromises we have made with
political power over time—with all the seemingly powerful
people in our lives who have ruled us through our acquies-
cence and participation around age, sex, race, nationality, class,
and the many other power arrangements we share with them.
This consciousness allows us to soften, to be less harsh and
rejecting, and to be more forgiving of others, as we reconcile
matters about ourselves that we'd just as soon forget. We
don't dwell on them, but we do recognize and acknowledge
them. As this capacity expands, it eventually involves reconciliation with those whom we formerly judged as unacceptable. It
will be challenging to imagine being this way with someone
we once saw as an enemy. Yet it is indescribably satisfying
once we experience it. Coming home to and collapsing the
Other into one with us, we move on from the ghosts of the
past.

In our compassionate embrace of ourselves, we let go of the
past as a player in the present. This is priceless. We cease being
bound to that experience by repeating it, over and over again,

day after day. Only when we do this for ourselves are we a fully realized person in the living moment.

As much as forgiveness includes letting go of that which has made our growth problematic, it does not remove the original heart injuries that we have suffered along the way, nor disappear them from our lives as if they never happened. They are part of us and will be so in one way or the other for the rest of our lives. As long as we don't become attached to them, but learn to accept and live with them in wholesome ways, they will serve as building blocks for a more mature us. Those primal wounds are part of us, even as they become transformed from sources of grief to the bedrock of our emerging wisdom and power. These injuries to the heart have put their stamp on the people we are and have become, and they need to be honored as such. We do so by learning to live with them as legitimate parts of us.

Our development is never in a straight line. It is always a combination of some steps forward, some steps backward, and many steps sideways, including elements of growth that we weren't even aware were occurring at the time. Because of the blessing of incessant change, we are always evolving, even when we're stuck.

As it is with the rest of life, we too are a child of nature, subject to Mother's laws of nonlinear change, tipping points, positive feedback loops, and other unexpected twists and turns in the road. We are a lot closer to where we want to be than most of us appreciate, as evidenced by the way increasing numbers of us are responding to this dying civilization with love and integrity. As children of nature, it is entirely conceivable that we could make an exponential leap from a lily pond that, while only half–filled with virtuous flowers today, we will find completely filled tomorrow.

But it is also possible that we will not realize our purpose because we continue to demonstrate a maddening attachment to behaviors that have long worn-out whatever use and value they may have had at another time, and are quite frankly contrary to living life as it presently is. There is no guarantee of eventual success for our liberating mission.

But by continually discovering and acting upon the awareness that we can live quite well without ego, thank you, we are at least on the right path, wherever that leads.

EQUANIMITY AND RESISTANCE

Seemingly disparate, even contradictory, equanimity and resistance are nevertheless each fundamental to accepting life as it is, and to acting appropriately to an unconditioned state of mindfulness that enhances and advances human liberation.

Equanimity would appear to be more simpatico with acceptance: quite simply, it is our state of being when we accept life for what it is at any given moment. Regardless of whatever else is happening, we remain calm, steady, centered and balanced. At least in that moment, we are immune to that which the Insight Meditation Center of Redwood City, California has called "the eight worldly winds of praise and blame, success and failure, pleasure and pain, fame and disrepute." In short, our behavior is not influenced by ego even when we are in the presence of "I."

As this suggests, it is not only in the negative experiences of life that we maintain an evenness of mind and temperament; equanimity also includes not being "carried away" by those moments that bring us great joy and happiness as well. In both instances, we maintain the person we are, and avoid falling prey to ego's volatile, unstable, exaggerated disturbances. We act as if it is all part of the passing moment. Which it is.

This is not to say that we anesthetize ourselves from our feelings. We wouldn't be accepting of who we are if we did this. Being robotic is quite different than accepting what is. Rather, when we are equable, we remain personally unattached from ego's judgments and opinions about what is happening. We are very much aware of our thoughts and feelings, and make note of them. And we naturally are aware of sadness or happiness, whenever a particular experience calls these forth. It is healthy that we express ourselves appropriately. But we forsake the temptation to convert emotions into the property of "I" and to hold on to them beyond their moment.

Equanimity arises when we can live as a free person in the presence of ego. That is the heart of acceptance, the essence of liberation. We should not misunderstand liberation as a state that arises when we are without ego, which would miss the point about the importance of acceptance to revolution; equanimity and liberation are not what we experience when we rid our lives of that which oppose this state.

The distinctive quality and unique contribution of acceptance to human liberation is this: it is the unconditional condition that must be present in order for us to be free when ego is present. Liberation is only real when we can live our lives as free human beings with life as it is, not necessarily as we might want it to be. Ironically, it is only when we do this, without trying to impose upon life conditions that it be otherwise, that we are able to realize—inadvertently, unexpectedly—the world we have wanted all along, a world that is good enough.

Given what I have said about equanimity as the embodiment of acceptance, it would appear that this leaves very little room, if any, to consider resistance as a legitimate behavior of such a practice. But just as politically-motivated activists mistakenly view acceptance of what is, including that which we rightly oppose, as a betrayal of the revolution, so too do we equally err in equating resistance to that which threatens to diminish the sanctify of life—including doing so to whatever extent is required to defend and protect endangered life—as a violation of living our lives with unqualified acceptance. In fact, standing up for life is an act essential to accepting life.

Contrary to what we may think, accepting life is not the same as submitting to the very systems of oppression that we oppose. Spiritual warriors and values activists are not passive in the face of evil. As it is with our political sisters and brothers, and anyone else with the courage to stand up to the diminishment of life, we resist when it is necessary.

Rather, what distinguishes activists who accept life is the way in which we go about resisting. Committing to the sacredness of life necessitates resisting that which threatens the existential integrity of another living soul. Defending our own and another's wellbeing, safety, and happiness from the threat or act of another that attempts to deny these necessities is integrally part of what it means to be an activist for human liberation.

However, when we do so, we don't resist with any purpose other than stopping the offending behavior. Our intention is not to go beyond this, to inflict harm, punishment, retribution, or to impose our power over the offending party. We refrain from Self-righteous judgment. Our intention is the way of peace, which means the manner in which we approach this task is nonviolent, both in deed and in manner. Rather than reflexively retaliating in the way we typically do in political society when faced with an assault on our own or another's life—tit for tat— we may step aside from or go around the threat, especially when direct confrontation will only exacerbate rather than address skillfully the situation we face; or we may use the aggressive energy of the other against them, or anything else of a nonviolent nature that prevents the threatened action from being consummated. Most importantly, we may choose to not make ourselves available for abuse when such a choice is viable, or even engage in accommodation or adaptation where possible as long as our actions—and this is crucial—satisfy our basic requirement of blocking the threat to life, and hence remaining a free human being in the process. What is involved here, in other words, is not an either/or proposition; like so much else in life, resistance is colored in various shades of grey.

When peace-oriented, we tend to be more imaginative and creative, not stuck in the standard ways of violence-oriented resistance. We're receptive to approaches that are less likely to perpetuate conflict. Since we have no ulterior desire to impose our control over the other, we are more likely to leave the engagement without the residue of revenge poisoning the outcome, which would likely create a new round of life-threatening hostilities.

However, while performed nonviolently, our actions do not preclude the use of physical force when required to stop the actions of another. The key here is located in Sharon Salzberg's statement; *"What is most important is the way in which we take action."* If our manner of resistance has the intention of inflicting harm, exacting retribution or punishment, or otherwise acting beyond the sole purpose of preventing the evil conduct of another, then this behavior exceeds anything that would be considered appropriate to a peaceful intervention.

Two critical, interrelated matters here are decisive in allowing us to resist the life-threatening other in a wholesome, moral fashion. The first is that we accept our adversary as an instance of life much like ourselves. In so doing, we are less likely to demonize them. Filtering our actions through a lens of acceptance makes it much more difficult to reduce the other to a one-dimensional fiend. Admittedly, this is especially challenging when confronted with behavior that exhibits evil intent, which is most likely to elicit behavior from us that is quite different from that of accepting the other as a fellow living being. As always, we are imperfect beings who are only committed to doing the best we can.

The second but closely related quality for a practice of principled resistance is to avoid personalizing the actions of the other.

Their life-threatening behavior must be resisted, to be sure, to honor and preserve the threatened life. But in a world of "I," confrontations and conflicts typically degenerate into personal struggles between egos, whose need to dominate and destroy eclipses a saner consideration. These interactions frequently go way beyond the needs of the matter at hand; however, when we successfully avoid taking the conflict personally, ego is removed from our behavior, and we are able to limit our resistance to getting the job done in a virtuous fashion. This approach distinguishes a practice of resistance based upon the bare bones of what is factually happening from its hostile counterpart.

Given the emotions involved in life-threatening situations, as well as our own state of spiritual evolution, we may not succeed in doing this, succumbing instead to our fears and engaging in the more primitive behaviors of ego. The ferocity of the other's assault may be too much for anyone but the exceptional amongst us to act in a wholesome fashion. In that case, we find ourselves resorting to a more bellicose resistance.

When this occurs, we must acknowledge our acts when we finally have some space to do so, see them for what they are, and with heartfelt sincerity forgive ourselves and, if possible, ask forgiveness of the other. As I have emphasized, accepting ourselves as the human beings we are, in all of our diverse, contradictory, imperfect ways, is one of the most important things we can do in this life as a human being, but especially as an activist. In a very essential way, it is this act above all that liberates us, for it goes to the heart of undercutting ego's reinforcement of our one-down status through blame and shame. In an instance of inflicting harm, only by allowing ourselves to fully experience our remorse can we forgive ourselves, as well as extend heartfelt apologies and requests for forgiveness to others, with appropriate grace and humility.

Important here is that we don't ignore an instance of violent behavior or excuse it with Self-justifications of "Oh, well, that's life," or "In order to save life, sometimes you have to harm or take a life." While there may be some truth in such statements, when we employ them or any other seemingly reasonable rationalization, we miss what acceptance in the face of evil is all about. The way to an increasingly consistent practice of nonviolent resistance is to take responsibility for ourselves and our behavior, and especially for any exception to our vow of nonviolence, no matter how justified it may appear to be at the time. Only then can we properly experience the grief we naturally feel in our hearts whenever we harm or destroy another life. This is central to honoring life as life.

Our purpose in resisting the expression of evil is not eradicating its perpetrator, but learning to live with oppressive others successfully as a free human being. This includes resisting in a moral, principled way those whose conduct would deny life. That is the task of a transformative activist. This is part of the path of liberation. We resist those who do evil but do so with the humility of knowing that they, too, are fellow living beings, and that we, but for the grace of God or a roll of the cosmic dice, could be them.

CHAPTER FOUR

RECLAIMING OUR POWER

TAKING RESPONSIBIITY FOR OURSELVES

While not participating in or otherwise supporting power relationships, it is critical we avoid the equally fatal error of dismissing the importance of power to liberation. To do so would be an instance of throwing out the good with the bad, a behavior not unknown to activists.

The difference between the two is that while political power is about dominating and controlling life, liberating power is found in accepting life as it is. Rather than going through daily life as an ego-appointed Self, we live life as it presents itself at any given moment. Regardless of circumstances, we are who we are. This is the power of being real. Not dependent upon a surrogate external to us, but rather something we do for ourselves—this is properly understood as *empowerment*.

But what brings empowerment to life, causing it to be actionable in our daily lives? At least three essential elements must be present. These are the fundamental states we must realize in our daily practice if we are to more closely approximate the empowered us. Being responsible for ourselves and our actions is one of them.

The willingness to assume responsibility for ourselves is the crucial benchmark of a true grownup, a spiritually mature person. It is not something another person can do for us, no matter how well-intentioned they may be. It begins, as it always does with matters of liberation, by accepting ourselves for the instance of life that we are.

Specifically, being responsible for ourselves can only occur when we are responsive to our heart values as virtuous human beings, as well as acknowledging the presence of ego and the oppressive/oppressed role it places us in. Assuming this level of responsibility affords us the power necessary to engage in a practice that exemplifies peace, freedom, and social justice. Only when we live without the stand-in of "I" and its false promises, are we truly responsible for ourselves and the living beings we really are.

Significant to this is our willingness to make choices in our lives—looking at today and asking ourselves, "Is this what I want to be doing today?"—no matter how circumscribed and limited they may be in our less than perfect world, *we act on this world*, anyway. I don't suggest that we aren't affected, and perhaps profoundly so, by our arbitrary circumstances or the travail of daily existence. These play a substantial role in our lives.

But to what extent, and in what manner is up to us? How we choose to respond to their presence is critical. We have the power of choice here if we elect to use it. Life doesn't have to simply happen to us; we can decide how to respond to the cards we are dealt. And while rarely, if ever, can we change our lives so as to eliminate the pain and suffering that go with being a human being on this planet, we can certainly learn to live with life in ways that allow us to be the good-enough human beings we are intended to be.

We have to forgo the practice common to Civilized humans, and especially those of us who serve as activists, of blaming others for our lives. Being responsible for ourselves entails no longer holding others responsible for making our circumstances better by changing *their* oppressive ways—something that we consider necessary to improving *our* general lot. People don't undertake genuine change through force and submission. Despite the oppressive role that others play in our lives, we nevertheless must accept responsibility for what needs to be done if we are to be free. We are responsible for our liberation, not someone else. And we exercise this responsibility by choosing how we live with the specific conditions and circumstances of our existence, the good and the bad.

Being responsible for ourselves, we cease giving our inherent power away to "I," or to all the embodied expressions of "I" in the world who want to control us. When we give ego less of our power, we also cease giving others our power—to take care of us, to live our lives for us, to dominate and control us in a variety of ways: even to liberate us. We empower ourselves by healing and closing the primal split that defines Civilized reality, and we begin to live as the whole beings that we originally are. Rather than make others responsible for our situation in life, we assume this for ourselves.

This includes taking responsibility for our role in our oppression. We cannot be agents of our liberation unless we are also responsible for our oppression, and this regardless of the fact that we are also *blameless victims.* By recognizing that in order for the oppressive situation to exist, we have to be present and participating by playing our designated role of the oppressed, and to bear this awareness without at the same time beating ourselves up: this empowers us to respond to it and *do* something about it. This consciousness empowers us to recognize that we are also responsible for our liberation, which is the step-ping stone toward acting on our liberation: being free.

This further underscores why trying to remedy our lives by blaming others is a fool's errand. It is almost always a mistake to try to force another to change their ways as a necessary condition for the life we want. Inevitably, as history teaches us, this will only result in conflict and a "resolution" that at best only seeds the ground for further conflict. As when it's raining, rather than shaking our fist at and cursing the dark clouds, we simply open an umbrella, come in out of the rain, and change our wet clothes—or come up with something else if those don't work! This is the behavior of a responsible human being when we actually live the changes we would like to see in our lives, behaving as the free human beings we can be anytime we choose to.

There are no shortcuts here, no half-hearted efforts to empowerment. Being free is not contingent on the world accom-modating us. It is not about changing life so it aligns with our vision of what we think life should be. It is being that liberated person, acting on the power we already have when we accept responsibility for who we are and the choices we can make.

Power is inherently benign. When it is the expression of heartfelt choice, exercised for its own sake, it is quiet and unob-trusive, even invisible. Responsible to the world we live in and to all the other living beings we share it with, it isn't the exer-cise of power that tries to force peace and freedom down the world's throat, or to be people we're not. We aren't trying to rid our lives of ego. Rather, inspired by and responsive to the moral murmurings of the heart, we simply are peace and social justice. That's all. That's good enough.

THE POWER OF POWERLESSNESS

The superb paradox of power is that it exists for us only when we finally accept our essential powerlessness. It is one of those delicious ironies, an awareness that most of us don't willingly see in our retreat to the usual defenses. We are more likely to stumble upon it when we fall on our face, and at least for a moment recognize what a laugh all this struggle is.

This is the moment when we cease trying to control the passing show we call life. This is empowerment, not being in control of life, but being with life—present in the moment of now, accepting life as it presents itself to us—we are truly free.

The wisdom of powerlessness defies the logic of traditional activism, as well as Civilization itself. Both rest upon the premise that we are free only when we are in control of our world. Only then can we impose order and structure—the way things *should* run—upon life.

Ironically, when we let go of this ego-driven need to exert power over our circumstances, we become empowered. We know this by the way we behave with another living being. If we surrender to what is the inescapable truth of our existence—our essential powerlessness—we finally *rejoin* our true nature, open and receptive, and in so doing become liberated.

At the heart of acknowledging our powerless state lies acceptance that we're here one moment and gone the next. We are then able to see that the only moment that really counts is the one we're actually living, right now. This is where the revolution of everyday life takes place. Not at some future time when the revolution has won and come to power. Simple, perhaps. But yet, as we know, not quite that simple either.

As I have discussed earlier, what prevents us from accepting our powerless state is our unwillingness to embrace our always-pending death and the wise counsel it has to offer us for how we live our lives from one moment to the next. Rather, we go about our daily existence in defiance of our momentary condition, postponing the only life we have to sometime other than now... acting as if we are in control of our lives.

But when we are guided by the fleeting nature of life we cease trying to control it, honoring not only that its impermanence can never be governed, but that the effort to do so is pure madness!

Accepting life as a moment-to-moment adventure and living our lives as best we can in approximation of this fact, we are unburdened of our millennia-long struggle to make our existence something other than what it is. A soul-rendering sigh arises from the depths of our being when we finally detach ourselves from this ball and chain. In itself, this release is empowering; our heart is emptied of the punishing load we had placed on it. Accepting this relieves us of the suffering that inevitably follows from resisting our fundamental powerlessness. The shoulds and expectations imprisoning life fall away. We *are* focused on the moment, and in so being, are lighter.

This awakening often occurs when we trip over ourselves in our effort to be in control. I remember very clearly an example of this in my life when I heard the disrespectful garbage that was coming out of my mouth with my children one afternoon and was both startled and ashamed to hear how unkind I was being. That was one of the life-changing moments in my life. My initial response to their "disrespectful" behavior was to be annoyed with being opposed, for treating me as someone less than I thought I was, a parent and adult who should be obeyed. It is not easy to face the truth of our powerlessness when we believe we are in charge.

But this can also be a blessed moment, a wake-up call to the complete absurdity of trying to control life. In this moment of brilliant consciousness, we become friends with our powerlessness, rather than continuing an existence of denial. We're not as frightened by it, not as defensive about being exposed for who we are. Perhaps initially we are rendered silent by our self-discovery about the fraudulence of "I," with only a silly smile of wonder on our face to testify to our dawning awareness. Or maybe we respond with a burst of laughter arising from our depths with such intensity that it stuns in wonder the attention of anyone around us. Or maybe, as was the case for me, we're just chagrined, and ashamed, and finally, apologetic, with a memory that has followed me—with laughter whenever I recall it—the rest of my life, to remember and build on.

However expressed, this moment of sanity can be absolutely hilarious. Recognizing the absence of control over our circumstances is one of the best jokes in the universe, one that can only be truly appreciated by laughing, not so much at ourselves, but at the undeniable clarity of the moment. With this heartfelt awareness we come to fully accept what has been in plain sight all along: we're not in control and never have been.

Appreciating the humor of the situation helps us to come to terms with our powerlessness. Humor allows us to accept our ego-centric Selves for the pretenders they are. It's the grease that lubricates the rusty wheels of self-acceptance, allowing us to see that, despite our efforts to the contrary, life happens anyway. Humor is most valuable here in lowering our defenses, breaking through the shield of Self-importance ego defends itself with, and bringing us to a place where it's okay to be one who is not in control.

In these situations, humor can be our saving grace, an expression from our depths that allows us to grow. Humor is the grease preventing us from getting stuck on what "coulda" and "shoulda" been, and to move on with what is. In a very important way, humor and laughter are ways we can painlessly accept our powerlessness: to let go of trying to be someone other than who we are.

Though often dismissed as less than consequential in the political world, or used to denigrate, mock, or hurt, humor is nevertheless a potential source of liberating power. At its best, humor allows us to enjoy a moment of acceptance—of seeing both self and Self. While humbling, this strength-of-character moment arises from the illumination of who we really are and the empowerment that accompanies this insight.

Becoming a person of heart liberates energies that have been suppressed to maintain the illusion of "I." These moments are exquisite. Releasing from the games we play with ourselves and others in an attempt to deny our basic truth creates a boundless sense of unclaimed space as expressed in our outburst of laughter. In these spontaneous, non-scripted moments, we laugh with the joy of what we see: humor undercuts our need for "I." It allows us to be serious about ourselves, while at the same time not taking our Selves seriously at all.

To suddenly embrace this fundamental fact of life, however, is challenging for so many of us, as evidenced by the lives of avoidance and denial we have lived through the years. After all, our (continuing) unwillingness to accept our powerlessness in this world creates stuck ego, the phenomenon that dominates so many of us and exerts a powerful influence in the world. In this moment of recognition we must embrace ourselves gently. We may laugh at ourselves for playing the fool for so long, but we do so with compassion: we laugh the laughter found in a deep, loving hug of acceptance.

It is important that we not forget the fear of non-existence that has blocked our recognition of our essential powerlessness for so long. It is precisely this awareness that we've been running away from all of our lives. In this moment of self-recognition, we also honor this fear as part of us. This awareness, embedded within our humor, opens the door to our intrinsic kindness and compassion with ourselves, as well as toward our fellow beings who are entangled in the same daily struggles of power and control that we are.

Letting go of "I" as our security blanket is existentially momentous, though in retrospect, as we continue to live our lives, it may not appear to be such a big deal. What we learn when we surrender to powerlessness is that the truth of who we are is something we can live with. We are not devastated with our discovery of ourselves as momentary sparks in the universe. When we finally risk stepping into the unknown, crossing that existential power chasm, we find that not only do we survive, we flourish, even if that means nothing more than being happy with whom we are. Which is also another very big deal.

No longer afraid of being out of control, we expand beyond ego, welcoming opportunities and possibilities we rejected as impossible at an earlier time, if we even considered them at all. We are empowered to act on them. Empowerment is ultimately something we do for us, a gift we give to ourselves.

Our experience of life becomes more immediate. We are alive in ways that we haven't been before. Whether we're doing the dishes, writing a poem, or driving to work, we are present, no longer compulsively imposing order and structure upon matters which do quite well without ego's intervention. Like a cloud that is forever shifting and mutating, we now have space, clarity, and energy we didn't have before. This is what it means to be living in this new, unclaimed space. In many ways, the same life. Just happier.

Despite the fact that our existence continues to be an unavoidable mixed bag, it is nevertheless a life we find worth living, one that we generally consider to be *good enough*. The ups and the downs are accepted for what they are, allowed to move on as they will when we are not attached to either. Being more selfless, we find life to be balanced, less extreme and volatile. We experience equanimity as a regular presence in our daily affairs. We show up every day with purpose, sometimes even passion, rather than going through the motions. Our actions have integrity and speak to the values they increasingly honor. We are just "regular" people: what you see is what you get.

In addition to the sense of rightness that acceptance of our ordinariness imparts, it also offers great benefits in our relationships with others. As we can interact with them without having to play a political role of one-up or one-down, we are people who help allow for wholesome interactions. When we speak and walk the truth of our hearts, we are able to do our part unconditionally because it feels right, and we do so regardless of how others behave. It is our reward, if you will, for being who we are. Life is experienced as something we value. Being congruent with ourselves allows us to be at home with the universe.

Despite the liberation we experience when we accept life, it does not protect us from the losses inherent to mortal existence. Interestingly, life continues to be pretty much as it was before we accepted our powerlessness, and in many ways is the same as it has always been. For the most part, there is not a dramatic difference. The changes are subtler: while we may still encounter conflict and discord in the political world, we don't add to or become ensnared in it; we don't rise to the bait, ego-compelled to contribute our unwholesome two cents. We understand that these aren't the problems they might have been for us in the past now that we accept that there is really nothing we can do about them.

When we accept our innate powerlessness, we now have the question of how we are to live with this truth. That is the key to human liberation. No longer struggling to make them conform to what we feel they should be, we recognize our lives for what they are, and therefore see clearly what is and what is not required of us. Without an agenda of obligations to accomplish, we can attend to what needs to be done in the present moment, for us, and for the world we increasingly care about. When things are not going well, accepting our powerlessness allows us to remain afloat and move on with our lives, knowing that this, too, will pass; when life is going well, however, we don't get carried away, clinging to the moment that we know is already passing. This is the power of no-power, the power of no-control: the power of surrendering to what is.

This power allows us to be responsible for ourselves in the end, not by behaving in ways expected of political society, but as beings harmonious with our interconnected existence: by finally accepting our true dimensions, we behave more modestly, more graciously with the rest of nature. We are regular people, no longer needing power over life to live our lives, to be someone. We are able to act with the only power we can ever know as human beings, the power of being real.

BEING ALONE WITH OURSELVES

As we tumble down the waterfall of birth into life, entering our first moments as individual drops of water, we experience ourselves as alone in the universe. This is a fact of human existence, one seemingly contradictory to our equally natural state of interbeing with the rest of the universe, but no less true for being so. The problem is that unless the social environment we are born into envelops us with a sense of our interconnection, this state of absolute aloneness pervades and dominates us, inducing a potentially debilitating terror, a fear of life. In this condition, we cannot tolerate being alone with ourselves. Disconnected from our inherent state of interbeing, we are alone with ourselves, powerless, with a profound dread of nonbeing.

Though last in our discussion of the three most important qualities Civilized humankind must possess in order to empower ourselves, the ability to be alone with ourselves is second to none in terms of its importance. For the realization and exercise of this capacity is nothing less than the ability to live without "I"—if not without its presence, then at least without the influence it exercises on the way we go about living our lives from one moment to the next.

Placing such an emphasis upon the individual person might at first glance appear to contradict, even undermine, my basic endorsement of the importance of interbeing to a liberated existence; it may even appear to be flirting with a variation of ego's radical individualism. Under the guise of promoting liberation, might this focus on the ability to be alone be yet another slick attempt on the part of ego to perpetuate a separate and independent Self?

Yet, as with other seemingly contradictory states, interbeing and individuality exist in perfect harmony, notwithstanding the tendency of Civilized beings to polarize them into separate entities. And it is precisely this capacity to be alone with ourselves —with the fact of our original and unique condition in the universe—that allows us to bear the concomitant tension between our individuality and our interbeing. Accepting our solitary state, without a dependency upon ego to do what only we can do for ourselves, allows us to act with the integrity of heart commitment. It is the acceptance of ourselves as a momentary presence, powerless to prevent our pending death.

Within the interconnected universe, there exist countless sparks of life, like so many stars in the night sky, affected by and contributing to the web of life. Each one of us is one of these unique sparks, no one identical to another. When all is reduced to its bare essence, it is we, these seemingly endless inconsequential sparks of light, who create the world we live in by the choices we make.

For one to be truly liberated, these are decisions that can only be made when we are alone with ourselves, despite the importance of the interdependent whole that we are part of. While what we choose and how we subsequently act are the product of many actors, both alive and dead, the choice is always ours alone. It is our responsibility.

We make these decisions all the time, every day, whether we're conscious of doing so or not. Moment by moment, they are the ways we respond or react to our situation. Regardless of the particulars, be they propitious, lousy, or garden variety no-big-deal, each and every one of us is making choices. This is so even when we're not making a choice, which of course is a choice in itself.

How we respond to situations—momentous or "unimportant"—contributes not only to the constant creation of the world we live in, but equally to the person we are evolving toward being. The absence of values constancy in our behaviors makes all the difference, as when we don't stand up for what we claim to value with the everyday reliability that is warranted, and are distracted instead by the laziness, indifference, carelessness, cowardness, or commotion that permeates so much of everyday life. We're much more disposed to getting along and going along with the prevailing norm, not sticking our necks out or "causing trouble," of giving in to what is expected of us rather than being true to what we know is right. We disempower ourselves because we are not secure in being ourselves, with being alone with ourselves, with the moral beings that we inherently are.

Despite the fact that we are all part of an interconnected whole, we are also ultimately alone, and must accept the responsibility that it entails if we are be liberated. To do so closes the circle of the dilemma we entered this world with and has haunted our lives ever since: of being so terribly on our own, ignorant of our connection with the rest of life, confronted with the dread of our always-pending death, absolutely disempowered in this political context. This state has challenged and often overwhelmed so many of us, causing us to seek refuge in stuck ego and its various political expressions, being a people of innate values who don't act on these values with the constancy required to be a moral presence.

When we are able to live with being alone, we are capable of being responsible to our heart values, no longer dreading the empty space of existence that we attempt to fill with "I." This hole is now whole once we live wholesomely with this emptiness. As with accepting our absence of control, we discover that not only do we survive, but we likely flourish as well. We discover that empty space is not something to fear, but to the contrary, is the fertile groundlessness that enables growth and transformation. We are authentically us, the shooting star that momentarily flashes across the night sky. The solitude we realize allows us also to be less influenced by the egos of others and by the ego-contaminated environment of our political world. To the extent that we are able to absent its influence in our choices and subsequent behavior, we live without ego.

In finally being at home with ourselves, discovering and accepting ourselves as the space beyond ego, we avoid the duality of selfish individualism and mass conformity, two sides of the same disempowered coin that has characterized Civilized beings. No longer is our capacity to be alone compromised by the political world we live in, with its demands for submission to external authority, the dehumanizing routines of industrial civilization, and the consumer culture that atomize our relationships into the alienated arrangements of what David Riesman once identified as "the lonely crowd." The solitude that comes with being alone with ourselves provides us with an opportunity to not only be present without "I"—it also allows us to be real with the rest of life.

EMPOWERED INDIVIDUALS, VALUES-BASED COMMUNITIES

Although understandable, it would be a mistake to suggest that empowerment of the individual is at the expense of the community. Our autonomy does not translate into living independent of the rest of life without consideration that our actions have social consequences. Being empowered includes being responsible for ourselves and our behaviors. We are cognizant of how our actions vibrate out into the universe, like rings in a pond radiating from a dropped pebble, however modest that may initially appear to be.

Furthermore, the power we realize by accepting our essential powerlessness is not one used at the expense of others. To the contrary, when we acknowledge our inability to control life and accept its/our impermanence, we recognize these as conditions we share with all living beings, as inexorable facts of life. Kindness and compassion emerge in our interactions as a consequence of this awareness, along with humility and modesty. With our earlier sense of separation and superiority receding, we're capable of seeing we're all in this moment of life together. As such, we also recognize that we both influence and are influenced by our human and non-human brethren in nature. Our acts always have consequences beyond ourselves, and are governed accordingly with this awareness.

And while the facility to be alone with ourselves is indispensable to our individual empowerment, it can also be misunderstood as being at the expense of the collective whole. There is a fine line between the person who isolates themselves from others because they are alienated from themselves, which causes them to be uncomfortable with their fellow beings, and one who is self-possessed, at home with themselves, hence, able to be with a variety of people in a diversity of situations. It is precisely this capacity to be relaxed with the person we actually are that grants us the power to engage in wholesome relationships with others, ones that are clean of Self. While interdependent with the rest of life, we are no longer pathologically codependent upon an ego and its human representatives in the political world to get us through life. Capable of being with ourselves, our relationships are not born out of neediness or insufficiency.

The origin of the societal irresponsibility that has brought us to this critical juncture, on this planet, at this time, rests significantly in our being stuck in our sense of being a discreet "I." In such a state, we don't have sufficient awareness of our interconnection to the collective whole, and therefore no sense of our responsibility to others. We remain blind to the fact that what we do every day and the state of the world cannot be understood apart from each other. We can only accept this awareness when we are empowered. This is a vital requirement for any society that hopes to successfully adapt to the unprecedented reality we are already entering, and to begin to move in a healthy, sustainable direction.

In equating individual empowerment with a viable social whole, I must not be misunderstood as advocating "rugged individualism," the mythological state Americans especially pride ourselves on as personifying who we are as a people and why we are the exceptional entities we claim to be. This representation of our national character—a people who can go it alone, not needing anyone else to meet our needs—is often presented to the rest of humanity to explain our country's preeminent position of power in the world.

In reality, this myth is nothing more than a version of the age-old illusion of an independent Self which Civilized human beings have spent lifetimes believing about ourselves, denying any interconnection with or responsibility for the rest of life. Given the overwhelming evidence of how we need and depend upon each other and the rest of the natural world for our daily lives, this conceit would be risible if it weren't for the sad and dangerous consequences resulting from our denial of such a fundamental fact. It is inconceivable that we could entertain the notion that we could survive for a moment on Planet Earth without the assistance of other living beings. Yet we do.

Individualism, rugged or otherwise, does not hold the essential social power that an empowered people possess. This enables us to develop the resilient, adaptive communities required for a transformative age. To the contrary, ego-driven individualism seriously impedes our ability to cooperate and work with each other in the manner required to successfully transition to the radically new normal we have already entered. We can only accomplish this unprecedented task through mutual aid, collaboration, and non-authoritarian social arrangements. These are efforts that only empowered individuals can undertake successfully, not the heroic actions of lone rangers.

As empowered beings, power is no longer an issue for us. Having reached such a state, we cease needing to contend and compete. We can afford to recognize our commonality and the benefits we derive from meeting our needs through mutual effort. Our awareness of our state of interbeing results in conduct that is responsible to others.

Further encouraging this tendency, people who are so empowered are less likely to be a problem for others. We don't take out on them issues that are our own, and when we have disagreements or conflicts, we are more likely to work things out, not allow them to fester or turn into nasty, unnecessary situations. Because we no longer have a need to be on top, we are accommodating and flexible, receptive to the points of view of others. Our ego, because of its diminished role in our lives, is not as threatened by the egos of others; with less of a presence in our lives when we're responsible for ourselves, "I" does not require protection. In brief, we are good neighbors, conscientious partners, true comrades, people of integrity that others can count on.

Not only do we become aware of our responsibility to the larger community, we don't interpret the other as a burden or infringement on our freedom, which is often the response of those suffering raw individualism. Without ego's participation, we're more willing to participate in the community dance where sometimes we lead and sometimes we follow, but where other times we just stand aside and be present.

Finally, what we also have going for us is that cooperation is not a foreign concept to human beings. In fact, it is a natural way of being, as has been demonstrated for thousands of years, despite what we may have been taught to the contrary by the ruling class version of human history.

Empowered members are a necessity for a truly peaceful community of free individuals. Built upon selflessness, we create the integrity and solidarity that brings and keeps people together out of choice and in ways necessary for a society where it is important that people get along.

CHAPTER FIVE

COMPASSIONATE MINDFULNESS

HEART PRESENCE

As is with everything else in life, acceptance does not happen in a vacuum. It, too, has a context. Only, in this instance, the context is mindfulness; that is to say, it is consciousness without context, space minus the contamination of comments and opinions, interpretations and concepts, ideas and judgments, illusions and mirages; it is awareness unfiltered. Mindfulness is being present in the state of now. And we can only accept what is when we are fully present in the present. When we are mindful, we simply see what is. As Joseph Goldstein noted, mindfulness is "like a mirror that simply reflects whatever comes before it."

Seeing what is, mindfulness is the necessary condition-without-condition of a truly liberated being. Being mindful, we cannot help but accept what is, "pleasant or unpleasant, just as it is," as Sylvia Boorstein writes, "without either clinging to or rejecting it." This state of acceptance produces the clarity necessary to engage in a practice of transformative activism.

Unlike political (prescribed) consciousness, where life is reduced to a shadow of its true nature in binary concepts and abstract representations, mindfulness is consciousness unbounded. Open to what is, it does not run away from ambiguity, paradox, or contradiction. It allows for the equivocal and inconclusive. As our original, non-linear, pre-ego condition, mindfulness is whole consciousness. It is space, empty and unspoken for.

To accept what is, we see beyond ego's interpretations of what is. To fully accept life, we must be mindful of what is happening right now, regardless of "I's" subjective reaction.

When we see matters objectively, we avoid taking them personally, therefore politicizing them. This is indispensable for a transformative practice. Being mindful, we are a selfless presence, a momentary flash of light in the universe. There is no sense of a separate and distinct "I" mediating life for us through the prism of an independent Self.

We don't live in our heads when we're mindful. Mindfulness is uncluttered consciousness, a state without the mental chatter typically occupying so much of our attention and energy. When mindful, we are not planning tomorrow or regurgitating yesterday, forever lost in our thoughts about what we think is real. We are quiet, instead, even still. We are simply observing the truth of the moment.

Rather than reacting to our situation with pre-recorded assumptions and beliefs, we see what we see, responding appropriately with behaviors both spontaneous and heartfelt, commensurate to the present reality. We operate beyond the confines of our politically designated box, cruising in the living moment, instead.

As this suggests, mindfulness is not a passive activity or an empty exercise; to the contrary, it is the necessary prerequisite for skillful, wholesome action. Thich Nhat Hanh observes that

"Mindfulness must be engaged. Once there is seeing, there must be acting. Otherwise, what is the use of seeing?" This is precisely what mindfulness is for the activist.

Seeing clearly is not sufficient. Being fully present in the moment does not guarantee we will do the right thing. Rather, as Joseph Goldstein observes, *"Mindfulness means something more than just being in the present."* As he goes on to say, *"a more complete or larger understanding"* of mindfulness is one that includes *"a further dimension,"* what he calls *"an observing power of the mind"* or *"reflective capacity,"* where we *know* that we are observing something.

But even that understanding is not fully adequate. Here we really get down to the liberating potential of mindfulness. For as Goldstein goes on to explain, there is yet a third quality of mindfulness based on the fact that we can be observing our internal or external experiences *"through a filter of many different mind states"* where we react to what we see—clinging to this, rejecting that—and where we identify with something and hence act out upon it. This is not mindfulness. We are observing and recognizing, but if the mind is not free of such mind states —*"free of identification with what's happening"*—then we are not mindful. Instead, we are reactive. Only in the moment when we are aware of these mind states and not identifying with them are we mindful, and thus liberated.

The significance of this is particularly important for activists. It is the moment when we are able to observe and recognize our unwholesome mind states and have the potential to avoid reacting to or acting out on them. We have choice. And when we choose not to personalize our experience, we are in a state of equanimity. This is crucial. Expanding our awareness so that we don't identify with corrupting states of mind connects us with what we have spent lifetimes denying and defending ourselves against—the *heart tendency* to be real.

Historically, we have suppressed the wholehearted expression of our innate heart values, though they are potentially actionable whenever we choose. We normally dismiss them as inconvenient, unrealistic, impractical, and too ineffectual to hold their own in the political world of force, violence, and other unprincipled behavior. As a result, they remain on the periphery of our awareness, hidden from view, when not suppressed altogether. We don't see them as necessary and practical in everyday circumstances.

We cauterize the truth with denials that we actually have a choice. We allow the values that we pay lip service to to be constrained by fear and laziness, cowardliness and indifference, reducing us to the status of the proverbial bystander when our moral stance is required. Especially in the seemingly inconsequential, easily forgotten, common moments of life that we take (mindlessly) for granted: our thoughtless response to our spouse or child, or our silence after hearing a racist comment from one of our best friends, or our potentially dangerous middle-finger gesture toward a stranger on the highway when they cut us off.

Mindfulness provides us with the choice that we did not know existed before we were awake. Without this awareness, we can only react to life, senselessly following the dictates of the political programming we have been conditioned by for generations. It is only when we are mindfully awake that we are able to break through this cage of unfeeling, mechanically repetitious behaviors.

With commitment and discipline, we are able not only to be truly mindful from one moment to the next, but also to be behaviorally responsive to the values that emerge and become increasingly prominent. Our deepening mindfulness nurtures our capacity for choice, an incomparable faculty we must exercise as a condition of being free.

We always have the potential of choice, of choosing what to do in every moment, when we are fully present. As this capacity develops, our potential to do the right thing is no longer limited to life and death occasions when the severity of the situation prompts the best from us. Beyond these exceptional moments, we have the potential to respond to ordinary everyday situations with comparable moral integrity. When mindful, we can recognize the choices we have, and relinquish acting out our usual patterns. Our enhanced awareness enables us to be increasingly skillful in our selection of our behaviors from an unfiltered sense of what is right.

This clarity empowers us. We choose this and pass on that, making choices fully conscious of our heart values. This is the consciousness of a moral practice, of behavior beyond good intentions alone, where aims and actions are united as one.

This is the foundation of a society characterized by peace, freedom, and social justice.

EVERYDAY MINDLESSNESS

Most of us exercise at least a degree of mindfulness as we make our way through the demands of our daily lives, though even here it can be challenging to be fully awake with the rudimentary requirements of the moment. We are easily distracted, spaced out, and just not paying attention. Often, we complete our tasks without actually being *there*. That we are seemingly "mindful" with the mundane details of our lives is largely due to habit and routine. More often than not, we are in our heads, operating on automatic pilot.

Though we can usually get away with performing our daily tasks in this manner, we are typically consumed by their details and the stressors they often entail. Despite our so-called "labor saving" way of life, we are busier than ever. Rarely are we still, quiet, relaxed. This hectic state removes us from being fully present. A charade of living in the now disguises an essential mindlessness that infuses not only what we do, but how we go about doing so. We get the jobs of daily living done, but often at the expense of ourselves and others by acting out the tension, resentment, irritation, anger, boredom, and absence of heart that characterizes so much of our rote existence.

In this situation, we can't afford to see what *is* through the eyes of our innate moral authority. We continue to live the very same lives that are contrary to our heart values, a way of life which has been killing us all along. As we demonstrate every day, this peculiarly Civilized human feat can be achieved by splitting ourselves in two and doing the best we can with this arrangement. We go about our lives in a mindless fashion so that we can perform what we feel we must do while not acknowledging, even recognizing, how we really feel. We can't do otherwise and still live the lives that have engendered a collapsing society. This is the mindlessness of getting by.

This also involves repressing dimensions of ourselves that are incompatible with living a mindful way of life. We push to the margins of our awareness, and beyond, any longings for a more authentic existence, one responsive to our passions, that feels *real* to us. Denying a life fully lived, we feel we can't be that person right now. This reality is located in that sentiment many of us think and sometimes express at one time or another: *Is this all there is to life?*

Operating on the surface of our existence, this industrial efficiency does not allow us to penetrate to an awareness of the moment, of *the* moment. Because we are not fully of the moment, we don't value its singular importance to our lives. We tend to treat the passing moments of our lives as throwaways, instants we hilariously believe can be returned to at another more convenient time. Everyday consciousness is not realized with the kind of focus and presence—the necessary integrity of being here now—that exists when we're fully alive. We go about our lives as if we have forever to live, unmindful of the only moment that we have, the living moment that is always moving on.

———

It is the exceptional one amongst us who lives with the awareness of the fundamental impermanence of life, who uses our always-pending death as a guide to living. The rest of us acknowledge our mortality at arm's length, as an abstract idea. In essence, we are in denial about its reality.

This is illustrated by the difficulty that we as a society have in accepting aging as another stage of life. From the adulation of youth and the billion-dollar industry around maintaining an eternally youthful appearance, to the sidelining and ware-housing of older people, death is not something that is readily integrated into most of our lives.

Life as incessant change—life as death—is a constant reminder that nothing stays the same. And while this is a blessing when things are not going well for us—a bummer when they're just fine!—it's largely something we're not mindful of as we go about the actual business of living. Rather, we attempt to defy this law of nature by shaping our lives into routines and patterns, repeating them over and over again. In this way, we create the illusion of forever. By living formulaic lives, we delude ourselves with an illusion of permanence.

But there's a price to pay. In our efforts to force life to conform to "I's" need for immortality, denying ourselves the rhythm of mutability, our souls dry up and our spirits burn at half-light. Existence becomes a mindless, well-ordered affair consisting of unquestioned behaviors. We sacrifice the verve and energy that naturally arises when we are real and operating on all cylinders, settling for a muted existence instead.

As a consequence, we require stimulation to divert us from

the gnawing sense that things are not quite right, that we're not really alive. We escape to drugs, compulsive eating, "shop-'til-we-drop" consumerism, spectator sports, workaholism, pornography, the ubiquitous screens, conspiracies, and religion. Along with all the other addictive surrogates we use, these distractions dominate our lives from the moment we arise in the morning until we go to bed at night, killing time before it kills us. We occupy rather than live our lives.

Failing as it does to address our fundamental need to be real, the "now" of distraction and denial prevents us from being mindful in the living moment. It numbs our awareness of the moment we're in, necessitating another jolt of unreality in order to transport us to some moment other than the present.

This is sad when we understand that a sense of wholeness— the existential integrity that can only be found when we are real —is what we're really looking for in our lives when we opt for its poor substitutes. Unfortunately, it is located in the very same moment that we're running away from. Acquiescing to a mindless way of life, Civilized beings become prime candidates for an authoritarian order.

MINDFULNESS IN THE AGE OF SOCIAL COLLAPSE

As there is no minimizing the importance of mindfulness for the realization of peace and social justice, so is there no substitute for its presence in our lives as we enter the accelerating stages of social collapse. We will need to adapt and prepare as best we can for what is essentially an unknown, but undoubtedly challenging, existence. Increasingly, we will discover we can no longer count on the way of life we currently take for granted. We will need to wake up to reality if we are to live our lives in the world as it is and is more and more becoming. Existence will likely be bumpy and unsettling, especially for those of us who remain attached to a dying culture, one in which we are unprepared, especially for the violence—nature's, as well as humanity's—that we are already witnessing at the present time. This will be unavoidable. To survive, we will be forced to learn and relearn ways of taking care of ourselves and each other, so that we can not only survive, but do so in ways that make survival worth living.

In this context, mindfulness is essential. We must be alert to our changing circumstances, from those which are suddenly in our face, topsy-turvy, as well as those which are subtle, almost imperceptible, but whose consequences are just as profound and dangerous, especially when not responded to appropriately. We must be flexible, light on our feet, a people who can be adaptive to unfolding circumstances without being in control of them. We must refrain from taking things personally and acting out on unhealthy sentiments, practicing instead a consistent morality with the world as best we can.

Only an approach that goes with the ebb and flow of life, skillfully and ethically, will stimulate a transformative practice commensurate to the change happening all around us. It is important that we maintain our composure in varied situations, even when this means not having a clue as to what is to be done next, but willing to just hang in there with the powerless moment, fully present and ready to respond. We do our best and forgive ourselves when we fall short. These are all attributes of a mindful presence.

Further, we must disabuse ourselves of the political roles we impose on ourselves and others, the beliefs and convictions that have guided humankind since the beginning of our recorded history. We can begin, at least, with what it means to be a man and a woman. In the world we're entering, we can't afford to act out these self-destructive roles of domination and subjugation anymore. Each of us will need all of our humanity to live in this new normal we are entering. As the pending collapse tells us very clearly, we must now take that step (that risk) into the unknown and be the grownup human beings we have resisted being for so long. We can no longer afford to postpone this choice.

To be mindful at this point in time means to increasingly get in touch with the incalculable pain and suffering that we as humans have visited on ourselves and each other down through the years, as is graphically illustrated by the cataclysmic events that characterize our world today. We will have to come to terms with the irony that, at the very moment we have achieved unparalleled scientific, technological, material, and cultural wonders, as well as unmatched political and economic power—a brilliant success by the standards of our Civilization—the world that has emerged from all of this splendor is in a state of unraveling and disintegration.

In no small part, this is a result of the amoral genius behind those achievements. To create our Civilized wonder, we have had to conceal from ourselves the consequences of doing so: the human oppression that has gone into building the American Fantasy is a perfect example. This is an act of unadulterated mindlessness. We can't allow ourselves to be truly aware of the greed and violence that informs our quest—the rape, murder, plunder, and enslavement that have been a leitmotif of largely white male behavior throughout Civilization's history—without, at the same time, giving rise to the moral dissonance such consciousness would alarm us to.

We created the mythology of America, instead, and the false consciousness that proclaims us to be the land of moral exceptionalism. We insist that, despite an occasional, unfortunate mistake, we are the nation of freedom and equality, the paragon of democracy. And while there is truth in this Self-portrayal of ourselves as a virtuous nation found in the many examples of citizens and communities which have responded selflessly to meet a crisis, and which have demonstrated the kind, generous, and principled conduct we're capable of, there is also much that our high school history texts left out of their glorious narrations of our past and present that seriously belie our national image. In that light, it might be a wee bit more honest, and certainly a stimulant of growth for the body politic, if the American Dream was portrayed as a work in progress, a developmental stage on the pathway to a society that potentially could live its professed values consistently in the everyday world.

Circumstances now mandate a transformation of the moral values we have always professed from an occasional practice exhibited during exceptional times to a daily practice that becomes a regular feature of our relationship with the rest of the world in both the momentous and the mundane. This challenge is particularly important for any of us who consider ourselves to be warriors of the human spirit and agents for human liberation.

This transformation can only be accomplished by allowing for the truth of our hearts to emerge through mindful contact, a practice which activates our moral center. It puts us in touch with our essential goodness, our innate capacity for knowing what is right. This capacity is crucial to our understanding of what mindfulness is all about.

Though it is apolitical in outlook and detached in action, being mindful should not be misunderstood as being bereft of values. Rather than being impersonal and clinical, mindfulness is selfless and heartfelt. Because of its unique ability to see beyond ideology, political stereotypes, and the personal agendas that circumscribe consciousness and mire our practice in counterproductive behaviors, we are heart-present when we are mindful. Being so influences us to act upon our potential for generosity, lovingkindness, and compassion, for exhibiting courage, integrity, and equanimity, for being a person of peace, freedom and social justice. We are the liberated beings who are able to engage other beings as activists of love.

To conduct ourselves in this manner with the greater consistency we require at this juncture, we must also allow our everyday practice to be informed by a mindfulness that is both whole mind and whole heart. Not only does this include naming what we see and connecting the dots of our existence, it also involves privileging such typically feminine attributes as instinct, intuition, sensitivity, and feelings that have typically been dismissed by our patriarchal Civilization. These are insights from the mind and messages from the heart that we frequently ignore because they are politically inconvenient. This is our loss because these same qualities are often critical to being mindful, and therefore are the pathway to doing the right thing in a given moment. They are part of what we need to both honor and consult, serving as the wise counsel to the choices we make.

When heart and mind are dancing effortlessly together as an interdependent whole, we can make choices compatible with being a moral human being. We cease tying one arm behind our backs and shooting ourselves in the foot, unleashing instead the full potential of who we are and can be. In these moments, we trust ourselves to be true to the person we are, at peace with ourselves and congruent with the universe. By accessing dimensions of ourselves that have long been suppressed and inactive, we become the powerful living beings we are meant to be.

The challenge we face in our efforts to live in a collapsing, post-Civilized world is a willingness to realize, in everyday fashion, the potential we came into this world with, and at times exhibit. This is the potential to be whole with ourselves and the rest of life. Some might call this *being love.*

Since it is through our daily interactions with each other that we create the world we end up living in, a practice informed by acceptance and mindfulness allows love to be out in the open, an active player in our lives, no longer shrouded behind a curtain of political conditionality. Rather than operating in a *quid pro quo* culture, love is expressed for its own sake, because we are no longer judged as good, bad, or, for that matter judged at all. We simply accept each other as good enough. This is unconditional love.

PART THREE
THE PRACTICE OF THE PRACTICE

CHAPTER SIX

CULTIVATING MORAL ACTIVISM

"When you do something, you should burn yourself completely,
like a good bonfire, leaving no trace of yourself"
—Chögyam Trungpa

SKILLFUL EFFORT

For all but the exceptional amongst us who are blessed with a seemingly instinctual capacity to walk the talk, translating our noble intentions into a consistent everyday practice is the challenge of our existence, especially living as we do in the political world that doesn't encourage or support such behavior.

It is not that we lack the potential moral capacity. We come into this world as inherently good people.

Nevertheless, the display of this quality is uneven and erratic, and all too often non-existent, as evidenced in the relationships of men with women, whites with people of color, bosses with workers, adults with children, and all other relationships based on political considerations of power. Their characteristic dominance in our world easily gives the lie to claims of the inherent goodness of human beings.

The problem for Civilized humanity is that our heartfelt, natural selves are all too often out of harmony with our everyday conduct. We know in our heads what is *right*, and while inconsistent and half-hearted, we do demonstrate that we're quite capable of acting in virtuous ways. The challenge for a transformative practice, therefore, is how do we behave as people of moral values from one moment to the next? For this is what is needed if we are to be a truly democratic people, living an existence of peace and social justice in a collapsing society.

Returning to the acute observation of Rebecca Solnit in *A Paradise Built in Hell*, who, while noting that life-threatening disasters often inspire the very best in us, asks *"how do we maintain this degree of moral presence—this essential goodness—in the absence of life-threatening catastrophes?"* How do we *"stay awake in softer times because we are ordinarily sleepers, unaware of each other and of our true circumstances and selves? Disaster shocks us out of slumber, but only skillful effort keeps us awake."* (My emphasis.) This is the heart of the matter for activists seeking revolutionary change that is actually transformative.

We cannot realize the liberated human existence that our inborn moral nature intends us to live unless we can resolve this fundamental dilemma of Civilized human beings: to close the gap between the people we are and the people we are. We're not trying to create a new personhood out of whole cloth; we possess the essential goodness we require to be an agency of everyday moral rectitude. What we need to do, however, is commit ourselves to a conscientious practice of the practice in which we cultivate behaviors of values constancy. This is the spiritual foundation for the liberated way of life we seek.

The remainder of this book addresses this issue in a variety of ways, but especially here in the two chapters of Part III; and more specifically, the question of *how* we can forge an everyday

practice of spiritual values that in turn allows for the *what*—
peace, freedom, and social justice—to actually exist in the
world.

NOWHERE TO GO, NO ONE TO BE

To begin a proper discussion about closing the gap between
intention and practice—that which has divided what we intend
to do from how we actually go about doing so—it is important
that we first correct the fallacy that there is some kind of divide
we must close in the first place in order to realize a union
between the two. This will undoubtedly come as a surprise to all
of you who have noticed that, on more than one occasion, we
have made special note of this dichotomy as the fundamental
problem in human relations: with each other and the world, as
well as with ourselves.

But despite the fact that we have found such a conceptualization helpful in framing the issue that revolution is faced with, as
well as the important truth about the existential gulf that
divides us from ourselves and from life in general, it is this
binary vision itself that is the fundamental impairment of our
Civilization. Through ego, its purpose to exact control over life,
and its creation of an "I" to serve as the instrument of this
quest, a dualistic vison of life emerges, which blinds us to the
fact that who we are and who we want to be are essentially the
same person. Both exist right now.

Ironically, the most revolutionary thing we can do is to let go
of this misguided idea of an either/or existence. In the real
world, there is no bridge to "there," and no "there" to get to. It
is precisely the idea of this split that undermines being liberated
right now. Rather than acting as if the revolution is already here
anytime we choose, and being the whole beings we really are,
we spend lifetimes struggling to replace that which we judge
poorly with what we believe we should be instead. This is not

the revolution. When our efforts are motivated by the conviction that who we are is not who we should be, or the world we live in is not good enough, we have become counter-revolutionary.

By so doing, we lock ourselves into other divisive concepts, such as "yesterday" and "tomorrow," which remove us from the present moment and the only reality there is. This is where the revolution of human liberation lives, if it lives at all. To paraphrase the classic Zen axiom, getting where we want to be begins by letting go of the notion that there is anywhere to go. Appearances aside, the issue we face is not one of creating a "new" us by shedding the "old."

As with life in general, we are a mixture of contradictory, paradoxical features that, unfortunately, we dichotomize into positive and negative qualities. Like ourselves, the world we would prefer and the one we live in are each expressions of the world as it actually is. They both exist, despite that throughout so much of known human history one has seemed more dominant than the other. The validity of this statement is apparent to us anytime we take a more expansive look at ourselves. While acknowledging our capacity for astonishing evil, we also give their due to the equally amazing civilized values most of us cherish and even exhibit at times.

We are essentially the people we need to be, right now: we just need to behave that way. The potential for being real is always present. Regardless of the infrequency with which we realize this capacity, or how diminished we may become over lifetimes of fear, violence, and habituation to the immorality of the political norm, or how we try to conceal the truth of ourselves from ourselves by gussying ourselves up with platitudes and false consciousness—regardless of all this, the potential for virtue nevertheless resides within us throughout our lives

Viewing our situation from this perspective, we see the issue is not one of becoming someone new, but rather one of moving ourselves off square one and returning to the natural growth of our original sane selves.

The good news is we're not starting from scratch. Though at risk, and for too many of us verging on realizing endangered status, being real is nevertheless not unknown to us. As I've maintained throughout, the values we require for a liberating practice are inherent assets of the heart. Their potential expression is always present. And at times are actually acted upon.

This is evidenced by the moral values being exercised by people right now, at least to some degree. If they weren't—if we were totally bereft of compassion and generosity, kindness and courage—we would have done ourselves in as a species long before now. While the absence of "common decency" in our everyday encounters with each other is often lamented, it is not totally lacking.

Additionally, because of its inherent presence, most of us have an instinctual need to give expression to the sense of goodness that resides in us. Doing the right thing is a necessary condition of maintaining a modicum of emotional health and wellbeing, of retaining psychological and spiritual integrity—a sense that we're okay. Though it can be expressed in ways that are quite contrary to our intention, the innate presence of our heart values engenders a need to see ourselves as good people. Even if *seemingly* inconsequential to the larger concerns of transformative change—things like holding the door open for another as we're passing through, helping a stranger to push their car out of a snowbank, volunteering to work at the church supper, or simply acknowledging the courtesy of another with a "thank you" and to respond with "you're welcome"—these gestures are important to being true to our natural goodness, and to holding on to at least a semblance of civility with one another.

These "small" behaviors allow us to see that, while not consistently expressed, our heart values are at least present to some degree. The problem is that we are not routinely generous and kind, unfailingly compassionate and empathic, unconditionally accepting and forgiving, dependably righteous and ethical, and characteristically the "good" people we are in our best moments. In order to realize the liberating existence we seek, we must be so not just in times of crisis, or when good will and civic responsibility are convenient, but especially during the more *normal* moments of life when we tend to be sloppy, careless, indifferent and mindless of what is happening around us.

But also as well in the more challenging moments—the ones that are uncomfortable, risky, or dangerous, the times when it's easier to retreat behind a curtain of know-nothing blindness than to be the stand-up person who does the right thing when facing an instance of gender, racial, class and state injustice. To be agents of the salutary change we seek is a matter of consistently exhibiting the righteous behaviors we're capable of, in all situations. Our failure to do so risks a fatal rupture with ourselves and our society. When we neglect to be the person of heart values, this allows for systemic oppression to arise, and to be constantly reinforced over time. It is the breeding ground of fascism. We must confront the individual psychosis and social barbarism that marks our history all too often. Although most of us are only a few degrees of separation from the potential to conduct ourselves in this manner, the fact that we don't is why we are on the verge of unmitigated social barbarism and collapse.

This shift from occasional expression to a committed moment-to-moment practice of the values we prize makes all the difference. To get to where we want to be, to return to where we inherently are, and to be who we've always (potentially) been, we must commit ourselves to a steadfast practice of the practice. We must strengthen and dedicate ourselves to qualities that are natural to us so that they become a more natural part of our relationships with the rest of life.

A SPIRITUAL PRACTICE

Because our relationships in the political world are typically corrupted by considerations of dominance and control, and, therefore, exist within a moral vacuum, the crisis we suffer from is ultimately spiritual in nature. This is another way of observing there is a marked absence of a reverence for life and a corresponding economy of loving kindness in our relationships with each other as we go about our lives.

By love, I'm not referring to the romantic variety, which is typically a conditional arrangement, one that is dependent upon a *quid pro quo* understanding where I will love you as long as you love me in return. It is a controlling love, one that is intended to bind one to their partner. This is possessive love where people are attached to, if not enmeshed with one another around "being in love."

Most importantly, it is not a relationship where we love the other for their own sake, independent of us. Unless the parties have sufficient spiritual maturity, they typically are challenged to extend themselves and adapt to and accommodate their partner when the normal vicissitudes occur over time. In many cases, the changes result in the end of the relationship; for however unspoken in the marriage vows, when we have attached ourselves to the other for the purpose of security and control, as we often do in the political world, their apparent loss through changes in one's partner ruptures the relationship, causing us to devalue the other.

This is not the case with spiritual love. While including features of romantic love, such as compatibility and sexual attraction, the strength of the relationship arises from the fact that the partners are valued by the other for the independent expression of life each one exhibits. Such a love is unconditional.

This is spiritual love, the love we have when we value life in each of its unique yet interdependent expressions for their own sake of *aliveness*. This love is founded upon our awareness and appreciation of life's momentary specialness, on our heartfelt gratitude for being alive—a sentient presence—in this living moment. Beyond the qualifications and restrictions of ego, independent of external contingencies or circumstances, this is an unmitigated joy of life.

Not only is this heart love missing in so many of our lives, but it has become increasingly tenuous right now in our polarized society. We don't love each other in the sense of making room for the other to exist, not only as the distinctive instance of life we all are, but also as beings just like ourselves, doing the best we can to live in this world.

In failing to see ourselves and each other for who we are, we deprive ourselves of the opportunity to appreciate our mutuality, and the feelings of compassion, generosity, kindness, and spontaneous friendliness that naturally arise. This is the power of spiritual love, to come together as the individual sparks of life we are in a state of interbeing.

The task before us as transformative activists in the making is to awaken our potential for this love and bring it to life as an increasingly consistent part of our everyday lives. And while there are a variety of ways of accomplishing this, most of us do so by committing ourselves to a spiritual discipline that accesses our inherent sanity through the intentional practice of values-based behaviors. This is what the practice of the practice is all about. Nothing less than a spiritual practice will do when faced as we are with the desacralization of everyday life.

Spirituality is about living our heart-centered values. It is the conscientious effort to include them in our daily lives. Spirituality is the way that we turn on the light we require so as to see our way through the unknown of the transformation we are here to realize.

There are different and equally valid views of what spirituality is about, but they all seem to be premised on the singular importance of love. They share the belief that the presence of love in our everyday life is necessary to live and honor the sacredness of life. The absence of the spiritual from an activist practice is at the core of our historical failure to produce the revolutionary change we have sought. A spiritual practice allows us to contact our inherent heart values so that they become a regular feature of our everyday practice in the world. Without love's presence, we are stumbling around in the dark.

When we engage in such a practice, we find that accepting life becomes self-evident. No longer do we try to change it to something it is not, discovering that the changes we seek are only found in the liberating understanding that life as it is is good enough. It is in that heartfelt acceptance of the potential for good that exists in most of us, and to act on that consciousness, that we are able to realize transformative change. For at the bottom of such a practice is our love for life for its own sake.

Though often thought of as existing above the mundane and material aspects of life, consigned to the special province of saints or similar otherworldly souls, the spiritual actually informs us common folks how to live our everyday lives. Not necessarily what we do, though this is important too, but how we go about doing so in the unfolding presence of now. In whatever appropriate form or expression the particular moment calls for, the spiritual summons us to be loving in our particular behavioral expression.

The soul of existence is not separate from the minutiae of daily living; to the contrary, it is when a spiritual impulse touches and awakens our hearts that our purpose in this world comes alive in our relationships with one another. Nurtured, supported, and encouraged, what we call the spiritual—the facility to love life—increasingly becomes how we present ourselves to the world every day.

COMMITMENT AND DISCIPLINE

It is not uncommon for Civilized beings to be faced with a serious challenge when we consider how we can raise our game in "normal" times to a level of routine excellence. Good intentions are essential, for sure; we have no chance without them. But they alone are not sufficient to carry the day.

To be spiritually transformative, we must be active activists. We must act on our good intentions, conscientiously and intentionally doing the practice, being the practice. Purposely so, we create a presence of liberation. This is the commitment and discipline we need to our practice.

We must keep in mind that when I emphasize the importance of acting on our good intentions, this also includes *not-acting*. There is a saying that instructs, "Don't just do something, stand there." There are times when our good intentions advise us that not-doing is the best way to act on our good intentions. Sometimes it is best to offer compassion to the other by withholding sentiments of how we know they must feel or advice for how they will get over their misfortune. Best practice is simply being present in whatever way is appropriate in a given moment, sensitive to what the other presents, and mindfully responsive, avoiding a prepared script.

Too often, and especially in the earlier stages of our efforts to develop a consistent values-practice when ego is still an active presence and likely to attach itself to our good intentions, we act when action is not called for. This is often because "I" craves immediate success so that ego can then claim it as its own. We are then oblivious to the importance of timing as a critical feature of acting skillfully on our good intentions.

We should be still and quiet instead, observing and waiting to act until the right moment arrives. Timing is everything.

To be successful, we must dedicate ourselves to a *practice of the practice* to cultivate a consistent expression of the values we inherently possess. Without a committed discipline of this kind, many of us will find it extremely difficult, if not impossible, to be the people we actually are and want to be. It is challenging to change ancient habits and forge new, more wholesome ones. As the Buddhist nun Pema Chodron put it, *"Remember that this is something we do not just once or twice. Interrupting our destructive habits and awakening our heart is the work of a lifetime."*

This will be uncomfortable, at least initially. We will not easily overcome the liability of the political world in our efforts to live the values of peace and freedom. More than once, we will be tempted to give up and resign ourselves to the old, familiar ways, settling for being the moral person of convenience we have been, rather than one of consistency.

We will have cause to discuss commitment and discipline throughout this work because of their importance to a spiritual practice and being a moral presence in the world. But there are three relevant matters of sufficient importance to highlight at this point: community, forgiveness, and intention.

To start, making and keeping a commitment to a values practice is greatly enhanced when made with other committed people. Though ultimately the decision as to whether we carry through with our promise is ours, and ours alone, there is no question that being in a community of comrades and soulmates who are also committed to a spiritual practice is both invaluable and perhaps necessary. This supportive presence helps us carry on when we've fallen short, to hear and accept what others have to offer about our practice, serving as a reality check and an important voice of accountability. Because we trust that they have our best interests at heart, we are able to accept that which may be challenging for us to hear. Despite their own share of human imperfections, they are people who are honest with themselves and with us, who tell us what we need to hear in a nonjudgmental way. Hopefully, they will be gentle but tough-love friends who manage to maintain the delicate balance between helping us toe the line of our commitment while doing so in the calm, nonjudgmental way of those who appreciate we're all works in progress. Being part of such a community provides the love that we don't get from our parsimonious political culture, but something we require to stay the course.

Secondly, our commitment to the discipline of the practice of the practice raises the issue of forgiveness and reconciliation, not only with others, but first and foremost with ourselves. When we commit to a values-based practice, we are not pledging to be perfect. We don't have to be faultless to realize human liberation; we can be less than perfect and still be a person of peace, freedom and social justice. In fact, it is only the one who becomes the other! We only have to do our best, as consistently as we can. This means that while accepting responsibility for our mistakes, learning from our errors, and becoming increasingly mindful of our words and acts, we forgive ourselves at the same time that we ask forgiveness of others when we fall short. The extra special bonus, of course, is that when we are able to forgive ourselves we are more likely to forgive others for their less than perfect behavior.

Finally, we must appreciate what it means to be disciplined. Certainly, such a quality is critical for developing a consistent values practice, one that can be counted on from one moment to the next. A now-and-then, "when we're in the mood" approach won't cut it, especially when we're trying to emerge from lifetimes of political conditioning. We must be purposeful in order to have our inherent heart values become regularly active. This means we must consistently focus ourselves on our intentions. However, this must be done mindfully. The only way most of us can activate a values-led way of being in a political society is by disciplining ourselves to a daily practice. We must deliberately and conscientiously pursue our heart's good intentions to realize our purpose in this world. We make a habit when we awaken in the morning of being grateful for the day we have been given, expressing lovingkindness to family members and friends, giving heartfelt attention to the beauty of nature, and to all that we typically take for granted and ignore. These are the important steps to the practice.

There is no substitute for employing mindful determination. That which we commonly call "willpower" is a capacity that most of us possess. In recognition of the conditions within which we operate, nothing less will do to help make our daily behaviors increasingly values-spontaneous, even instinctual over time, as they evolve to a more natural expression. Linking our will with our intentions is necessary if we are to forge a revolutionary transformation.

However, this approach is not without its dangers. There is but a razor's edge of difference between using our willpower in service of being disciplined and using it in *striving* to realize an ulterior purpose in the Self-interests of "I." Nowhere is this truer than with our commitment to our egoless heart values.

Whenever we act conditionally, we're no longer acting without ego. Only when we act unconditionally, without being in the service of a goal (no matter how virtuous), ironically, are we able to realize our purpose. This is accomplished when success and failure are not our ultimate concerns, but just making the effort to do the right thing as best we can. It is in the actual doing of virtuous behavior, regardless of outcome, that we have succeeded in that moment in being a liberated agent of change.

We recognize the distinction between a conditional and unconditional act when we see them in action. Unconditional discipline is not harsh or inflexible. While purposeful, the act is also gentle and kind, flexible and accommodating of what is in its application. Despite helping transform us under challenging circumstances, the discipline that is needed is voluntary, not mandatory. We are not driven by the lash of ego to achieve some goal. The effort involved is performed for the sake of an awakening heart. A clear indication that we are on target is evidenced by not beating ourselves up when we "fail," and are able to forgive ourselves.

In this way, our discipline within a values practice melds into an expression of the practice in itself. This is the only way we can move away from old habits and begin to try out new ones. Though seemingly contrary to the expression of values for their own sake, there will be times, especially early on, when they will be awkward and stiff, more in our heads as good ideas than full-blown, uncontaminated sentiments from our hearts. Our practice will be performed with a "should" prompt, reminding us of what we want and are committed to do. What we do may not be done unconditionally, spontaneously. It may be done because we think that it's the right thing to do.

This is OK. In this moment it is the right thing to do. Don't judge this action harshly, or better yet, judge it at all. No matter how the *right* behavior is expressed, we are doing the right thing, whether we do so spontaneously or with a prompt from our conscience. Even if we might judge ourselves as "hypocritical" and "phony" because what we do is not something we feel like doing, but do so anyway because it is the right thing, all expressions—"real" and "false" alike—of doing what we know in our hearts is right contribute to our growth on the path of liberation.

As with ego's contribution in general to this process, our development as moral beings doesn't necessarily follow a straight and narrow righteous path. To force it to do so is to submit to ego's mechanistic logic of the way things should run in life. As long as we can accept this kind of relaxed and flexible discipline, we discover one day that we are doing the right thing without even thinking about it. We're just doing it.

RETURNING TO MOTHER

> Some keep the Sabbath going to church —
> I keep it, staying at Home —
> With a Bobolink for a Chorister —
> And an Orchard, for a Dome —
> Some keep the Sabbath in Surplice —
> I just wear my Wings —
> And instead of tolling the Bell, for Church,
> Our little Sexton—sings.
> God preaches, a noted Clergyman —
> And the sermon is never long,
> So instead of getting to Heaven, at last —
> I'm going, all along.
> —Emily Dickinson

A spiritual practice begins when we come home to Mother: when we finally embrace nature as us. Much as we did before we became a Civilized race, when human beings were one with the whole of nature, and as some indigenous people continue to be today, we must respect—more, *love*—Mother as the life force that She is.

Returning to nature as simply a part of it, thus recognizing our state of interbeing, ends our ancient, matricidal power relationship: mankind over Mother. This starts us on the path of a truly transformative revolution. Not only does such an act address what is really Civilized humanity's "original sin" of dissociating ourselves from life, it helps to undermine the other power relationships that have grown from this primal one. We are liberated through our reunion with our natural selves and, in turn, become a force of liberation.

In a practical sense, nothing better cures us of our radical individualism and brings us into the light of our essential oneness with all beings than healing our apocalyptic breach with nature. Doing so, we recognize that we're not on our own in the sense of not needing anyone or anything in order to live, and have in fact been totally dependent upon others for our daily existence all along.

This intelligence softens our hearts so that a sense of gratitude is released toward life and the manifold instances of care from others over the years up to and including the present moment of now. We become one with and appreciate the efforts of these countless "others," our mothers and fathers, friends and neighbors, farmers and teachers, factory workers and bureaucrats, all the people who made, delivered, and repaired our material goods; the birds, animals, and fish; the plants and woods; the worms, bees, water, air, soil, rain and sun, all of which have provided us with the sustenance, shelter, and necessary wherewithal to survive. And, of course, we are grateful to women everywhere, who have made countless sacrifices on our behalf so that we might live. We accept the fact that we wouldn't be here now if it wasn't for all of them. So conscious, we are flooded with a love for life; a heartfelt solidarity with all sentient beings arises.

As we come to recognize and appreciate the web of life we're inextricably part of, we awaken to nature as something we must cherish and protect. In so doing, we let go of the mechanistic worldview that has allowed us to exploit the natural world and to instrumentalize its expressions because we failed to attribute any inherent value to Mother beyond how we could use Her for our own Selfish purposes.

Gratitude arises in its place, which is a most important response to closing the gap with the rest of life. Thankfulness and appreciation are expressions of humility that allow us to return to our rightful place in the universe, letting go of our sense of superiority and entitlement to domination, being and becoming one with the many, no longer striving to be above it all. This consciousness further encourages the sunset of our sense of a separate Self, transmuting instead into a compassionate commitment for the wellbeing of all beings.

This emerging attitude begins to eclipse the long history of our antagonistic, exploitive behavior that has characterized our relationships with the rest of life over the years. It is absolutely essential to transforming these fraught interactions to ones known for their expansive values. Albeit each of us are unique expressions of life, we come to appreciate the universal aliveness that is the common feature of existence, the thrust and instinct, the pulse for life that we share with all other living beings. As with ourselves, the ant and the elephant naturally want to be life: to be their essential ant-ness and elephant-ness. Our awareness of this quality expands our solidarity with and love for life, allowing us to recognize that we're all in this business of life together.

Perhaps most crucial to our re-discovered relationship with the rest of life is that it allows us to value our kin in nature in a way that we hadn't before. As a consequence, we grow into a commitment of no-harm toward all sentient beings. In significant part, this arises from our recognition that our guaranteed mortality is what we share with the rest of life. This awareness cannot help but cause us to respond to "others" with the warm heart of commonality.

Taking the life of another, therefore, is no longer done unmindfully or without conscience. We recognize the instinct for life in all living beings, no matter how small or seemingly inconsequential they may appear to our Civilized eyes. Life is life; to live is as valuable to the fly as it is to us. To assume otherwise is Civilization's conceit. When we value another's life in this manner, we acquire one of the most profound developments we can have on the road to spiritual transformation.

It goes without saying that we can only do this when we no longer allow ego to act for us. Our reunion with Mother goes a long way toward advancing this prospect. It is then that we see that life alone is what ultimately matters, not the control and domination of life. Through the pursuit of power, money, status, and the acquisition of material goods, ego has distracted us from the plain truth of the value of our momentary existence. This remains our pattern until we learn to live with our inevitable passing, graciously and courageously, in the moment of now where our pending deaths are always waiting for us.

Beyond simply intellectualizing about our relationship, reconnecting with Mother doesn't occur until we actually spend time *in nature*, being with Her. Not to exploit or abuse, but to hang out with what is essentially our home as well. It is only in this way that we can get out of our heads, with our mental constructs and abstract musings, and actually be (with) nature, "wasting time." Not being productive by using nature for some ulterior and profitable purpose, but quietly observing and listening to her many expressions. We are with nature on Her terms and for Her own sake.

She is a great teacher when we allow ourselves to be one with her and engage with Her more fully through our senses as living beings. We learn to listen, smell, taste, and feel Mother's expressions without having to put a name to them. We engage in direct perception and open awareness of Her majesty. No longer objectifying or commodifying nature into discreet pieces of data or product, we are less inclined to exploit and abuse that which we are now in silent communion with.

When fully present with nature, we become aware of the incessant change taking place all around us when we enter the woods, sit in a field, climb a mountain, or wade in a stream. These changes are usually subtle from one moment or day to the next, but they can also be sudden and dramatic, as Mother is perfectly capable of exponential leaps. This ability to be in complete contact becomes even more possible the further we are away from Civilization, alone with the rest of life. If we allow Her to do so, She takes command of us, not necessarily in the shock and awe fashion of our industrial Civilization, but more likely as a quiet astonishment because of Her sheer presence: the evolution of a flower from first bloom to total glory to dry husk, the inexorable changes in the seasons, the dance of death that a once vibrant leaf performs as it falls randomly from a tree, the meanderings of a snowflake as it wanders in its own anarchistic way from sky to earth. Without Civilization to interpret what we're experiencing, we are essentially a human being in a non-human setting, the domain of many other living beings —but no longer our home, at least since the time of our hunter-gatherer ancestors. This awareness can evoke many different feelings and emotions, but in one way or another, being with nature can bring us back down to earth as well as send us off to the stars.

It is liberating to simply watch a bird or a spider, a tree or a plant, as it goes about its business, without having to analyze its activity into concepts and knowledge; to just be, instead, with the dance, music, and stunning beauty, unobtrusively, that we're blessed to be part of. If good fortune smiles upon us, and we are mindful in the moment, we witness relationships and interactions between nature's beings—or even are part of one ourselves. We observe acts of care and love between others that our Civilized minds had not previously allowed us to consider. Together with deeds of egoless killing and death that take our breath away with their matter-of-fact ferocity, inspired by the needs of survival and the instinct of being alive, we allow our curiosity free rein, without judgment or an agenda to necessarily accomplish anything useful, and certainly without any desire to do harm. Perhaps as a result, we are a little more modest, a little humbler then we were before we left our buildings and went into the fields, the woods, the streams, and the mountains.

There is much we can learn from Mother when we do this; practical stuff, for sure, that is the basis of a sustainable existence for those of us who are open to being taught. But at least as importantly, this kind of receptive contact puts us in touch with nature's beauty and magic and sheer awe, imparting a sense of how we are part of this with all other sentient beings. A peacefulness settles over us when we begin to discover this new relationship with what was previously the alien "other." A quiet moment arrives. We realize we don't have to dominate or struggle to be someone we're not when we come to this state of calm acceptance. We just have to be one with who we are.

Despite our dependency upon Her, we have historically neglected to attribute value to Mother beyond that which we can extract and profit from. Our objectification and commodification of the natural world has reduced soil to dirt, insects to pests, plants to weeds.

But nowhere is our failure to act upon our responsibility for the stewardship of the natural world more evident than in the behaviors that have brought about the sixth mass extinction, which is well underway. In so doing, we have befouled the only true home we have. We are busy cutting off the limb from which we precariously hang on to over the eternal abyss, and have cursed ourselves, perhaps, to extinction.

We've also driven thousands of species to the edge of annihilation and beyond. A 2014 study by the World Wildlife Fund (WWF) found the total number of wild animals has plunged 50 percent in the past 40 years. The WWF estimated populations of vertebrates have fallen by an average of 60 percent since 1970. Over the past 20 years, there has been a 90 percent plunge in the number of monarch butterflies in America, and an 87 percent loss of rusty-patched bumblebees. According to a 2019 report by *Biological Conservation*, the world's insects are hurtling down the path to extinction, threatening a "catastrophic collapse of nature's ecosystems." More than 40% of insect species are declining and a third are endangered. This represents a clear and present danger not only to the production of our food, but to many other living beings that depend upon insects for their diets.

A report by the Institute for Public Policy Research (IPPR) perhaps best summarized our assault upon the environment when it wrote that "Human-induced environmental change is occurring at an unprecedented scale and pace and the window of opportunity to avoid catastrophic outcomes in societies around the world is rapidly closing." It raised alarm not only about climate change, but also other human activities tied to declining biodiversity, ocean acidification, land degradation, high levels of phosphorous and nitrogen runoff, a waning ozone layer, and air and land pollution. Considering all these factors, the IPPR report concluded that "we have entered the age of environmental breakdown."

In light of the horror of this ecocide, it is obvious that our relationship with the natural world must immediately change, not only for our own survival given our absolute dependency on all that we're willfully and mindlessly destroying, but for the sake of all the other living beings who we're killing in pursuit of economic progress and insatiable quest for convenience. This requires radical departures from what we have taken for granted and consider to be our God-given right! It also involves the spiritual dimension of making friends with the soil and insects, the infinitesimal members of Mother's family, and by assuming a mindful, compassionate, more modest place in the larger scheme of things.

In order to do this, we must relinquish the primary illusion that Civilized human beings are above and outside of nature. We must abandon our efforts to be in control and instead accept the humbler dimensions of being but one of the universe's infinitude of sentient beings in the web of interbeing.

GRIEVING OUR LOSSES

  Significant to walking a spiritual path, as we reconnect with Mother and cultivate a heartfelt commitment to the sacredness of life, is seeking forgiveness from Her for the crimes against nature we as a Civilized species are responsible for, however "innocent" we may insist they have been. For most of us this expansion of our awareness is painful and difficult. There are those of us who will protest that we haven't cut down trees, or extracted "resources," or blown off the tops of mountains. What we overlook, however, is that the lives we have lived as a charter member of our industrial consumer Civilization have been built upon and sustained by the violation and murder of Mother. Accepting our responsibility for the resulting material privileges is a necessary step on the road to recovering our humanity and accomplishing spiritual transformation.

  Vital to this process is learning to grieve what we have lost—and are continuing to lose—due to the heedless acts of us and the rest of our species. Doing this, however, requires us to reach the depths of acceptance. This is challenging because it involves exposing ourselves to the most vulnerable area of our being—the fear of death—and to be touched in our most sensitive place, our hearts.

  Unable to accept our momentary existence, we deny death's reality as part of life, as well as the benefits that await us whenever we recognize its constant presence in our current lives. This is the wisdom of Don Juan's advice to Carlos Castaneda, *"to let death be an advisor."* It is ironic, indeed, that for all the energy we put into avoiding and denying death, it is only by accepting it that we benefit greatly from its life-enhancing lesson to live our lives in the present, as if we are breathing our final breath. This causes us to act in the moment with whole-heartedness, knowing it could be our last.

By suppressing the need to adequately grieve, we distort and exacerbate the experience of death and loss. Rather than sparing us the pain and suffering that comes with any significant ending, it secures a hold on us. Our unfinished business only attaches us to that which we avoid and deny. Rather than allowing for the growth that naturally occurs with its acceptance, loss becomes an impediment to healthy growth. The failure to grieve radiates throughout our lives, informing every moment of loss—incessant change—that we experience. Our resistance to it becomes our habitual way of dealing with change.

This characteristic is most commonly observed in the way we typically handle various endings throughout our lives, especially with significant relationships such as spouses and lovers, family and friends, and others who touch our hearts. We don't give their endings their proper due by honoring their importance to us. Rather, we avoid grieving the loss, denying its import. For the most part, we hold it at arm's length, or try to fix it with new relationships or similarly distracting activities.

The failure to grieve properly prevents us from realizing and fully expressing the compassionate, generous impulses that naturally ascend—including to those whom we've lost—when we fully accept loss because it shuts down our hearts. Denial closes us off in order to protect us. As a result, not only are we unable to extend ourselves to others, more basically we block ourselves from our innate capacity to express love and our need to receive love. We disempower ourselves from the power we have to develop towards the grown-up human beings we are intended to be.

Properly grieving loss assumes particular poignancy in our time, when so much of the world we take for granted, and the way of life we thought would last forever is disappearing right before our eyes. When we consider the accelerated death of sentient beings due to human behavior, we appreciate why some are stating we've entered a *"period of hospice."* This is the reality of climate change.

But unless we can properly grieve the losses that have already occurred, from the daily extinction of species and the rapidly vanishing glaciers to the disappearance of the coral reefs and the collapse of our fish stocks, we will not be able to realistically deal with this catastrophic event. When we allow ourselves to experience these losses on a gut level—to meditate upon these tragedies so they move from our heads to our hearts —climate change becomes less an abstract issue for us. Only when grief is fully experienced does the new normal become real.

Rather than embracing the heart of the matter, we are responding to this unprecedented trauma as a mechanical problem that requires a technological fix. This is not to suggest that solar panels and electric cars are not important. We must stop using fossil fuels, and fast. But when we limit ourselves to industrial interventions, being sustainable becomes a matter of creating a green variation of the same ego-driven capitalist industrial paradigm we presently live under. No matter how we try to disguise this fact, approaches built from political power result in the murder and exploitation that we as a species have inflicted on each other and other living beings for millennia in the name of our Self-proclaimed superior Civilization.

In essence, values ungrounded in the sanctity of life produce climate apocalypse, as well as the legacies of patriarchy, white supremacy, and capitalism. When we are caught up in the urgency of solving the climate crisis as a matter of preserving the world as it has been, we ignore the domination/subjugation paradigm underlying our industrial civilization. Bemused by it, we have yet to understand that while our civilization has created our unprecedented material wealth, it has also led us to our present dead-end predicament: the wholesale destruction of our environment and countless sentient beings. We remain blind to such matters as the extraction, exploitation, and extinction of Mother's bounty and the centuries-old attempt to establish dominion over nature, while leaving unquestioned our assumptions about a society built upon corporate profits, consumerism, and a perpetual growth economy of impoverishment and exploitation of the many for the sake of the astounding wealth of the very few. By limiting our vision to renewable alternatives to fossil fuels, we're devising industrial solutions for more basic human problems and the spiritual crisis that underlies it all. We need to be thinking beyond fixes.

In his book *Eaarth: Making a Life on a Tough New Planet,* Bill McKibben notes how the astronauts of the 1968 Apollo 8 mission were ecstatic when they looked back at the earth from their position in space. One of them noted that it appeared as *"a grand oasis."* But, McKibben goes on to write, *"we no longer live on that planet"* (his emphasis). In the four decades since *Eaarth* was published in 2010, *"That earth has changed in profound ways, ways that have already taken us out of the sweet spot where humans so long thrived. We're every day less the oasis and more the desert...It's a different place. A different planet. It needs a new name. Eaarth."*

It is precisely this loss that we must honor and grieve, for only then can we experience the depths of our crisis. Only then can we appreciate what's really at stake.

Joanna Macy and Chris Johnson write in their book *Active Hope, "If we felt the pain of loss each time an ecosystem was destroyed, a species wiped out, or a child killed by war or starvation, we wouldn't be able to continue living the way we do...The losses continue because they aren't registered..., they aren't seen as important. By choosing to honor the pain of loss rather than discounting it, we break the spell that numbs us to the dismantling of our world."*

As challenging as this is, we must experience ourselves in

the face of what we have done (and are continuing to do) to our Mother and to each other. We must contact the despair and rage, sadness and guilt, fear and pain we naturally feel at such a moment of recognition. We must allow our interconnected selves to suffer this moment of what we are doing throughout the sentient world. This opens us to be in touch with our compassion and love. Only when we accept this responsibility can we then ask forgiveness and do what must be done.

"The reality is that you will grieve forever," Elizabeth Kubler-Ross and John Kessler tell us in their book, *The Five Stages of Grief. "You will not 'get over' the loss of a loved one; you will learn to live with it. You will heal and you will rebuild yourself around the loss you have suffered. You will be whole again, but you will never be the same. Nor should you be the same, nor would you want to."*

Through the experience of grieving, we are able to move toward a truly regenerative, transformed way of life. We integrate our losses into our lives and suffer their demise so they can make a valuable contribution towards where we go from here. Beyond the unexpressed, heartfelt feelings that we have protected ourselves from lies the exquisite love we have for life and all its infinite representations. Here, in our undefended hearts, lies our strength. As with our vulnerability, the exposure to which we have looked to "I" to protect us from, so too is the undefended heart our true source of power.

CHAPTER SEVEN

MEDITATION

Reconnecting with Mother and grieving life's inevitable losses are essential steps to creating a committed, spiritual practice. They are basic to being and acting as people of values. Both center us in the most essential realities of our existence: the first in our interconnected, interdependent nature; the second with life's momentary character and the inevitability of loss and death. By coming home to nature, we heal the original separation that divided us from ourselves and the rest of life; by grieving, we accept death as part of our lives, always present, thus enabling us to live our lives in the present. In both instances, we open ourselves to our hearts—to life itself. We liberate our inherent moral values.

There is a third dimension to our spiritual journey, however, essential to the first two, which makes possible *how* we go about the business of being a values-guided spiritual warrior. This is the practice of meditation, the intentional cultivation of transformative mindfulness where there is an observable connection between its daily practice and ethical conduct.

Meditation is the heart of the practice of the practice. It nurtures mindfulness as our everyday practice in the world, facilitating our awakening and expanding awareness of the present moment that allows us to be real. Development of a regular meditation practice cultivates the ability to see clearly what is in our hearts, beyond ego and its tendency to limit our vision by attaching us personally to phenomena with its judgments, opinions, cravings, and aversion. It puts us in touch with our direct experience. With persistence, meditation enables us to not only see what is, but to translate that growing awareness into actions and behaviors that are commensurate with that sight.

Chogyam Trungpa Rinpoche summarized this practice precisely: *"The practice of meditation is not so much based on becoming a better person, or for that matter becoming an enlightened person. It is seeing how we can relate to our already existing enlightened state."*

At its best, meditation is a *don't-know* perspective, what Shunryu Suzuki termed "beginner's mind"—an attitude of openness, free of preconceptions. Not-knowing is rooted in the present without a concern for what will happen next or what occurred before. When fully present with what is, we bring this essential "beginner's mind" to our encounters with life from one moment to the next.

Seeing what is, unadorned and unexplained, is the necessary condition to acceptance. The two are actually the same: we cannot accept life for what is if at the same time we are blind to it at any given moment.

This state of being allows us to act with moral intention and loving purpose. When we are in a meditative state of mindfulness, we are naturally open to our hearts and the values therein. In this moment, we are suffused with a consciousness of the blessed experience that life is. To *know* life in this way is to love life. It could not be otherwise.

I have been meditating since my first retreat at the Insight Meditation Center in Barre, Massachusetts in 1980 with the wonderful teacher Joseph Goldstein. I accidentally stumbled into this practice with no other purpose than a curiosity based on what friends had told me.

However, this was also a time in my life when I had become particularly disenchanted with traditional (i.e., political) activism after being engaged in anti-war and social justice struggles over the previous 15 years. I was increasingly uncomfortable with what seemed to be a confrontational and adversarial activism that was focused on defeating whoever was designated as the enemy, rather than creating the alternative to what we opposed through our practice. I was embarrassed by the destructive, hurtful words that came out of my mouth, and by the behaviors I saw myself displaying. But I was also confused as to what the alternative might be, since it seemed to make sense to treat the enemy as the enemy because, as their deeds plainly testified, they were undeniably bad people doing bad things to others.

In retrospect, it is apparent that I was ripe for Buddhism, especially with a practice that emphasized proactive, life-affirming values and behaving in a compassionate and loving way with other sentient beings. Since that watershed experience, I have found the discipline of meditation most relevant to my growth as a human being and an activist. I want to quickly emphasize, however, that notwithstanding the modest spiritual growth I have made over time, I am still a work in progress, as anyone who knows me can testify to! Nevertheless, Buddhism and meditation, in particular, have been life-changing experiences for me.

I also found that, as with almost anything in life, we cannot grow as skilled, values-oriented activists without making a commitment to the practice. In the earlier days, I was an inconsistent meditator and therefore did not grow as I might have otherwise. Fortunately, this has changed, and I discovered the benefits that can be realized through a more disciplined approach. I found that maintaining a commitment through daily practice is key to realizing mindfulness over time and cultivating my intrinsic heart virtues. There is no substitute for an intentional effort. As Joseph Goldstein noted in *A Heart Full of Peace*, *"To embody our commitment to morality, we need to pay attention to what we do, waking up to our actions of body, speech and mind."* To realize this kind of spiritual mindfulness, we must practice. Pointing to the direct connection that exists between mindfulness and morality, Goldstein went on to observe that it is the *"regularity of practice [that] effects such a transformation."*

To nurture a values-based practice in the everyday world, we must commit ourselves to doing the best we can. This is our baseline. If we are serious about being activists of human liberation, this is what we try to do as consistently as we can. Doing our best is a commitment appropriate to our purpose of living an increasingly moral life. By accepting that we make mistakes and have shortcomings, we come to understand that if we commit ourselves to doing our best, reliably and dependably, it will invariably elicit the best from us. This is good enough.

Meditation is typically done as an individual activity. We'll get into that practice in greater detail shortly. But first, I want to underscore that meditation is enhanced and reinforced when done in a community of similarly inclined people, known as a *sangha* by Buddhists (an affinity group might be the name applied to a similar gathering by non-Buddhist activists). There is great value to being in the presence of people with whom we share values about the sanctity of life, as well as our mutual intention to grow our practice with them.

Attending retreats (self- and teacher-directed alike) is invaluable for the growth of our practice. There really is no substitute for them if you want to grow your practice. Additionally, listening to talks and reading relevant books and articles is helpful to increasingly draw us into a culture of meditation. Having books and articles on bedside and coffee tables that are open to significant passages, as well as slips of paper upon which we have written meaningful quotes, is also useful in making the practice of meditation a presence in our daily lives. It is through this variety of activity that meditation becomes not just something we do, separate and distinct from the rest of our lives, but more and more our way of life.

In the beginning, we may meditate for only 5 or 15 minutes a day. If that is what we can commit ourselves to, then let that be where we start. This will cultivate our meditation, providing we are consistent with our practice each day. There may even be a day here and there when we don't meditate, or when we are too busy to do so. But this is not a problem as long as we are committed to the practice. More than anything else, it is our commitment and the constancy with which we follow through that ultimately count. This is how we develop a habit of mindfulness in a world of habitual mindlessness.

At some point, we extend ourselves. Commitment grows with practice. Regularity breeds longer, more concentrated periods of meditation. It becomes a wholesome routine, one we intentionally seek and choose voluntarily. We give ourselves a nudge, a push, meditating 30, 45, even 60 minutes in a single sit. We find we have the time and make time for doing so. It will happen naturally as part of our everyday lives.

But growing a habit of meditation is also challenging, more so than the preceding description might lead one to believe. We will encounter obstacles that we must learn to live with as we nurture the practice. They will otherwise throw us off the path if we don't apply our meditative practice to them.

Interestingly, while we may not appreciate them as such at the time, these hindrances can also be gifts that strengthen and mature our practice if we work with them skillfully and do not fall prey to their seductive, ego-inspired natures. After all, we must remind ourselves that developing a practice of meditation, and particularly the capacity to see life for what it is, is not in the best interests of "I." Representing as it does the potential evaporation of ego's illusions, and hence its own demise, this kind of salutary growth is a direct threat to ego, one that it will respond to with vigorous resistance and clever distractions. "I" has a personal investment in interpreting our boredom, fatigue, or slow progress as statements about how inept and feckless we are, or how worthless the practice is, tempting us to call it quits.

But things don't always proceed the way we might like them to. In order to avoid succumbing to "I's" enticements, we must gently but firmly disabuse ourselves of the expectations that we, as products of an easy on/easy off, throw-away culture of convenience, have understandably and unavoidably brought to our practice. It is unrealistic to expect that the development of a consistent practice would be all smooth sailing. This is not the way life unfolds. We will continue to contend with the long-held habits of a political culture, always trying to seduce us where we're most vulnerable, preying on the same habits of half-hearted or close-hearted behavior that has been our problem all along.

More importantly, we must avoid building our practice on the false promise of a finish line that will tell us, *"It's over, we've been successful, we can ease up and stop now."* That's not what meditation is all about. We know we're in trouble once we realize that our efforts center on the achievement of a goal, or that we're a failure if we don't reach a preconceived objective. The practice of meditation is not about successful endings. It is an activity without end, doing the practice of the practice for its own sake, being present unconditionally. It's a lifelong process of being here now in the moment as it is, without any expectation that it should be otherwise.

We must be clear-eyed when we make this commitment to a practice of the practice. No doubt, it can be challenging. It won't necessarily meet our expectations, provide instant gratification, or be something that we feel like doing on any given day. We can expect a variety of hindrances to challenge our commitment. But as I have said, these difficulties are blessings, facing us with challenges that are very much a part of the meditation itself.

Rather than giving in to the desire to quit, this is an opportunity to look at what is causing meditation to be so difficult for us in this moment. We meditate on the meditation, looking mindfully at what is getting in our way. This will provide insight into the mental conditions and their ensuing behaviors—the apathy, laziness, restlessness, indifference, and general half-heartedness—that not only drag our spirits down and impede our growth as meditators, but also interfere with doing the right thing in the larger scheme of our lives. It is important to sit with whatever urges flight, not so we can better intellectualize about it, or even overcome it, but rather so we can shine a light on it, waking up to and becoming conscious of that which is typically unconscious. With a nonjudgmental attitude of compassionate curiosity, we accept that we're bored with the practice or find it frustrating and impossible to do. But instead of fighting or fleeing from it, we just sit with it, let it be what it is without judgment or expectation. By not identifying with it as "I," we find that, like everything else in life, it lacks solidity. Eventually, it passes on, especially if we avoid acting out on it or allowing it to have more influence in our lives than its insubstantial existence would warrant. At least for the moment, we are liberated.

Most of us must work at developing a regular practice of liberation if we are to consistently express our values in the everyday. While we are blessed with the heart-potential for such conduct, thus starting with a necessary foundation, our history is nevertheless replete with instances of behaviors—from those we accept as "normal" to those we can still be horrified by—that clearly show that the exercise of ethical and moral conduct is all too often the exception rather than the rule. As important as they are, good intentions are not sufficient by themselves. This is especially so when they bump up against "political reality" and we feel the need to compromise our values in order to avoid potential conflict or inconvenience to our daily routines.

The values that serve as the foundation for peace and freedom have atrophied over time through political habituation and calcification, even though they are grounded in our essential sanity. As such, we cannot take for granted our ability to be liberated souls without committing ourselves to a daily effort to act that way. Short of an unexpected intervention by a divine province, the conventionality of "I" is too powerful to allow us to otherwise get to the heart of the matter. Ego will struggle mightily to avoid its demise in our efforts to move on with our lives, employing all of its clever, seductive wiles to convince us we cannot live without it.

To untangle ourselves from the coils of "I," we must nurture a more consistently wholesome practice that gradually acquires a life of its own. A daily practice of meditation is vital to this process of becoming less Self-conscious and more selflessly heart-oriented.

Admittedly, it is a bit ironic that, after advocating that we move beyond characteristic behaviors, we now advocate developing what can only be termed as a new daily *habit*, albeit one consciously chosen and committed to voluntarily upon the basis of our good intentions. While it is true that, in the face of engrained behaviors and institutionalized conduct, we must engage in a daily practice of this kind to cultivate wholesome behaviors, we need to keep in mind that habitual behavior can also degenerate into mindless activity.

But our perseverance rewards us by enabling us not only to become more aware of the obstacles blocking our practice as

meditators and our growth as human beings, but to also see—
often after the fact—the other benefits of meditation. These do
not usually arrive with bells and whistles during a sudden
breakthrough; developments of this kind are typically gradual
and not realized right away. This is a profoundly deep process in
which there are no final results. However subtle its expression
may be, when we intentionally cultivate mindfulness through
meditation, our potential for compassion, lovingkindness,
courage, integrity, generosity, and forgiveness surface and begin
to inhabit us.

Why is this? As I argued in the previous chapter, mindfulness is the pathway to being real; it is the nature of mindfulness
to put us in touch with our hearts. By its very nature, mindfulness is an inclusive consciousness, not only of our "outside"
reality, but most importantly of our "inner" reality. When we are
mindful of what is, we cannot help but feel more generous
toward ourselves and experience heartfelt compassion toward
others. Behind the masks we wear and the roles we play, we
discover the suffering human beings we all are in our struggles
to live with the burden of ego that our kind bear: the obstacle to
being real.

With mindfulness, the defenses that protect our hearts from
being vulnerable and authentic in the political world melt.
Mindfulness, exercised moment-to-moment through meditation, brings our hearts out of the shadows into the light and
warmth of day. With this consistent focus, these values are more
likely to assume their rightful, more conscious place in our lives.
We become our heart values. Increasingly in touch with our
hearts, we are touched by life.

Not only surfacing through mindfulness, heart values also
are reinforced, expanded and deepened when we take our values
out into the larger world beyond meditation. As with those
ominous features of climate change that understandably frighten
us, this is where nature's positive feedback loop and exponential

proclivity is operative; only in this instance, it works for the home team! Together with meditation, moments of inhabiting our values off the meditation cushion compound our practice. This happens not in a nice, neat linear fashion, but in an irregular manner—slow and subtle, or perhaps as a sudden, unexpected leap—much in keeping with the nature of life itself. The more we are able to be mindful of life as it unfolds before us during our meditation, the greater the likelihood that we will accept life for what it is when we're out in the larger world, and thus exhibit behaviors in our daily practice that are suffused with the values of a free human being.

There is nothing automatic here, and we can't take for granted that what we "exhibit" during a quiet meditation session will necessarily translate into corresponding behavior in our noisy, distracting lives. Nevertheless, this deeply powerful practice of meditation is a proven way to develop mindfulness and the values of a liberated people. It promotes the kind of compassionate awareness and behavior we need to function skillfully in our efforts to create a successful transition from the world collapsing all around us, and to prefigure the world we are entering.

FOLLOWING THE BREATH

The essence of meditation is to be consistently mindful of what is present in the passing moment, and not become distracted by the products of a busy mind, which labors to define what reality is for us. While this can be done in several ways, many of us meditate by paying attention to our breath as it rises and falls; breath in, breath out.

We simply observe our intake and outtake of breath, breath in, breath out. We try to be aware of the nuances of our breath as it changes during the course of the meditation from shallow and deep, fast and slow.

Because breathing is the most important thing we do to sustain life, focusing on our breath serves to remind us about the impermanence of existence—here one moment, gone the next. Becoming mindful of this most basic fact of life not only grounds us in this essential condition to being alive, it also wakes us up to what is real.

Meditating is usually done by sitting by ourselves, or with others, in a quiet space to maximize the conditions that will best serve us to practice mindfulness. We either kneel or sit on a cushion, a small bench made for meditation purposes, or on a chair, depending on our physical comfort. The important thing is that, however we sit, we do so in a comfortably straight but not rigid position.

There are other ways to meditate that can complement our sitting position. Walking and standing meditation are common variations. But in fact, there are almost as many ways to meditate as there are daily human activities. We can do so, for example, while standing in line to check out our groceries, eating a meal, taking a shower, laying down, waking up or going to sleep —almost any activity in which we are deliberately mindful in the moment. We become more meditative (which is to say, mindful) in other parts of our lives as our practice grows deeper and we are more committed to and more accomplished in the practice. Ultimately, this is what meditation is all about.

We further strengthen our practice by being mindful of the interstitial space between breaths when we're not breathing. This can last a millisecond or longer, when life is suspended before the breath resumes. It is especially important to be mindful in this moment because this is the empty space of freedom, the open space of an unfettered heart. It is the residence of a liberated existence where we operate as an awake and empty being.

Meditation on the breath serves no other purpose than itself; there is nothing else we need do. The rising and falling of the breath—the very essence of our life—is the basis of our practice. Breath in, breath out. Meditation requires we simply focus on our most fundamental reality as it expresses itself, from one moment to the next. Breath in, breath out. Life doesn't get any simpler than this, though mindfully following the breath can be a most challenging exercise, as the rowdy, unruly mind can instantaneously kidnap us. We will improve over time when we increase our practice and the mind has had time to settle down.

Our meditation can be enhanced when we include meditative exercises. These reinforce the intentionality of our efforts, especially with cultivating and strengthening specific behaviors we wish to have as regular companions to our behavioral expressions. This can be as simple as beginning each session with a prayer stating, *I wish that all living beings be free of pain and suffering and that they all know peace and happiness, health and well-being, joy and ease of being.*

From there, we can direct loving kind thoughts, first to ourselves (*May I be happy, may I be peaceful, may I be free of pain and suffering*), and then extending these thoughts towards other living beings in general (*As I want to be happy, so may all beings be happy, etc.*), including loved ones and friends (*As I wish to be free of pain and suffering and to know peace and happiness, so, may my wife be free of pain and suffering and know peace and happiness*).

This exercise expands when we direct these sentiments towards people we feel neutral about. And it becomes especially powerful when we focus the prayers on people in our lives with whom we are angry, have hurt or have been hurt by, or are otherwise in conflict with. Envisioning the face of the other as we express lovingkindness toward them makes the exercise all the more compelling.

Such is also true when we apply such intentional behavior towards asking for and extending forgiveness: *If I have hurt or offended anyone in thought or deed, I ask forgiveness. And I freely forgive anyone who may have hurt me.* Again, this exercise assumes greater power by asking forgiveness of a specific person we have offended, and by forgiving another who has hurt us, especially when we picture the other as we express these words: *Just as I forgive myself for having caused harm, so do I forgive my father.*

What is important to keep in mind is that the expression of this feeling is no less valid when we direct lovingkindness and forgiveness toward ourselves, the one person who so many of us feel is the least deserving of such sentiments. But as noted earlier, the behaviors we wish to have for the world cannot be real until we embrace them for ourselves. Though this may seem Self-serving and suggest another instance of our meditative efforts being hijacked by ego, the fact is that unless we can take care of ourselves by extending to ourselves what we would offer to another, we have nothing of value to extend to them. Expressing lovingkindness and forgiveness to ourselves is the journey we travel as agents of liberation.

These exercises may appear to be hokey and contrived, which they are in a way. After all, what do a bunch of nice-sounding words expressed in a private moment of meditation add up to, especially in a world where such sentiments are often insincere, hypocritical, and little more than politically oriented, Self-serving affirmations?

Though modest and largely invisible—until its influence is bumped into in retrospect—exercises of this kind are nevertheless important because they regularly bring to mind the values we are trying to strengthen. They help reinforce the habit of the values-grounded practice we're creating. That is the significance of acting intentionally, something I will expand on below when we discuss right conduct and right speech. By consciously eliciting such thoughts, we become more aware of these life-generous values. It helps in our efforts to stay in contact with our hearts. By purposely bringing values to mind, they come to the forefront of our consciousness over the course of our everyday lives and are therefore more likely to be a part of how we approach and interact with other beings. Speaking from my own experience, I have been struck by how over the years I have become more spontaneously aware of appropriate values in the very instance of their relevancy, and hence choose to act upon them.

Performing such exercises in an interconnected world carries weight, however indeterminable their effect may be. Everything counts when we're all part of a whole. Though modest, putting loving kind sentiments out into the world has transformative influence.

Meditation is essentially an exercise in being awake in and attentive to the passing moment. It cultivates presence in the present. In so doing we avoid becoming attached to rising and falling phenomena, not interrupting the flow by grasping this or rejecting that, but just letting it be and to pass on as it will.

One of the beauties of the practice is that it is not one step removed from our lives. That is to say, meditation is not only a rehearsal of liberation, it is liberation itself. It is a practice to develop mindfulness, to be sure, for a practice we hope to embody when we are out in the world. But it is also the real thing. Moments of struggle, lapse, and forgetfulness that occur notwithstanding, it is being fully alive in the living moment as we sit on our cushion, breathing in, breathing out. When we are totally aware of and focused on the breath, we are in touch with our original nature.

It's so interesting that when we are mindful of something as basic as the momentary breath, something we are usually unaware of and take for granted, we are also in a moment of complete freedom. What the practice of the practice is ultimately about is not only realizing the liberated state, which we always potentially can do, but helping extend the liberated state from one moment of freedom to another, consistently throughout our day.

Breath in, breath out. There is nothing else that we need to do. Breath in, breath out. Life doesn't get any simpler than this.

As is often the case with matters that are very simple, mindfully following the breath also has its challenges and difficulties. This is especially true when we're just beginning as a meditator. At least from the standpoint of maintaining constancy from one breath to the next, we may find we all too often lose the breath. This varies from day to day, and within an actual session itself. Rather than performing the "simple" task of following our breath, we discover we've zoned out—busy planning tonight's dinner, perseverating on an unpleasant incident that happened at work, nodding off to sleep, or otherwise being consumed with the infinite array of mental chatter which seems to have no purpose other than to occupy our minds, distracting us from our breath. Achieving consistent mindfulness is challenging. How easily we lose focus, becoming swept away by the needs of "I" calling the shots. We can be easily sidetracked by a "monkey mind," as it's often called by meditation practitioners, that refuses to be still. Rather than let go, it continues trying to seduce us with its enticing diversions and entertainments. Our commitment is tested. We can be tempted to quit. We don't seem to be getting anywhere.

This is all exacerbated if we enter this practice with expectations that we'll be new people, completely mindful and accepting within 30 days, or our money back! It's not just that anticipations of this kind are a recipe for disappointment, by their very future-oriented, nonpresent nature. While we may very well enter this discipline with the admirable purpose of improving our daily conduct—to facilitate greater congruency between our heart values and our actual behaviors—we must at the same time do so unconditionally, without any hope or expectation of accomplishing anything at all. This appears to be totally contrary to achieving a desired purpose: what's the point if not to have a goal we succeed at? But while meditation is rightly associated with commitment and discipline, to be successful at meditation it is important that we meditate without the goal of attaining anything! Unconditioning a conditioned mind can only be accomplished when performed unconditionally. The doing of meditation is its own reward and is most effective when it is done for its own sake, without ulterior purpose or ego. We are not on the way to somewhere—as Chogyam Trungpa put it, *"rather, one is on the way and one is also at the destination at the same time."* Meditation's gift to us is, as I stated at the beginning of this chapter, that there ultimately isn't anywhere to go, no one to be. We are already there, and we are who we need to be. Simply being mindfully present in the living moment brings us full circle.

Another delight of meditation is that at some point, we discover we actually enjoy the practice in its own right; the very act of doing it is a pleasure. While the calm and empty state it produces is subtle, beyond conceptualization, we generally experience it as a sense of well-being, a feeling akin to what we might experience when being fully in and with nature. We are one with ourselves and our world. Characteristic of itself, this quality does not announce its presence dramatically. It's a quiet, unassuming state of existence, something we may intellectualize about in retrospect, though not in the moment when, by definition, we are egoless. At one and the same time, it's no big deal and it's really quite wonderful.

Meditation also has its dangers and potential pitfalls. For one thing, we can just as easily become attached to this feeling of "bliss" as we can with any other phenomenon that entices us with happiness and well-being. Meditation can be addictive, something that we turn to and use to escape from our lives, rather than to engage with our world. In this way, it is potentially much like drugs, shopping, or anything else we use in order to evade living life.

This trap is especially important for activists to be aware of. After all, our purpose is to take our meditative practice off the cushion and bring it out into the streets. While it's great to become so skilled a meditator that we experience existential peace, this can become a Self-indulgent exercise if at the same time we aren't bringing the facility of meditation to our relationships with others. An effective activist doesn't participate in the practice of the practice simply for our benefit alone, nor do we sacrifice this essential work on ourselves in the service of others. We do so for both.

One of the sure signs that our meditation has been expropriated by ego is the emergence of a sense of superiority over our fellow beings, which can develop when we're wrapped up in our personal transcendence to the exclusion of the larger whole. The feeling of having achieved something that differentiates us from others exacerbates our separation from the rest of the world. It indicates that ego is haunting our practice, undermining the compassionate, generous, social nature of transformative activism. Rather than bringing us closer to a practice centered upon our interconnectedness with all beings, such an outcome achieves quite the opposite: it intensifies our egocentric view of life.

Hubris or humility—we are always on the razor's edge as we practice the practice. This underscores a fundamental reality about meditation: even with its potential to strengthen and develop our inherent virtues, it is also possible to become the captive of "I," to be just one more notch in ego's gun belt. Rather than promoting selfless behavior, meditation can be something else we become attached to. How could it be otherwise, given who we are, living in the world we do?

Another of ego's traps is to become doctrinaire about the breath, clinging to the notion that meditation is exclusively about staying with the breath from one moment to the next. Only the breath is relevant. Only the breath is real.

There is truth in this assertion, but what is important here is that it is not the only truth. While concentrating on breath is useful in developing the space of mindfulness, a rigid adherence to this can put us at war with our restless minds, causing us to harshly judge and suppress unwanted thoughts and emotions because they interfere with our focus on the breath. Specifically, it provides no room for the busy-minded distractions of ego we experience while sitting on the cushion, trying to follow our breath. As a consequence, these unwanted products of the mind end up as evidence of our failure as meditators, to be discarded in our quest for the holy grail of breath mindfulness.

Again, the challenges we encounter in meditation are gifts to our growth. Rather than quashing these impediments or attaching ourselves to and mindlessly spinning out with them, we acknowledge them for what they are and bring them to full consciousness. Despite being the mind products of "I," hence not real, they are nevertheless tangible in that they are present to us right now. Being unreal is who we are in this particular living moment, and this is as important for us to be conscious of as we are of our breath. These impediments we experience define our lives for us as ego identifies with them, at least until we shine the light of spacious awareness upon them and recognize them as the ephemeral phenomena they are.

We benefit greatly from seeing these moments, naming them for what they are: "planning," "blaming." "punishing," "hating," "fantasizing," "lusting," "romanticizing," "regretting," and so forth. We forgo perseverating on all the endless words we attach to these thoughts and feelings, but we do not deny their existence. Rather, we view them dispassionately, letting them come and go without comment, and gently return to our breath. This is the insight of *vipassanā* meditation. We expand our awareness of what is, and in so doing are much more present in the moment.

In naming our experiences, even when they're "unreal," we loosen the grip of ego. Naming our experiences beyond the meditation room is equally important, where seeing things with clarity and without interpretation or judgment has a salutary influence on our everyday interactions with the world. Speaking truth to what is, observing and noting, we behave with the detachment and equanimity that is present whenever we refrain from personalizing our behaviors. We take the steam out of ego, denying its source of power—our identification with what comes to pass. At least in this moment, we don't buy into the fiction of "I." The ego construct we previously identified as Us, and which served as the basis of our personality, we now recognize for the fraud it is. We let go of it; we are unstuck.

To the extent that we deflate "I's" significance by observing phenomena without judgment, we create space within which to live our lives as free human beings. Before all else, meditation is space. It is this singular quality of unnamed, unclaimed, unspoken-for space enabling us to see without ego. Meditative consciousness means being aware of the real world. In this state, phenomena are fluid and supple; with our insight into ego mind, we can choose to avoid becoming stuck in them. Distractions will simply pass through as we accept them for the unsubstantial phenomena they are. This space is why a meditative approach to the world we seek is so vital to our practice.

Unattached, we are able to gently bring our attention back to our breath, whether on the cushion or out in the world. Breath in, breath out. Expanding our awareness and seeing matters for what they are is as powerful and righteous a moment of mindfulness as if we had never lost the breath in the first place.

With meditation, "success" is committing ourselves to a continuing process with its inevitable ebb and flow, just like life itself. Although it is a practice of focusing on our breath, meditation is also about *losing* and *returning* to the breath: awake and asleep, real and unreal are but two expressions of what life is all about. Being mindful is being mindful, whether of the breath or whatever distracts us from it. Ultimately, being conscious of ego's workings allows us to follow our breath and move along the path of liberation.

This demonstrates how forgiving the practice of meditation is. Meditation has infinite capacity to absolve us of our "I"-perceived "failures," which is one of its most blessed features. It allows us to lose our breath and become lost in our mind-products without judgment or punishment. Its practice does not require us to feel guilty, or to blame ourselves for some Self-identified error. Success and failure are but two arbitrary sides that "I" imposes on an otherwise indifferent process. Meditation works just as well when we recognize and acknowledge the workings of ego as it does in its "pure" moments of selflessness, following the breath. It practices what it preaches: no political agenda, no right and wrong. It is solely the awareness in the moment of now that counts. All we must do is be mindful of whatever *is*. In so doing, we are rewarded for both "failing" and "succeeding." Mindfulness is mindfulness. Meditation is meditation. Being present is being present. That's why it's the walk of the talk.

RIGHT CONDUCT

"Each and every action is our practice,
because some quality of heart and mind is being developed."
—Joseph Goldstein

Though always threatened by the possibility of being colonized by "I," the practice of meditation has the potential of deflating and reducing ego over time. As our awareness of the present moment expands, the narrative feeding our constant (re)con-struction of the Self has increasingly less space to exist. Opin-ions, concepts, interpretations, and judgments lose their energy and fall away. As we deflate "I's" significance by observing without judgment, we create emptiness to live life as a free human being.

But this can only happen if we take our meditation out into the world and have it wrestle with the messy realities of our momentary lives. This is when our practice becomes down-to-earth practical.

But as with meditation itself, acting on our values in an everyday, consistent manner is not something that can be performed half-heartedly, left to chance, without commitment or discipline. We are kidding ourselves, and not giving the political world its proper due, if we believe otherwise. We cannot simply assume that having the right intentions alone is sufficient for the practice we want. While they are the all-important first step to doing the right thing and absolutely necessary for our even-tual success, good intentions by themselves are not enough. They must be acted upon intentionally, at least until they become spontaneous, habitual, and are one with our being. Only then do they translate into actual behaviors. We must purpose-fully bring the values of our meditation into our daily practice with others. In the political world, right conduct and right speech won't happen otherwise.

Meditation is essentially a solitary activity. Even when performed in the company of others at a retreat or as part of a meditation group, we are essentially alone with ourselves. This is central to experiencing the stillness of the mind and body which we require to be one with ourselves. Being alone provides the supportive context to cultivate the values crucial to a whole-some activist practice.

In light of this, there would appear to be a serious contradic-tion between engaging in a meditative practice that requires quiet and solitude in order to be successful and acting as an agent of human liberation which, by definition, involves relationships and interactions with others, along with the inevitable turbulence of the political world. At first blush, anyway, this seems to be adverse to spiritual development.

Yet becoming a spiritual warrior is incomplete if one doesn't include this outer work with the inner work of the practice of the practice. Meditation is very important, of course; our *inner work* is essential towards accomplishing what must be done. But it is insufficient, not only in serving as an agent of liberation, but for our own transformation as well. We are incomplete without doing the *outer work*.

As we mindfully reconnect with ourselves on the cushion, we become aware of the presence of our hearts. In so doing, we begin to open ourselves to the world we're part of, the one we've been closed off from in order to protect and defend ourselves. We cease being isolated and separated, becoming more transparent and genuine in our contacts with others. Becoming so open, we are less heart-withdrawn and more available to the possibility of love, especially for its own sake. At least on our meditation cushions, we begin to see ourselves and our fellow beings in a more generous, forgiving, accepting light. Our hearts smile in our awareness of goodness and begin to recognize this quality in others.

But this state does not easily thrive, nor necessarily survive, when we are out in the world. While the potential for an expanded consciousness is being nurtured by our practice of the practice, we must not assume that it will automatically translate into corresponding behaviors once we move off the cushion. The equanimity we thought we had developed can suddenly evaporate in the blink of an eye. Much as our busy minds can throw us off balance, our encounters with the larger world can impact our momentary behavior in a mindless fashion, with consequences that extend beyond ourselves. As important as disciplined meditative exercise is to cultivating a mindful social practice, the former will not automatically result in commensurate right conduct, especially when we are up against the power of the political culture we live in, and in light of the imperfect, politically-conditioned beings we are.

This consideration may give us pause about going out into the political world, as it has for many spiritually-oriented people. We may be tempted to stay clear of political involvement, considering its well-earned reputation for being corrupt and Self-serving, bereft of integrity and principle. We may prefer, instead, to continue pursuing personal enlightenment, fearing that we could otherwise become fatally compromised by politics' moral dirtiness.

But if human liberation is to be realized, we who seek peace and freedom must be out in the world exhibiting behaviors relevant to being free and peaceful. We must live our lives as the liberated beings we have the potential of being, and do so while swimming adeptly and virtuously in the muck of the political world. Our "new" world is birthing within the "old" that is dying; together, they constitute our world of the present moment. This is the world that is especially suited for the spiritual warrior.

As activists for transformative change, it is precisely in our relationships with others outside of the meditation room where a practice of liberation comes full circle—where we forge in the furnace of daily reality a practice of revolutionary mindfulness. Only when our work on the cushion becomes meditation-in-action with everyday people, when our practice of the practice is integrated into our moment-by-passing-moment lives, does liberation come alive. To do this, however, it is necessary in the first place to make the kind of commitment to right conduct which is compatible with the heart values that form the basis of the practice of the practice.

Although meditation is routinely performed in an environment of quiet solitude with only our busy minds to contend with, where losing the breath does not threaten dire consequences, taking our meditation practice out into the streets and communities where we live involves greater exposure and risk. Out there, we are unprotected, transparent, vulnerable—we are who we are in reality. The practice of being selfless, without ego to guard and defend us, is very challenging, even for those of us who have been meditating for years. We often are uncomfortable being real with others, as accustomed as we are to being "I," seemingly in control of our lives. It is daunting to just be ourselves, out of control.

Additionally, it's more than a question of our own fallibility as human beings. It is also the other person and their own potentially provocative, Self-serving behaviors that our naked selves must respond to with split-second skill and wholesomeness. It would be one thing if all we had to deal with were fellow selfless beings, who were compassionate toward and accepting of us. How much easier it would be to risk being ourselves if life was peopled with grown up human beings!

But that's not necessarily what our relationships are about in the political world. We are all members of the Civilized version of our species who have egos and are involved in power relationships. As such, not only does "I" accompany us when we go out into the world, we inevitably encounter the "I" of others as well. This is the core of the matter: can we serve as living expressions of liberated human beings, while at the same time still surviving in the world as it is? How we respond to everyday variations of this significant fact of life speaks volumes to this question. Quite simply, what is critical at this time is not transcending ego. More realistic (albeit challenging, to say the least) is learning to live with our own egos and those of others as a free human being. That's what liberation is all about. Despite having to practice moral behavior in a political world with "I" more or less our constant companion, we must nevertheless accept our situation for what it is while committing ourselves to a practice that, in terms of its everyday behaviors, is beyond ego. This will take courage, integrity, equanimity, and other virtues to essentially surrender to our hearts, surviving as well as thriving in so doing.

The great advantage of a committed meditation practice is that while we may not transcend ego, we can be aware of its presence and acquire insight into its workings and the influence it has in our lives. These are no small matters. With our expanding consciousness, we have the necessary space to see what is real and what is hallucinatory; we are then better able to choose how we behave in any given situation, and to specifically choose skillful behaviors. At the same time, our behavior in the real world of political relationships also serves to further our practice of the practice, reinforcing and strengthening fledgling habits.

This is where the rubber meets the road—where our resolve is truly tested. Ultimately, meditation is all about leaving the cushion and dealing with life as it is in the real world. We act mindfully in the moment and on the basis of the values we are increasingly aware of and committed to. As a consequence, we choose not to act out as "I," but to conduct ourselves as the inherently values-based, liberated beings we are.

Just as our lives reproduce our political world from one moment to the next, so do we reduce ego's impact on our behaviors when we are mindful in the presence of "I." We deprive ego of its influence when we are able to stay with our breath; we minimize its effect when we choose to act selflessly in the world. Behaviors that are salutary in and of themselves as expressions of peace and freedom help to cultivate a habit of such conduct in our next moment, much as with any habit we develop.

One way that we can better guarantee the successful expression of our values in our everyday lives is by committing ourselves to a voluntary code of conduct. Much as following the breath can help discipline mindfulness while meditating, a code of conduct can help us do the right thing out in the world. This is a self-created statement of our values and principles, a promise we make to ourselves defining the behaviors we desire to consistently practice.

This can be especially effective when our vow is shared with others who we trust to keep us accountable in loving, nonjudgmental ways. By making our intentions publicly known, we more effectually make possible their actualization; they and we are then more transparent and intentional.

At its best, a code of behavior serves as a voluntary guide for our conduct. It is both the vision of, as well as a flexible road map to, the society we aspire to live in. While not a guarantee of anything—after all, a commitment is only practical to the extent we live our lives by it—following a heartfelt code is but a degree or two of separation from the spontaneous expression of the real thing. In fact, if we didn't know the difference, we would swear they are the same! As with our awareness of the breath, a code can become *habit-forming*.

A code of behavior is really nothing more than a pledge to ourselves to do the right thing the best we can. Placed on our desk, bed, or meditation cushion, the code serves as a continual reminder of what we have committed to. Bringing greater resolution to our practice, it evolves over time, adding behaviors we are especially sensitive to and want to work on. Essentially, it is a vow to behave toward others as one of us, with heartfelt camaraderie and friendship. Principled solidarity with other living beings is always significant to a practice of right conduct.

Perhaps we dedicate ourselves to it every morning upon rising. After expressing our gratitude for being alive in this incredible world, and for anything else we are thankful for, we recommit ourselves to a practice of right conduct and right speech.

This is even more powerful when we focus on a specific behavior, entering the day with a promise to be particularly mindful how we interact with others. Perhaps we focus on someone who is particularly challenging for us, who we want to be more skillful with, more compassionate toward. To recommit ourselves daily to listening to the voice from our hearts is a powerful stimulus to doing the right thing over the long haul. Especially in the context of the everyday is this true, when the seemingly most inconsequential word or deed can contribute to a web of routine decency.

Developing reminders helps us follow through on our intended behavior. This can be a thought, word, or phrase from one of our spiritual guides that we leave on a post-it on our bathroom mirror or bedside table; an alarm set with soft chimes on our phone; or something to read or listen to that inspires us before we turn out the light at night. It can also be as simple, yet profound, as remembering our breath at various times as we go through the day, with its associative connection to the heart and the values therein. Reminding ourselves helps us to be mindful in the moment.

These prompts assist us in developing a more consistent practice of doing the right thing in a world that, for all its noble rhetoric, doesn't do a good job of modeling or supporting what we as a Civilized people claim to be. In this context, our *code* is not a list of do's and don'ts; these are behaviors that don't require explanation or justification. Compassion is compassion, kindness is kindness. They defy being spelled out and categorized (*"This act is compassionate; this act is not kind"*) in a document that is then used to pass judgment on ourselves or to evaluate another. There's no mistaking behavior from the heart.

Even when we forget or fall short, being conscious about our promise to act upon our values is helpful. A moment of unwholesome behavior has the potential to also be a moment of liberation to the extent that it reminds us about our commitment. To experience ourselves as embarrassed or ashamed, and to not ignore these natural sentiments of the heart, is a helpful nudge for awareness and growth, as long as we don't punish ourselves for being "bad" in the process.

Ideally, we go into the world with the intention to behave with integrity, to live by our professed values as best we can. That's all we can do. That's all we can *ever* do. But it is good enough.

RIGHT SPEECH

Although as much a behavioral expression as any physical deed, speech is not always given the attention it deserves as one of the most potent actions human beings exhibit. Speech is significantly related to power relationships, especially those based on gender, race, class, and age. In the political world, speech is second to none in enforcing domination and control. Words are frequently weaponized to silence or put one in their place just as easily as a gun. Using speech in this deadly manner is a behavior that is unfortunately not unknown to activists, and male activists in particular.

Becoming mindful of what comes out of our mouths is especially important for those of us who wish to have a positive effect on others. A careless, sloppy word can completely wipe out the positive example we might have been until we put our mindless foot in our mouths.

The good news is that, despite this engrained behavior, it can be remediated and improved to the point where it largely becomes a nonissue. As with other behaviors, we can become sufficiently aware to make an intentional choice whether to say something or not, and to forgo altogether talking as if on automatic pilot.

We can also learn the important art of active listening, where we are an engaged presence without having to comment on what someone else has said or take exception to it when it contradicts our beliefs. Listening with a mind empty of "I" is a mindful act, one attentively focused on what the other is saying, unburdened by our own thoughts and opinions. This skill is especially imperative for activists in that we often learn of matters or viewpoints we weren't aware of before and which contribute greatly to what we're trying to do. I have long been struck by the fact that many of the suggestions or ideas I have contributed to a discussion in my role as an activist or community organizer are those I've heard from someone else at another time.

Listening without commentary is also a great way to learn about the other. Displaying interest in what they have to say, especially by asking questions that prompt further revelation, also helps render a more complete picture of them. The judgmental boxes we may have placed them in fall apart the more we learn, permitting us to appreciate the variety of their humanity.

Active listening is a most positive way to build relationships. In so doing, we are valuing the other, something that too many of us suffer a serious deficit from in political society. Active listening communicates to the other that they are worth our time and attention.

This is enhanced when we share with the other about ourselves, but only when the timing is right, and not interrupting the flow of the other or responding to ego's need to take over the conversation and say something. Engendered by honest expressions about ourselves, revealing our common humanity adds to the growing trust that is necessary to any worthwhile relationship.

Being skillful in our speech also includes allowing ourselves to pause before blurting out what happens to be wandering through our minds in the moment. Through a meditative approach, we can teach ourselves to consider what we are about to say, to be aware if it is redundant or unnecessary, hurtful or destructive, or simply Self-serving, or worth saying at all. With that kind of clarity, we relax ourselves into the conversation and limit ourselves to what contributes in terms of both content and manner of delivery. Often a question to clarify what the other had to say, or an additional observation that is relevant and contributes to the discussion, will suffice. We'll know that we're on the right track not only by the way others respond, but by our own sense of ourselves at this moment. If we are willing to consult this quiet intelligence, we always know at some level of our being when our values are awake and alert, beyond ego and its judging mind, or whether we're just being a jerk.

Engaged listening is especially important when serving as facilitator of a discussion where the purpose is to give everyone an opportunity to express their views, but also to achieve some kind of consensual closure. The inherent wisdom of what action to take will emerge if we are tuned into what is being said, not busy composing our own speeches. This practice involves patient, nonjudgmental listening, as well as the skill to accurately summarize the salient points of the conversation to hopefully arrive at a consensus for any next steps. Needless to say, these skills necessitate the ability to deny "I" a place at the table. This is skillful listening in action.

In general, *right speech* also requires a level of commitment similar to the kind we make for our physical behaviors. That is, we pledge ourselves not to cause harm to another sentient being by using words to threaten, intimidate, harm, frighten, humiliate, or degrade. In a world where we are so often divisive with what we say, where our words are uninformed by wisdom and compassion, speaking from a platform of lovingkindness will do much to advance peace and harmony in our interactions with each other.

We also apply this consciousness to eliminating what at first may appear to be a more innocent kind of discourse, but which in its own way is equally pernicious. This is the common practice of gossip. Invariably steeped in judgments, gossip is a Self-serving exercise in talking behind another's back that denigrates the subject while elevating "I" at the expense of the other. As unconscious as this may be at times, it is always an act of poisoning the mind—ours and others'.

As we come to recognize that so much of what we as Civilized humans give voice to is little more than advertisements for our Selves, we see the wisdom of not saying anything at all until we have something worthwhile to offer—words that are honest, kind, helpful, and appropriate to the moment. Though this may involve a lot less talking, silence is often the most effective speech of all!

"MASS PRACTICE"

Everything in your life situation becomes part of meditation,
which is an enormous demand.
—Chogyam Trungpa Rinpoche

The expansive quality of an activist practice is essential for activists to both appreciate and embrace. All too often, our practice has a much narrower focus. Confined to what we call our "mass practice," our efforts largely center on those we define as "oppressed."

While this purpose emanates from a heartfelt place, our "mass practice" suffers from this limitation, as it reduces our activism to a variation of the bifurcated lives we commonly live within political society. The practice is a part of our lives, but does not become embedded in our entire everyday lives. When we restrict ourselves in this manner, we are only part-time activists.

Most importantly, we undermine the potential of a values-informed practice. Through the development of a more inclusive, righteous practice, our capacity for compassionate mindfulness, and our awareness of our greater interconnectedness, enhance our potential to assume greater responsibility to the whole of life. An activism of human liberation is not simply an activity we set aside and attend to as a compartmentalized activity, as one of several discrete things we do. It is not confined to the meetings, the rallies, the demonstrations, the direct actions, but is instead a way of life, influencing and shaping all our relationships with our families, strangers, work and school mates, friends and enemies alike.

When a values practice is not organic to our lives, we end up committing the fatal error of treating the revolution as an event that is separate and distinct from the rest of our lives. It loses its moment-to-moment presence. Beyond those we have designated as the "oppressed" or activist comrades, we don't bring the values of a spiritual practice to the rest of our daily lives and our everyday relationships. This is because we fail to see that "the rest of our lives," with their mundane routines largely peopled by the same folks we see most days, have the same value and importance as our "mass practice," where the "real" revolution with the "real" people will take place. In this way, revolution loses its crucial distinction as an everyday affair.

Our practice suffers proportionately, diminished or ignored altogether. "The rest of our life" lacks the moral sensitivity essential to a revolution of everyday life when we live less mindfully, often reproducing the very same power dynamic in our interactions with others that is at the core of what we are working to change through our "mass practice."

Relegating our lives into separate parts is a major disempowerment for activists, undercutting such critical social practices as building community, mutual aid, and solidarity. Our specialized focus tends to isolate us from other activists and their own discrete issues. "Mass practice" tends to silo our particular political concern, promoting the kind of division that unfortunately typifies activism all too often. Not only are the individual concerns of our groups separated from one another, preventing us from collectively acting upon the root causes our entire individual causes share. They can also lead to the kind of ego-based, internecine conflict so often characteristic of activists, where we end up spending our time and energy fighting each other over our differences, depriving us of the support and strength we could realize if we recognized ourselves as comrades engaged in a common struggle.

More importantly, by viewing our "mass practice" as unconnected to the rest of our lives, we undermine what a meditative liberating practice is all about: the re-joining of humanity with the rest of life. If it is to have its salutary effect, activism is not a practice that is only performed for some people, but not for others. Rather, it must be part of everything we do, and with everyone we encounter from one moment to the next. It is us and our lives. It's what we're doing right now!

To be on the pathway to liberation means to be someone who is ethical and moral in the *entire* real world, exhibiting those values in our daily behaviors commensurate with being free, peaceful, and just with everyone. As with meditation, activism must be in all moments and aspects of our lives; we must extend our practice beyond our *official* activism to include all moments and sentient beings, as best we can.

This importance is borne in the cauldron of everyday relationships—our "private" lives—that often fall outside of official activist practice. They consist of our most personal and heartfelt associations with our spouses, partners, significant others, parents, and children, as well as our close friends—in other words, the very people who are perhaps the most deserving of experiencing our best "activist" selves. If we don't do the practice with them, then with whom do we practice?

Daily life is the soul of our existence, the heartbeat of who we are. It is where politics is born and liberation lives. Given its crucial importance, the momentary unfolding of everyday life presents us with endless opportunities and challenges within which to be mindful, accepting, and responsible. It is where the practice of the cushion resides when we're off the cushion.

As we know, personal relationships provide a rich stew of issues and needs, baggage and habits that go to the heart of our own ego's stuck-ness. Not only do we have to contend with others, we must also do so with those people in our lives with whom we are most vulnerable—those we are most personally invested in, dependent upon, and enmeshed with. These are the people we are attached to, and who are attached to us.

Given the level of exposure we have to these intimate others, we are always traveling in potentially treacherous waters where an unwholesome word or unskillful act can, if not crucify, at least inflict needless suffering. Personal relationships are challenging due to the ease with which we can become lost in harmful behaviors. All too often they involve not interactions of free, compassionate and loving kind human beings, but of exchanges where we are locked into the other as part of a Self-fulfilling power dynamic. In this scenario, the participants are stuck in codependent relationships, each seeking to have the other satisfy needs they don't take responsibility for. Toxic behaviors consistently arise, whose visitation on the other can become the basic script of the relationship.

While this is not true of all personal relationships, which certainly encompass a broad spectrum with many variations, the fact remains that in the political world, dyads of this kind are basically Self-centered, intended to serve the controlling/dependent needs of "I." This is natural in a world of stuck ego. It is also tragic, because "I"-motivated behavior is always the death of true love, the betrayer of lasting friendships, and the fatal obstacle to egalitarian relationships.

But as problematic as it is to have their ego and ours in each other's faces, these special relationships also present a priceless opportunity. For the only way out of this otherwise no-exit cul-de-sac, and to otherwise enjoy a healthy, sane relationship, is to surrender—intentionally leave our egos at the door of our inter-actions. Once "I" is no longer a player, our behavior choices are much more nourishing and exemplary.

Potentially, these are ego-smashing relationships because they often cut to the heart of our stuck-ness. Given our relative intimacy with the other, these connections can reach the raw meat of our hearts, threatening our idea of Self, thus raising the possibility of its dissolution. In the face of being real, our choice is to either respond in typically defensive ways by reasserting the primacy of "I"—or to give up, surrender, let go, and relax into the other (and ourselves) for who we are. In so doing, we are able to lend expression to our capacity for attributes of a liberating relationship, the necessary humility and compassion.

This can only be done through purposeful effort. We rarely surrender unless our backs are against the wall and we feel we have no other choice. For some of us, it may take a choice of no-choice to make this choice.

For others, however, surrender can be approached with the same kind of commitment and intention we bring to our medi-tation. As with the latter, we can make a point of being mindful in the moment. Rather than blindly acting out, we can make room for ourselves and our choices by being meditative in our interactions with the other.

Mindfulness involves space. This is the context of a successful "mass practice" of everyday life. Operating within this expanding space allows us to *be* the revolution. The benefits are life-changing, not only on the "personal" level, but the "mass," as well. A salutary dialectic goes back and forth between the two, informing them both. In the process, the two become one; the destructive dichotomy typical in everyday life dissolves. If only for a millisecond, a meditative practice provides us with the latitude to observe what arises for us in our moment-to-moment interactions, an invaluable insight for all our relationships. Rather than reacting blindly to the needs of ego, this awareness is the space we require to respond with a wholesome behavioral choice.

Even such a simple thing as noting our breath—in out, in out—during a moment when we experience an agitated, threatened "I," provides us with the time we need to let these states pass as they will, allowing for the room that follows, and the possibility of the liberating choice that mindfulness provides. In this nanosecond version of the classic wisdom from mom to *"count to 10 before doing something we'll regret,"* we speak less; what we do say is expressed without harm or malice. It is clean. Though we are always present and engaged, there are times when we do nothing at all.

Rather than reacting back and forth with "I," surrendering ego at the point of contact is both the most loving act we can extend to another living being, as well as a gift we give to ourselves. For activists, it is the golden highway to a successful "mass" practice, as well as to sustaining personal relationships.

MODESTY AND HUMILITY

Developing a commensurate sense of modesty and humility indicates that the practice of the practice is beginning to make real the behavior we require to be relevant agents for transformative change. This is the inevitable result of immersing ourselves in grieving our losses in life, returning home to Mother, and engaging in a committed meditation of the passing breath which cultivates right conduct and speech. Such activities all lead in one direction: the acceptance of life for what it is and the demise of a stuck ego. This is human liberation.

In following this path, a magical change takes place. We return to our true proportions and dimensions. We come down to earth. We are who we are, no longer trying to be more than that. Accepting ourselves for who we are, we become embodiments of modesty and humility. This is the true condition of a spiritual warrior.

Not only does this state of being allow us to be much more effective agents of peace and social justice, but it also offers us a priceless gift. With humility, we experience an enormous sense of lightening. No longer carrying around the burden of "I," we relax into who we actually are. When we arrive here, the obvious modesty and humility in our lives speak for themselves. They require nothing more than their simple, unadorned presence. They are what they are and who we are in each particular moment.

This is the incalculable blessing that comes with being real. This is the grace of living life as it is without having to be anyone other than who we are.

PART FOUR
BEING FREE IN THE WORLD AS IT IS

CHAPTER EIGHT

THE WAY OF THE TRANSFORMATIVE ACTIVIST

"The greatest gift you have to give is your own self-transformation."
—Lao-Tzu

As we enter the final part of this book, my purpose is to render as concretely as possible what has preceded it into practical ideas and suggestions for how an activist of transformative change might be a liberated human being in this world of political relationships and "I"-centricity. What I have to offer is not a definitive listing of qualities and characteristics, or even ideas that are original with me. Rather, they are intended as stimulants for your own creativity and imagination, to be contemplated as we enter this unprecedented world of human transformation in a collapsing Civilization.

A. Guiding Principles

ACCEPTANCE AS TRANSFORMATIVE CHANGE

The key to being an activist of transformative change is our acceptance of life for what it is. In so doing, rather than devoting our energies to trying to change the world to conform to some concept of the way things should be, we increasingly devote ourselves to being and living the peace, freedom and social justice we want by expressing our love for life through behaviors informed by our inherent heart values. In short, we are the revolution of everyday life, and especially as it manifests in the myriad of relationships and interactions we have with the world.

These values are the essence of our morality, the guiding light of a transformed existence. By taking responsibility for ourselves in this manner and acting with the compassion, kindness, courage, and integrity that the self-evident logic of our interconnected status commands of us, we selflessly serve other sentient beings in their efforts to be liberated.

Transformative activists accept that life is less than what we might want it to be. But we also know that life is forever changing, that it is a permanently impermanent condition. Life is however we find it at any one moment, fluid and unpredictable. It cannot be pinned down and confined to some ideal; its very nature resists this and any other definition.

That is why for the transformative activist there is no perfect world to pursue; there is only the living moment and how we choose to respond to it. Because such a world does not exist, the closest we come to the ideal is to live successfully as a liberated human being in the world as it is.

Not trying to change the world means that we do not try to change others. Despite the baggage we have been carrying around with us as "activists," where practice was one of making others change—especially those whose oppressive behaviors result in so much pain and suffering in the world—we go about the business of change by actively being the world we desire through an everyday values-informed practice.

Rather than change others, we want our practice to be of service to them. However that may be expressed, in dramatic gestures or more often than not, through quiet, unobtrusive acts that in both cases don't call attention to themselves, we want to be responsive to another in a manner appropriate to the circumstances. Personifying acceptance of ourselves in the ways we act with others, thus able to accept others, we invite and provide space for others to do likewise, foreshadowing in the present the liberated life we seek. In this way, we are useful to others as they walk their own paths. Accepting ourselves/accepting them —that quintessential act of love—is our potential gift to all living beings; this is the very best that we can be as activists of the human heart.

We don't have to force change for we know that change is happening all the time We only have to be present in the flow of now, mindfully alert to the passing moment when a word, a deed, no matter how modest and unassuming, even unnoticed, would be the right action to advance our collective liberation: both theirs as well as ours. In this way we are serving the cause.

In the end, transformative activists understand that our task is not so much about creating a new game, as we had thought at one time, but how to accept and play the game we're already in. Doing this skillfully and wholesomely is our task. Just as acceptance serves as our exit from the blind alley of "I," so is it also the open door to where we want to be.

THE PRACTICE IN EVERY WORD AND DEED

As we've stated, a revolution of everyday life is a practice where how we act today prefigures "tomorrow." This is the only way a liberating transformation is ever realized.

To do this, an activist makes an intentional effort to weave our practice of the practice into our daily behavior with others so the values being cultivated on the cushion are further nurtured and realized in the words and deeds exhibited with others. Over time, everyday practice becomes the practice of the practice.

Everything counts in a practice of liberation: from the way we wash the dishes in the morning to how we take out the garbage at night, from the way we greet the neighbor next door to the quality of our encounter with a homeless person on our way to a restaurant, from taking exception to the sexist comment of a male associate at work, to not letting pass a racist joke when we're with the guys at the bar, from apologizing to a child for treating them with disrespect, to greeting the trees as we encounter them on our walks—we intentionally bring a values-conscientiousness, as best we can, to our daily lives in everything we do.

Everything counts. There are no moments that don't help to create the liberating culture within which we live; they all contribute to the larger scene we're all part of and that we help to shape though our acts. It is the quality of our presence in these countless moments that not only enables us to be free, but also helps to provide the space that extends this possibility to others. Moral consistency from the individual heart informs the nuances of quotidian existence that allow a culture of heart to arise and increasingly characterize who we are as a people. *This* is revolution that is transformational.

It is important to understand that a more consistent, day-to-day performance of values-directed behaviors will not necessarily eliminate those forces in life that are oppressive and destructive. Given the almost infinite variety of human beings we are, we can be confident that evil—socially acceptable, as well as universally repellent—will remain. We have no control over others, as much as we have tried to exact it. It doesn't work.

We are not working toward some Utopia, which, as Riane Eisler informs us, in her required reading *The Chalice and the Blade,* literally means "no place" in Greek. Instead, we are working toward what Eisler defines as "pragmatopia," a reasonable, everyday way of being for the imperfect human beings we are. This is another way of saying that we live as a liberated human being in the world as it is. We do our best, not by trying to be paragons of virtue, but by being true to ourselves and by our example encouraging others to do likewise.

THE IMPORTANCE OF HOW WE DO WHAT WE DO

Everyday practice is not only a question of what we do, but also *how* we go about doing so. As important as the former is, it is ultimately the how of our practice that determines whether or not what we do is truly transformative. Peace is not peace when it comes out of the barrel of a gun, no matter how the shooter may insist his act is necessary for peace; the spirit of generosity is undercut by expecting a *quid pro quo* from the recipient; and courage, while usually implying physical action, may be simply a matter of doing nothing while being fully awake and present. The Buddhist nun Thanissara summed up the issue well when she wrote, "it is not so much what we are doing, but the quality of presence we are 'doing from.'"

Regardless of the apparent virtue of what we do, the business of how we behave is always a matter of whether we can act without being Self-serving, glorifying ego. Can compassion be compassionate minus heart? Just the form, and not the substance? Can it be performed for its own sake, without expectations attached to it? The answer to these questions speaks volumes as to the difference between a transformative practice and one that is the same old thing dressed up in moralistic clothing.

In short, the values that arise from a practice of acceptance are not matters of doctrinaire "correctness" that can be spelled out into edicts of Right and Wrong. Rather, they are morally informed behaviors because they are unconditionally offered, congruent with the circumstances we find ourselves in at a particular moment, and expressed in a manner that is fully attuned to our hearts and the best interests of the other that we intuitively understand when we are fully present with them. They are the consequence of a consensus between a mindful mind and an awakened heart.

How we express ourselves is the litmus test of our behavior. It is the look in the eye, tone of voice, body language—the *feel* of what we're about, which speaks to our true intentions and whether our act of apparent virtuous behavior is truly one of moral quality or just a charade.

Having said this, however, there is a key exception that needs to be underscored because of its importance to our spiritual growth. Especially in the earlier stages of this process, we may act with virtuous behavior that is not spontaneous or heartfelt, but is done anyway, not as a phony or hypocritical act designed to fool the other as to our intent, but because we *know* that this is the right thing to do. Doing the right thing is always the right thing even when it's a mixed expression of a conflicted heart. We know this to be true when the other responds to our gesture with obvious heartfelt gratitude that allows our heart to experience genuine pleasure in their response.

However we may have stumbled upon this less than spontaneous act performed more out of knowing, rather than feeling, what was right in the circumstance, this in no way lessens its value, if in fact it was the right thing to do. It is only suspect when we know that what we did was not for the benefit of the other, but to serve our own purposes. There is nothing perfect about transformative behavior.

CORE RELATIONSHIPS

As I've argued throughout this book, what renders Civilization so distinctly and characteristically uncivilized for all living beings (including those who are one-up) are the power arrangements that have dominated human relationships from the very beginning. This absence of a moral foundation—the one we insist bestows upon humankind the mantle of superiority over all other sentient beings—gives the lie to our claim of being truly civilized.

For this reason, activists who are committed to transformative change need to focus on our everyday relationships. These are second to none in providing not only the necessary agency for, but also the living example of the revolutionary change we seek.

It should be kept in mind that I will be addressing relationships of gender, race, and age in the voice of a white male adult. While this leaves out other, equally important relationships (e.g., those of class, sexual orientation, not to mention Mother, Nature Herself), it does allow me to concentrate on three that are basic to human liberation.

I feel it is necessary to underscore who I am—a white adult male—as I begin to discuss transformative change in the context of people who have especially suffered oppression in our society, in order to emphasize that I recognize that I am a member of humanity who bears predominant responsibility for this oppression. Not only is this so for the sins of my gender and race, past and present, and the privileged position of power that this status has gratuitously bestowed on me, but from a more personal standpoint, for the very behaviors I have exhibited throughout my life that reflect, however unconsciously yet no less decisively, my possession and exercise of this unmerited power.

Hence, even more than the book in general, what follows in this section truly reflects myself as a continuing work in progress.

THE EVERYDAY RELATIONSHIPS OF MEN AND WOMEN

As we begin this discussion, I have to admit that I find it very hard to dispute the contention that white male adults are, if not exclusively, at least largely responsible for the state of our world, and have been throughout history. It's not my intention to argue that case here, only to ask you, especially my fellow white males, to think about this. A reasonably undefended review of the past leads inexorably to the centrality of patriarchy, and the domination of men over the rest of life.

Nowhere is this more striking than in the apparent synergetic relationship between nature and women, and the attempt by men to conquer both. I don't believe this is a coincidence, and feel the effort to dominate and control women probably occurred at the same time, if not before, Civilized humans began their assault on Mother with the birth of agriculture some 10,000 years ago.

This belief is underscored by how much closer women and nature are to the essence of life, especially its renewal through the birthing of new life that continues the eternal cycle of momentary existence. As men, and regardless of how responsible many of us are in the care and nurturance of the progeny we help produce, we are nevertheless one step removed from the life-creating process. Men don't carry the child through the pregnancy as women do; men don't provide sustenance through our nonfunctioning breasts, or experience the monthly menstrual cycle that makes this creation possible. We don't birth the child.

In this sense, men can appear to be powerless, at least in our own eyes, which may result in gender-specific insecurity. This could well be the origin of the original power-trip of our species: the acting out of our existential anxiety through our attempts to dominate and control women in a variety of personal and systemic ways that employ social, psychological, sexual, and physical violence to achieve this purpose. Through our habitual practice of acting-out on them, this has been our way as men when we are not able to come to terms with feelings that threaten our sense of Self. These, in turn, have become institutionalized by the rules, expectations, customs, and habits of the patriarchal world these behaviors have created.

In essence, therefore, the domination of men over women is a classic instance of what power relationships are all about. The dominator attempts to establish its control because we suffer a generalized inferiority that exacerbates our original fear of non-existence. However men may express this power over the world, and over women in particular, there is always this sense that behind the curtain of bravado, machismo, and terrible violence that attempts to lend credibility to our pose of being in control, lies a fundamental anxiety and insecurity about ourselves. We cannot accept that we are good enough as the people we are, and that we don't have to constantly "get it up" to prove otherwise.

That is why, despite the presence of race, age, class, and the almost endless examples of other power arrangements that characterize our hierarchal society, it is patriarchy, the relationship between men and women, that is the original and most crucial social arrangement to maintaining our political society.

It is also why, though both sexes are born with this capacity and women are particularly socialized to express heart values, the latter gender is the vanguard of the revolution of everyday life. The transformation of this power relationship to one that is predicated upon love-morality—traditionally the province of women—is the basis of the liberation for the entire human race.

Transformative relationships must be intentionally approached because power arrangements, such as patriarchy, are so deeply embedded within the existing structure of our society and the fiber of each and every one of us. Good intentions are of course essential to get the process going, but only commensurate actions will eventually carry us forward.

The good news is that notwithstanding our bluff and bluster (and unfortunately our various ways of defensively acting out) to the contrary, many men really want to be the people of heart and loving partners we can be. We don't readily admit to this for fear of being labeled a "pussy," "fag," or some other put-down by other men to keep us in our place.

But we're not starting from scratch: what we want, what we're really looking for, is already here. It just needs to be recognized and accepted by men, and, of course, acted upon. Which is tricky when we've spent lifetimes denying our feelings, struggling to maintain the semblance of control by exerting dominance over our world by any means necessary—for most men, this is the home, wife, and children—and experiencing the spiritual and emotional crippling that accompanies the burden of an ancient patriarchal culture and conditioning. It is not easy to forsake our power and privilege, and just accept being who we really are.

There are at least two remedial practices that men can undertake in addition to the practice of the practice. One involves learning how to be more wholesome with women, and the other is to do the same with men. With women, men must first disabuse ourselves of any notion that the transformative growth we hope to cultivate in our relationships is somehow women's responsibility: to teach us, to nurture our potential, to mother us along. It is important that we don't saddle our commitment with the expectation that women must help us to finally realize our humanity, to make us more complete human beings. This is not their job, though god knows, they have been doing their best to serve precisely this role for eons! As it is, they have enough to do in coming to terms with being a woman in a patriarchal society, and the part they play in perpetuating and sustaining patriarchal culture.

Once we're able to do this, men can open up to women in ways we are presently defended against. As is commonly observed, men are typically much less vulnerable and transparent in our interactions, closed off to our feelings, removed from our intuitions and instincts. We don't value this realm of subjective knowledge as women do, therefore we go through life minus awareness of an entire dimension of life as it is, of the truth we could discover in our personal experiences with the living moment. It is not that this potential doesn't exist for men; it's that we are systematically discouraged from inhabiting this feature by our families of origin, and the larger society we are part of, especially by other members of our gender who dishearten its expression—often in violent, certainly ostracizing ways—whenever we cross our "feminine" border and our behavior is seen as threatening.

No, we learn from women by doing what we must to open ourselves to them: by making ourselves more available to them, more receptive to the real people they are, although they have become invisible to us because we see them as sex objects (which they may collude in by making themselves more presentable to us), when we see them at all.

Men must interact with women in those everyday ways that we typically remove ourselves from and are generally disrespectful about. We do this by demonstrating interest in what women have to say, what they're interested in, what they do, even when foreign to our masculine ears—as it can be until we come to appreciate them more for who they are and value their thoughts and perspectives. In general, we must be a quieter presence, less active and domineering, asking more questions, making less statements.

While women are also concerned about the "larger issues" of life, and can talk as intelligently and insightfully about them as any man, they are socialized to be more in tune with the everyday, which men often dismiss as boring and unimportant. At the heart of the everyday are relationships, which many women value for the supportive and caring arrangements they are, as evidenced by the energy and attention often put into close same-gender friendships. Relationships are seemingly more natural for women than for men—especially those that they are engaged in for their own sake, with displays of compassion, kindness, and other heart qualities and are often less transactional than they are for men. This is not because these abilities are unique to women alone, but because the socialization of women has allowed for and encouraged the expression of these values that we all potentially possess, but that men typically devalue.

To be helpful and of service to others are attributes that have also acquired an oppressive dimension under patriarchy, embedded as they are in the female role that women are expected to play, as well as the under-paid (and often unpaid!) work they have been largely confined to. Despite being expropriated and used to subjugate women, these inherent virtues can be liberated and practiced by all people, men and women alike, once the male foot is removed from the neck of women and men begin to value them, rather than oppress.

It is their relationship skills and values-affinity that so recommend women for positions of leadership they could potentially occupy in a liberated society. Interestingly, this is a capacity that is demonstrated in the management of a home and family, which is no easy job, as any man who has served a term as house-husband and stay-at-home dad knows! Despite male denigration of these "domestic" skills when compared to the hard-headed, unemotional ones that men insist are their province (and the ones we insist are required for running a business or nation), it is speaking to the obvious when we observe that the virtuous qualities women often exhibit are so critical for the peace, equality, and social justice a transformative society exemplifies.

The second practice men must engage in is one that deals

affirmatively with our own sex. We must stand up to the concerted, often virulent, albeit largely unconscious efforts of men to keep men in line: *to act like a man.* To overcome this, we must place a special emphasis on the importance of accepting ourselves for the complete human beings we are, including those qualities that are considered feminine. We must cease being one-down to ourselves.

This is our fundamental task as men, which is especially important in our relationships with other men. Here we compromise, selling ourselves short, for fear of not appearing to be a man in the company of other men. This is apparent in the homophobia many of us suffer from, making us particularly vulnerable to archaic taunts from our peers that we're *queer:* less than a real man, more like a woman.

Being real is important in all the arenas of our everyday. This ability and willingness seem particularly vital with our brothers because men play a critical role in enforcing and reinforcing not only the gender-specific role women are expected to adopt, but our own as well. Going against the grain of what it means to be a man in our society is challenging, to say the least.

But we don't need to make grand gestures to assert our multidimensional selves; we must only allow ourselves to express—to be—the person of values we are. And in so doing, we'd be surprised to see how, when our potential for compassion, appreciation of beauty, capacity for gentleness, and untapped lovingkindness come out into the light of day it is favorably received, not only by women who have long waited for their male counterparts to emerge as equals, but by at least some other men who perhaps only needed another man to show —to risk being—himself for who he is to consider being themselves, as well.

A supportive men's group can be helpful, though one to approach with care. These groups can devolve into sessions where the men are still stuck in their competitive roles with one another and more interested in scoring points by trying to prove how "woke" we are, rather than just being awake.

An effective group is one that accepts who we are, including the residue of our patriarchal conditioning and toxic masculinity that we are struggling to evolve from. In such a group, men support all men and refrain from judgments or better-than-thou behaviors. We learn to love one another, and to openly express that love, an extremely challenging act for many of us because of our homophobic fears of how this behavior might be interpreted by other men.

But the gateway to egalitarian and truly loving relationships with women is in opening our hearts to and with men, and coming to terms with those inherent values we have long denied ourselves. Becoming increasingly at home with men—with ourselves—we are much more likely to be comfortable with women to the extent we cease having to be one-up to them.

Another virtue of a well-functioning men's group is the potential for compassionate accountability. With a gentle and caring approach, the group can raise issues about the behaviors of members that breach our defenses so as to be heard and accepted.

As with women, our relationships with men improve substantially when we are finally able to recognize each other as the people we actually are. At this point, it is stating the obvious to emphasize the importance of relationships to the quality of the world we live in. But this acquires even greater weight when we finally come to understand and appreciate the significance of the arrangements between men and women, and the revolutionary potential they possess. Once both sexes, but especially men, begin to move toward a consistent practice of heart-inspired relationships throughout our daily lives, the critical dynamic between women and men will serve as the foundation of remarkable transformative change.

Alas, this is only true when men do that which would seem

most obvious if we are truly committed to a transformative practice, given the incessant violence that men routinely visit upon the world, and particularly on women, literally from one moment to the next. Whether with our bodies or our speech, our customs or policies, men must cease the various acts of violence and harm we employ to keep women in what our society insists is their "place." When we make this change, when we men consistently behave in this most elementary manner instead so that women no longer have to fear the eruption of misogyny through either a raised fist or a raised eyebrow when they walk down a street or enter a bedroom, men and women both will know that we're on the pathway to liberation. Not only will women be increasingly released from the fear of men; men will experience the special pleasure of living and loving alongside women who are no longer afraid of us

LIVING WITHOUT WHITE SUPREMACY

Whites are my people, they are my tribe. I am a member of the White race.

Only when we come to this understanding of who we are, as White people, and are able to own such a distinction, are White activists able to begin our transformative journey toward racial egalitarianism and come to terms with our corrupting state of White supremacy.

White people must start with who we are. The first thing is to recognize that while historically we haven't seen ourselves this way, we are a race. We are the White race. As White people, we go through life on this planet oblivious to the fact we are a race like every other.

Instead, we have viewed ourselves as being outside of race. Unlike the races of color, we are the non-race, above and beyond race—at least in our eyes, certainly not in the eyes of people of color!—distinguished by the fact we have no color.

It is our singular lack of pigmentation that allows us to assume from the beginning of life that we are the normal, the *civilized* representative of homo sapiens, while the rest of our species, as evidenced by the color of their skin, are decidedly less: *ipso facto*. White supremacy positions them as sub-human, innately inferior to Whites, closer to animals than they are to us who, because we are white, are considered the full, complete, *civilized* embodiment of human beings.

Looked at dispassionately, it is as if this mindset was birthed and nurtured from the desperate need of a fragile, shaky sense of personhood, and clung to over the years as if our lives depended on it, a White DNA that feels threatened with extinction if not guarded against and protected from people of color. This is so vividly apparent at the present time in the United States, where the ascendancy in sheer population numbers of BIPOC (Black Indigenous People of Color) folks that is poised to overtake whites very shortly has elicited an absolute terror amongst an appreciable number of White Americans.

Another crucial truth that members of the White race must come to terms with is that we have benefited immeasurably, and continue to do so—economically, socially, and legally—from this racialized arrangement, whether that be the system of slavery that created the capital for growing the American industrial giant, or the practice of discrimination that followed "emancipation" in employment, housing, health care, education, civil rights and almost any other area of life that has kept Black Americans in a state of social inequality, maintaining and reinforcing the phenomenon of white privilege that has always been the reverse side of black subjugation. We White folks overlook this fact because we see our great, great, great grandparents as "innocent" Northerners who didn't rape and lay the whip across the backs of slaves they didn't own. And today, we White liberals who claim that we don't have a racist bone in our body and that some of our best friends are people of color disavow responsibility for the cruelty and terror our White brothers and sisters have perpetrated against African Americans and Native Americans since at least 1619 overlooking the fact that we benefit every day, and in so many ways, from the privileges we enjoy that their actions made/make possible. To be a White person in the richest country in the world, which even the kings and queens of old could only imagine, but that we as White people take as our due, has enmeshed us inextricably into a society of exclusivity that legitimizes lawlessness and entitlement. The fact that so few of us comprehend, much less appreciate, that we are the recipients of an unprecedented economy and material bounty that has been provided to us through the oppression of African Americans, and other people of color, as well as the genocide of Indigenous people, is just one of the many reasons why White people need to be reminded all the time, and deeply humbled by the fact that, indeed, Black Lives Have Mattered... To US.

We have begun to be aware of what prompted such a watchword. Through the epidemic of wanton killings perpetrated by police that the presence of videos has helped educate us about, we have gradually awakened to the ubiquity of violence in the everyday lives of Black people. Unlike a Black man, for example, I have come to see that, as a White man, I can walk out of my house on any morning with no concern about being physically, emotionally or "legally" assaulted because of my skin color as I walk down the street, tending to my own business. Or unlike a Black parent, I don't need to concern myself with conscientiously educating my children—especially the boys—about how to properly conduct themselves when approached by a cop.

Because of our Self-designated "superior" racial status, Whites assume an unbridled authority over BIPOC humanity, personally and institutionally, one that we exercise with indiscriminate violence in order to maintain our control. As if it is our God-given right to not only rule, but to do so lethally—

personally and institutionally, to take the life of a nonwhite person anytime we feel threatened by their existence.

So fragile and insecure are we in our whiteness, our privilege is only maintained by stoking the flames of abject hatred toward Black people. We inadvertently yet dramatically expose ourselves when we project on to men of color our inner demons: the dread of a Black uprising we claim is lusting to murder us, to rape *our* (sic) White women, and from whom we have to protect ourselves through an intentional policy of terrorizing Black people—but especially men—with slave patrols, torture, lynching, beating, raping, imprisoning, and government-sanctioned murdering, not even to mention the racialized justice system.

As horrific as this violence is, it only "makes sense" within the larger context of racial oppression, the formal and informal domination of Black folks through all kinds of dehumanizing policies and practices that seriously compromise their access to the basics of life—food, shelter, employment, health, education, self-respect, and in general, "life, liberty and the pursuit of happiness," as guaranteed by the Constitution. It is only within this intimate yet ubiquitous everyday oppression that the private and state violence it begets can be adequately appreciated. Nowhere is this more clearly seen than in the violence that exists amongst Black people living in predominantly poor, Black communities.

But this intra-community violence, often cited by Whites as evidence of the "inherently" sub-human, violent nature of people of color, is more accurately understood as deflected aggression. This is the consequence of the rage that accumulates when a people are subjugated to systemic inequality and lack a viable outlet to respond to their oppression. It is only *safe* for Black people to act out against their own people, in their own communities, because of the severe reprisals they can expect from the dominant White person, they can literally get away with murder of their own kind. This is because of what the Black scholar and activist W. E. B. Du Bois has called a "peculiar indifference" that White America has toward Black-on-Black violence, another instance that demonstrates how in this racialized culture of white supremacy, Black lives emphatically do not matter.

The irredeemable nature of race relations that one cannot help but feel is where matters sadly stand between Blacks and Whites. It was captured by the writer James Baldwin when he said, *"I will flatly say that the bulk of this country's white population impresses me, and has so impressed me for a very long time, as being beyond any conceivable hope of moral rehabilitation. They have been white, if I may so put it, too long…."*

What is to be done? How do White activists respond to the profound and pervasive existence of White privilege in such a way that it cuts through that which has kept us apart and offers transformative possibilitiesW instead? As before with the subject of dismantling patriarchy, it is not the responsibility of Black people to cure the White race of our disease. This is not a Black problem. It's a White problem. We need to be the solution to this problem ourselves. We need to do something.

Right intentions, of course, are important. But speaking here directly to White readers, we need to consider, for example, what it means when after marching in the streets all day chanting "Black Lives Matter," our sisters and brothers of color go one way to their homes, and we go another way to ours; that all we may have in the way of connection and relationship until we encounter each other at the next demonstration is a "Black Lives Matter" sign we stick in our lawn. As White activists seeking transformative change, we need to stretch those good intentions beyond the old and familiar, beyond our comfort zone to a level of commitment where we begin to have the backs of our Black sisters and brothers not only during times of protest, but in the hours and days before and after these episodic events, when their lives are threatened with violence or further impoverished by an unjust system—when we could be a real ally, a friend. This kind of involvement requires everyday relationships with one another, the kind we may have with some of our White friends and neighbors, but that most of us do not have with Black folks.

In the racially homogenous areas of this country, it's not just living in the same neighborhoods, where proximity to one another is a matter of being next door or just down the street, and where the barrier of physical distance is greatly reduced. As propitious as this would be (and it should be taken advantage of whenever possible), it is not realistic for many of us, White and Black alike, and frankly it is impossible in numerous instances.

Our challenge, therefore, is to figure out ways we can come together, be together, have something other than the often one-dimensional (at best) relationships we have now, where we hang out together, spend time in each other's homes, get to know each other: having a beer or cup of coffee, a play date with our kids, watching a ballgame or having folks over for dinner; going to the movies or out to a restaurant, or whatever, just talking about things, everyday things and sometimes serious matters, doing the common, everyday things with each other that friends usually do with one another.

This schematic representation distorts the real-life process involved in the creation of relationships with people "not of our kind." They won't happen overnight, given the long history of charged, toxic associations we have with each other as the White race and the Black race. They will take time and patience, flexibility and accommodation, consistency and commitment, imagination and creativity.

It may be a small act like regularly attending the services of the church that the African American community attends. Or frequenting a bar that Black folks patronize. And seeing what happens: a smile. *"Hi, how you doing?"* Engaging in normal conversation. Mentioning something about the stress of the holidays, or your kid's birthday that's coming up; the score of the game on the TV, or TGIF. Taking an interest in the scene you have entered, with the people who are there. Being open to whatever the opportunity provides.

I don't have the answer; I don't think there's a magic wand, or some hot water we can pour over the scene that will produce instant relationships; I'm just riffing on the possibilities that are always present.

And I realize, given its profound systemic nature, with roots that stretch back for millennia, that relationships alone are not the whole answer to White supremacy and racial subjugation. There are also the institutions of racial oppression—the non-existent jobs, the redlined housing, the voting suppression, the school segregation, the food deserts, the discrepancy in health care, and more—that impact Black lives like a sledgehammer to the gut. These need to be addressed.

And for that reason, active, committed support of Black power movements, such as BLM, is critical. This is the other side of building relationships of integrity with BIPOC who are part of our communities. We must stand with our neighbors of color.

But it is only the everyday presence of transformed relationships that we nurture with each other that, by eliminating its social basis, ultimately erodes the *legitimacy* of the systemic racism that holds people down. The growth of meaningful relationships with BIPOC folks, where Whites become increasingly conscious of and progressively cease acting out our privileged caste, will begin to wear away the building blocks of superiority in speech and behavior, the foundations of racist institutions that are both created and perpetuated by quotidian acts of hated, violence, and cruelty. By eliminating from our race's collective behavioral repertoire those individual, everyday acts that allow White supremacy to be real, and replacing them with acts of acceptance and compassion instead, the system of racial oppression will be progressively diminished. Without our active participation, this system cannot be supported.

IT ALL BEGINS WITH OUR CHILDREN

Unquestionably, the socialization of Civilized human beings to become the political people we are rests in the way we are raised by our parents and the larger world of adults. To one extent or another, this is done through a power relationship, in which younger people are categorically one-down to older people simply by virtue of age and the assumption of universal adult superiority because of that arbitrary feature. As a result, children are expected to submit to an authoritarian, hierarchical arrangement that is all too often capricious and arbitrary, not to mention violent, in an effort to maintain its rule of authority that is simply based upon the unfounded assumption that adults "know better."

Now there is no question that as children, we require the care of adults, especially around our basic needs, as well as acquiring knowledge about the dangers of the world, and how to avoid them.. But in a political society, this necessity becomes the rationale for a more dominating, controlling relationship that transcends its legitimate purpose to encompass one that trespasses upon a child's integrity. By imposing arbitrary rules and regulations, however unintended, which serve only to maintain adult authority at the expense of children learning and doing for themselves, we cramp, if not suppress altogether, a child's potential as an autonomous living being.

A transformative society loves their children for their own sake and honors their presence in a variety of ways: listening to what they have to say and incorporating their desires and wisdom into decisions we make about them; reality checking with ourselves and our partner about whether the way we handled a situation was done in the best interests of the child or whether it was merely to assert our authority over them; apologizing to a child when we're wrong; always giving them the space they need to grow and become the being they are when it's not at the expense of their safety. Adult love doesn't stifle or suppress, but rather is curious about and tuned into the child for who they are, open to accepting them as a unique expression of life, and not trying to change them into what we, the adults, would want them to be. In this way, *raising* a child is as much an experience of growth and development for us, the adults, as it is for the children we care for and hopefully guide to a wholesome maturity.

Children require us to be grown up human beings in our relationships with them. Their behaviors can be challenging as they experiment and push the boundaries that are endemic to becoming a fully realized person. Their perceived "misbehavior" can be threatening to an adult whose sense of Self requires them to have more control of the situation. In the end, and as it is with all relationships, the only way adults can appreciate children and be of genuine service to them in their development is by parking our egos at the door every time we interact with them.

Activist Relationships with Activists

ACTIVIST SOLIDARITY

One of the central features of transformative activism is that it is founded on a consciousness of interbeing. We move beyond the ego-dominated, individualistic ways of political practice where the baleful influence of our narcissistic civilization is killing us, towards one that emphasizes the wholesome alternative of compassionate solidarity. This is essential for negotiating life in this era of extreme polarization we live in and the dangerous unraveling that is occurring all around us. It is only when we recognize our common needs and purpose that we come together and act together.

For transformative activists, relational skills are the heart of a skillful practice. Wholesome relationships are the bricks and mortar of the existence we're trying to create, whether that be in our households, neighborhoods, communities, or the larger society.

But despite our best rhetoric to the contrary, relationships are not necessarily the strong suit of activists. Too often, we revert to adversarial and unskillful behaviors with anyone who opposes us or takes exception to what we stand for. Rather than employing a more compassionate approach, we engage in power struggles in an effort to impose our version of what should be on the other, usually with an attitude of Self-righteousness.

This is unfortunate and self-defeating, but not terribly surprising when this kind of behavior is directed at those people we designate as our enemies. Understandable, perhaps, but conduct that nevertheless inhibits a practice that is intended to be progressive.

What is especially startling, however, is how activists so often display this conduct with our allies and fellow activists, people who are also engaged in struggles around human liberation. Rather than being collaborative and mutually supportive, these relationships are frequently mean-spirited and nasty-competitive, where people not only refuse to work together, but actively oppose and undermine each other. Too often we don't unite in common purpose and effort; instead, we allow ourselves to become ensnared in territorial disputes, bitter disagreements over the interpretation of some arcane point of doctrine, or dragged down in the mire of personal backbiting and character assassination. Rather than work out our differences, which is one of the hallmarks of relational maturity, we take refuge in the silos of our particular causes.

Conduct of this kind only replicates some of the worst behaviors of the social order we're trying to influence in a more positive direction. Such is the nature of this contradiction, it is not unusual for an outsider to look at us and wonder who our enemy really is. In these moments, we are hardly the living examples of the revolutionary solidarity we are calling for.

This fatal contradiction between what we sincerely say we stand for, and the behaviors we exhibit, is the curse of our kind. Whatever awareness we had of our interconnection with all beings disappears in these moments of internecine conflict between professed comrades. It is really nothing more than a mirror image of the polarizing behaviors that beset the larger society.

This is doubly disappointing when we consider that especially now, given our current crisis, activists must work effectively with—not against—each other. We give lip service to the importance of "solidarity forever," but we don't act as if we want it enough to break the ancient habit of trying to dominate and control the revolution. The old practice of power politics has insidiously infiltrated our practice, short-circuiting our transformative intentions and replicating some of humankind's more unsavory tendencies in the process.

When this arises, we must make a special effort to recommit ourselves to a conscientious, values-based practice. Through a contemplative discipline such as meditation, we can come to see not only ego at work, encouraging the very behaviors that undermine our purpose, but also help us to intentionally focus on ways that counter its influence. A practice of compassion and lovingkindness toward our fellow activists that acknowledges they too are fighting the good fight, along with recognizing our commonality as living beings, can help us to appreciate the practical wisdom of working together.

As with so much of our practice, activist solidarity must be approached conscientiously and pursued intentionally. We cannot leave it to chance—as history demonstrates, it won't just happen. A hopeful scenario toward building solidarity includes organizing social gatherings with other activists that embrace conversations about how we might bridge our differences and work together. This is hopefully followed up by devising plans with each other for how we might come together around a common effort or project. To successfully realize such a state will increase our strength and influence exponentially and, not incidentally, provide a positive example to the larger community.

Building relationships is vital to a practice of transformative activism; doing so amongst fellow activists is invaluable as a practical way to advance our common purpose. To the extent that it also enhances our collective presence and strength, solidarity relationships are also a strategic necessity.

THE AFFINITY GROUP

Although operating at a more intentional level, affinity groups are another example of activist solidarity. Along with similar assemblages known as tribes and resilience circles, they range in size, but operate best when limited to that which its members find comfortable and when they meet the agreed-upon purpose for which the participants came together. At a minimum, an affinity group that is centered around a transformative vision engages in a practice that is based on peace and non-violence, gender and racial equality, as well as other life-affirming values. They generally consist of fellow comrades, people who at least some of the members have known previously, and who also have a sufficient relationship with one another to feel that they trust and care for each other. It is within this kind of social arrangement that participants can enjoy the solidarity of kindred spirits.

This isn't to suggest that the several disparate individuals come together as a united monolith. There is commonality, of course, as I've suggested in the preceding remarks, but also differences that surface which weren't apparent or seemingly important at the beginning. But a strong affinity group recognizes early in its development that before all else it is about relationship-building, an ongoing process that involves coming to care for and trust one another in ways that couldn't necessarily have been anticipated prior to the group's formation.

As a consequence, a successful affinity group learns to hang together, to risk being open and transparent, and to work differences out in ways that don't lose sight of each other's value. To do this, the participants involved have to both tolerate and be patient with a non-judgmental group process which is planned for in the beginning and made part of the group culture. This is incorporated into a weekly meeting during which not only is the business of the group discussed, but personal issues and relationships, as well.

In this way, activists grow through trial and error, successfully negotiating the changes, differences and tensions that naturally arise over time between human beings, especially those who are involved in the intense work of activism. However necessary, creating a safe place for each other in such a milieu doesn't necessarily make what needs to be dealt with more comfortable. But it does make possible a culture of trust that can arise when members consistently treat one another with kindness and compassion, and certainly without judgment.

As this suggests, when affinity groups are successful, they are vital for the support they provide individual participants. This is important for activists who otherwise live in the largely individualistic social environment we all do. Here, in the affinity group, we can find confirmation of our viewpoints and validation of our practice. Members come together around a commitment to a practice of values, though our understanding of them evolves over time through shared and at times unexpected experiences. Unlike the outside world, where being opposed or unsupported for our point of view and activities is not uncommon, these are sanctioned as legitimate and worthwhile by the affinity group.

This is not to suggest that reality check-ins and individual accountability are absent. To the contrary, because they are performed within a culture of honesty and trust, where people exhibit an acceptance of one another, these are also times that allow us to get to the heart of a matter. Being real is only possible when it comes from a selfless place, and it is clear to all concerned that there truly is "nothing personal" in what is being said. Rather, as best as we can do in our spiritual and moral growth, it comes from unconditional love and respect.

Activism is not easy. Our chosen calling can be fraught with tension and stress, failure and disappointment, and at times physical danger, all of which can result in burnout, cynicism, and despair. Potentially, the affinity group can serve as an antidote for these occupational hazards. It can provide the support and nurturance we require to keep going as well as to be effective in our efforts.

Notwithstanding our sincere desire for a new world, we remain carriers of ancient oppression and a way of life that has acculturated us in "I" since birth. We bring with us habits and patterns of behavior deeply embedded for most of us that don't magically disappear with our membership in the affinity group. Despite our commitment to a values practice, these older ways of behaving will leak out at times, especially when matters are stressful and solidarity erodes under the continual physical and emotional proximity to one another. It is hard for many of us who are one-down to empower ourselves, despite the support, nor is it any easier for those of us who are accustomed to being one-up to relinquish our privileges and control regardless of the constructive, non-judgmental assistance we receive from our comrades. As it is for most human beings, it is challenging for activists to live an enlightened existence. It doesn't happen automatically, nor without anguish and a few tears along the way.

Nevertheless, the challenges to being an activist are best dealt with in the company of people we trust. We need relationships with people who are also committed to being open, to lowering their defenses, to providing the honest and compassionate accountability we require to develop an everyday practice that enables us to accept a variety of situations and people with relative equanimity. We can't accomplish this growth by ourselves; as transformative activists, we recognize we cannot go it alone in the political world and hope to be effective. Living in this debilitating culture, we need the company of others to do the work of activism over the long haul. We won't survive (much less thrive) otherwise.

If the creation of the group has been approached mindfully, where members feel safe and accepted, people will hopefully have anticipated the challenging times and built into the nascent group culture regular meetings where they can honestly talk about themselves, each other, and the group in an atmosphere revolving around their values. They will also create other opportunities, especially those that promote fun and joy, that help to oil the gears of relationship building. In a very real sense, such gatherings could serve the affinity group as a collective version of the practice of the practice, where important individual and group issues are aired, and done so in a skillful, mindful manner. This would allow us to engage in both the inner work of the practice of the practice, as well as the outer work of being actively involved with others in the larger world outside of the collective. In this context, the well-being of each member is always a priority. Taking care of ourselves and each other in loving kind ways is essential to demonstrating similar behavior in our activist practice.

In order to craft an effective group in which all members feel valued, the decisions that guide the group must be consensual. A successful affinity group guarantees through its practice that all members have a voice in how the body operates, and ensures decisions are made in which everyone agrees to the final result. In this way the group also serves as a model in the larger community of how participatory democracy might work.

In operating in this collective fashion, however, the group takes care not to diminish or sacrifice individual expression for the sake of fashioning a group consensus. This is the fear of those who prize the sanctity of the individual and resist any perceived subservience of the latter to a group will. As any of us who have ever been part of such groups know, a skillful and creative dance between the individual and the larger body must be operative to realize the strengths of each. While it is understood that in the end the collective expression prevails in order for the group to function effectively, it is equally agreed that the collective expression is arrived at through a process that allows for and encourages the decision which eventually emerges to be the result of the interactions of all members, and that it is not is imposed on any.

For example, consensus decision-making typically has three ways to vote—thumb-up, thumb-down, or thumb at half-mast. At half mast, the member is indicating that while they are opposed, they will not block any decision to go ahead. Thumbs down, however, does signal the person is blocking acceptance. When this occurs, a discussion ensues in which various points of view are aired with the purpose of finding common ground that will lead to some kind of resolution that all the parties can live with. This process enables a consensus to arise through the give and take of the individuals involved, often by uncovering a position agreeable to all that didn't exist in the beginning.

Affinity groups must also be mindful of the power dynamics of the larger society of which we are all intimately a part, especially when it comes to the gender and racial composition of the group. Intentional efforts are made, for example, to rotate leadership positions and to the alternation of group jobs; as well as to subtler but powerful concerns like the amount of time each person can hold the floor; using a talking stone or other object to determine who can speak; creating understanding about not interrupting or being judgmental of another; only talking again after others have had an opportunity; and so forth. Regular check-ins about the flow and conduct of the meeting and the state of the group in general are conducted so that the group can assess how it is doing.

As important as the affinity group is for people to come together around a common values perspective, it should be emphasized that it is not a private group, or a secret society walled off from the larger world of which it is a part. Quite the contrary, such a practice would spell its death. Rather, through its activism in the larger community, an affinity group that considers itself transformative is inclusive of others in its collective workings and activities, open to expanding so as to include others who are committed to a values practice (or, if size is a consideration, helping to start a second group).

Along with the examples cited above, inclusion and transparency also suggest how in its own modest way, a transformative affinity group, with its emphasis upon relationships informed by heart values, serves to prefigure the society we are helping to create.

THE ACTIVIST COLLECTIVE

A living collective or intentional community of activists is an affinity group whose members live together, sharing property, possessions, and the responsibility of paying the monthly bills and attending to the chores of daily life. The group commits to doing so in a sustainable, resilient, equitable, democratic way, and in so doing serves as a living example of these practices in the larger community of which we are a living, active participant. Like the affinity group, all are committed to human liberation, to living the heart values as if the revolution has already taken place.

Almost all of that which was described in the preceding section about the affinity group applies as well to the intentional community with the significant difference that the members live with one another. This is important because unlike the affinity group, whose members are often scattered over a town or a region, the collective is usually based within a single large dwelling located within a particular geographic neighborhood or community. Ideally, the collective would be made up of people who have lived in the larger community most or all of their lives, hence are very familiar with each other.

Living in this manner provides the intentional community with the advantage of being physically situated in, and therefore more accessible to and involved with, the people of a larger community who are the focus of their practice as activists. Because of our physical proximity to our neighbors, we are more likely to become involved with them and the life of the community. This is critical to our integration into and acceptance by the larger community, allowing us to better demonstrate how everyday working people can adjust to the demands of a collapsing society in order to survive, perhaps even thrive, in these apocalyptic times.

Central to our integration into the community is the socialization that the collective members do, individually and as a group, in a variety of ways. We will discuss this at greater length in the next chapter about communities and community organizing. Suffice it to note at this point that without a doubt, our purpose is to get to know our neighbors and for them to become familiar with us. While we hope to serve as living examples of moral values in our daily interactions, we go about doing so by being sensitive to and observant of the mores and customs of others, while being true to ourselves at the same time.

This can be quite tricky, as it is with human beings in general. It becomes particularly challenging when the behaviors of others confront us with instances that violate our own values around, for example, gender and racial equality. There is no hard and fast formula for how to respond when these moments arise, as they most inevitably will; each situation and relationship will require its own unique response.

As a general suggestion, however, avoid responding to the offending other in a way that rejects them as a fellow human being, or in a manner that communicates that we are superior to such behavior. Instead, we should frame our objection as something that personally offends us in whatever way that it does. This by no means guarantees that the gentle but direct confrontation will not result in embarrassment, hurt feelings, and perhaps even anger that impairs an otherwise budding relationship. The fact that we can deal with these situations with a wholesome expression of honesty and acceptance does not preclude the risk involved in so doing.

As with the residents of the larger community, the members of the collective will not be living off our nonexistent trust funds, or our daddy's inheritance. Because of financial necessity, as well as our values, we will most likely secure property we can afford in a working or middle class part of town. We will be working jobs to earn the money we need to pay the rent/mortgage, buy food, and keep the lights on—in other words, dealing with the same inescapable responsibilities that significantly define the energy, time and, most of all, choices that the people of our larger community have, but while doing so in creative, sustainable ways that enable us to be increasingly self-sufficient.

For instance, the matter of the collective's basic income needs can be approached in a number of ways. An example is for one or more of us who have employable skills to acquire a part- or full-time job that earns sufficient income to cover basic household expenses. Another way might be for us to organize ourselves into a worker's collective who hire out to perform a variety of part-time jobs such as fruit picking, gardening and landscaping, data entry and IT, substitute teaching, home repair and maintenance, childcare, house cleaning, and so on.

Being dependent on outside income is particularly onerous when we're trying to become increasingly self-sufficient. That is why it is important that time and energy be devoted to reducing this need wherever possible by focusing on such endeavors as the growing and storage of food, and the maintenance and repair of home, car and clothing, so that we are less at the mercy of this dependency. This involves removing ourselves as much as possible from the consumer culture that makes so much of our earned income seemingly necessary, spending more time engaged in physical labor which the highly touted convenience we supposedly gained by spending lifetimes "working for the boss" had liberated us from. Real work in which we are increasingly taking care of ourselves, meeting our needs by our collective physical and mental efforts, is the trade off to working for a living.

Making the collective increasingly self-sufficient in very practical ways is also intended to demonstrate to the larger community how this can be done, not only by people who live together, but also by neighbors. For this reason, the collective is an open house to the larger community in the sense that neighbors are encouraged to become a part of and share the benefits of the work involved in a particular project, so that, for example, what begins as our collective's garden might expand to include the folks next door and down the street, and perhaps eventually into a network of community gardens, herb/health gardens, green houses, cold frames, root cellars, canning circles, and buying clubs. Over time, this approach might grow beyond food to include other needs (like childcare, ride sharing/community car, tool and machine sharing, etc.). As part of their basic commitment to community service, the collective's members work with and help interested residents to initiate and sustain these projects.

Through our living example, transformative activists can demonstrate how the work involved in the necessary, everyday affairs of maintaining life (cooking, laundry, house cleaning, childcare, etc.) can be done cooperatively, and in a non-hierarchical, gender and age-free manner for the benefit of all. This way of life will not be easy to adjust to, involving as it does some personal sacrifice and adaptation. Patience and perseverance, along with heavy doses of lovingkindness and an acceptance of all for what each of us can contribute and bring to the collective table, are a must. Otherwise, we will not be successful.

But there are also great benefits to joint, cooperative labor, especially as the old normal, fragmented, isolated way of living breaks down and becomes less efficient in the new world of societal collapse we are entering, where a more collaborative approach demonstrates its superiority. The tasks of everyday life that are presently so time-consuming and unrewarding when performed by individuals (usually women) in solitary households become more satisfying and easier to accomplish when done as part of a group effort—cleaning the house together, preparing the evening meal—and are done because they are centered around the care and welfare of everyone. Helping to make us more resilient and sustainable, meeting the everyday needs of all, and making us less dependent on the corporate world are perhaps the most satisfying experiences that an intentional community of activists can undergo. In its modest way, it is the living revolution.

Needless to say, this approach to everyday life defies the radical individualism that most of us have been brought up on, and that will likely continue to exist, at least to one degree or another, through our constant companion of ego. Realizing a non-authoritarian, non-hierarchical, cooperative and sharing way of life, such as I have tried to suggest here, is not second nature for most of us. Accomplishing this vision will not likely be realized overnight; our efforts will take time, and there will be setbacks along the way. As I said earlier, the pathway to liberation is characterized by two steps forward, one step backwards, and many steps sideways.

It should also be said that what has been offered in the preceding remarks is but one of many ways that creating an activist collective can be done. In no way is it intended to be a definitive blueprint that any and all should follow. What I've provided here is intended only to suggest possibilities involved with an activist collective. In many ways, it is schematic and idealistic, without all the challenges in attempting such an effort. There are many ways to create such a body, none more valid than the others, and all dependent upon what its particular members bring to the table. They all will—and should—reflect the individuals involved, as well as the particular circumstances they are faced with. As with the affinity group or, for that matter, any of the specific ideas I have presented in this book, the collective should not be seen as a project that follows a linear direction. Like everything else, they come to life as part of a process that is uniquely their own.

But in the same way as an affinity group, an intentional activist collective is all about building values-based relationships. These relationships are the bottom line of transformative activism. While we certainly don't enter such a project having all the answers, and perhaps have little more than a commitment to live our values as best we can—not as missionaries or saints, but very much like the regular folks we come to live with —we discover that when we're open to it, we learn from and with our neighbors as together we engage in what is nothing other than an ongoing revolution-in-progress.

Transformative Practice

DANCING WITH THE DIALECTIC OF WITHDRAWING AND CREATING

We flow around,
pour over,
seep under,
or evaporate and rain down
on the other side.
—The Activist's Tao Te Ching

The importance of everyday life is best appreciated when we recognize it as our source of empowerment. This is where we exist; moment by moment, this is where we make choices for ourselves and the kind of life we live, whether done consciously or not. The quotidian is the crucible of our existence, where we can be proactive agents, acting with our values within the forces and conditions that operate on us and help define what our choices are, that we in turn influence. Or we can opt not to do so, allowing ourselves instead to simply be acted upon, blown about in the wind like some disengaged leaf-of-chance, an easy mark for an authoritarian power.

Creating the life-affirming alternative is essential to a revolution of everyday life, but it is only one half of the liberating equation. At the same time we are doing this, we must also engage in a conscientious practice of withdrawing our participation from this toxic and dehumanizing way of life. Creating and withdrawing are nothing more than two sides of a single process, each providing necessary support for the other. It is a dance of skill, timing, and intentionality, informed by a moral vision of what is best at any given moment. As we create the alternative, we naturally withdraw from that which we find unacceptable, and as we withdraw from the present system, so do we build what we need in its place. This is the dialectic of withdrawing/creating, creating/withdrawing.

Decreasing our involvement in a way of life that we have lived and taken for granted since we were born is easier said than done. It is not as impossible, however, as we may initially fear once we commit to this purpose and begin to act on it, becoming increasingly mindful of details that we had been blind to. The latter are particularly challenging because most of us are enmeshed in socially conditioned behaviors. From this unenlightened perspective, it seems so much easier to remain stuck in our unliberated state, reinforcing and reproducing our own enslavement.

But this fate is not fixed in stone. Even though it is mindless and involuntary, it is also the result of choices we make.

This is where transformative activism comes in. We can, for example, choose to significantly reduce our hypnotic attachment to the consumption of the material world and its coinciding plunder of nature and exploitation of our fellow human beings by choosing to live a simpler existence. By doing this, we can also choose to evolve away from the daily grind of jobs we hate, and hate ourselves for doing, accepting that the only reason we do them is to make the money we believe we need to buy the things we have been habituated to want. The payoff enables us to not only keep showing up to these lousy jobs, but to also throw away what we bought when it's no longer new and replace it with fresh crap.

Though this vision runs contrary to the conventional view of what "the good life" is all about, we can choose the real deal through a more modest material existence, one in which we spend and possess less, which we can afford with less dehumanizing work. This lifestyle might be successfully attempted alongside folks who have similar desires and needs, who share a common vision of wanting to live a more satisfying, more enjoyable day-to-day existence, and who are willing to pursue this through an increasingly collaborative, community-centered approach to life: a perfect example of the withdrawing/creating dialectic in action.

It is challenging to detach ourselves from the barnacles of material accumulation that have affixed themselves to us over lifetimes of acculturation, or from the co-dependent conviction that we have to "work for a living." Unless born with a silver spoon in our mouths, we understandably accept this conclusion as an inescapable fact of life. The only remedy for this affliction of Civilized human beings is to approach it with intentionality, with a felt desire to do something about it, regardless of how impossible it may initially appear to be.

As this example underscores, we must pursue in tandem the two interconnected goals of withdrawing our participation in the culture that is enslaving us while creating and living the alternative in order to experience success. These two sides of transformation cannot be done separately without losing the support they each provide the other. Without withdrawal, we don't have the space, time, and energy within which to create alternatives; and not forging the alternative deprives us of living the liberating change that supplants what we have withdrawn from.

Our initial steps consist of modest efforts we can reasonably take, like making conscientious efforts to reduce our cost of living to essential items. By doing so, we discover that with our new purpose of living a simpler existence, at least some of the "things" we thought we couldn't live without are now no longer necessary, while other things we do need we can share with neighbors or through a cooperative collective that we help to organize. Simplifying our material needs allows us, in turn, to take work with reduced hours and/or reduced pay that our new lifestyle can afford, and is otherwise not opposed to our values. These changes may leave us with enough time and energy to pursue our passions and fall in love with life once again.

As idealistic as this all may appear to be, it is also a realistic possibility if we are committed to making it happen through intentional effort. Admittedly challenging, and something we may not readily embrace until it becomes a felt need in a collapsing society, its success largely depends upon us, our intentions around realizing change for ourselves, as well as our willingness to make the choices and commit the efforts of what is involved.

There are many things we can do gradually that don't require a lot from us. We can minimize the energy and support we give to the national security state and its corporate sponsors, for example, through conscious choices and the actions that we take. As we absent ourselves from the militaristic and consumerist way of life, one step here, one step there, we find more and more that we can break free of bonds that have ensnared us to an oppressive existence, unobtrusively, invisibly, though done in plain sight. We might cancel Facebook and Twitter, withdraw from television and other mass media that tell us what's going on in the world and what to buy; we might refuse to participate in Black Friday, do fine with used clothing, and provide more of our own food through gardening, farmers markets, the reduction or elimination of our consumption of meat (especially from factory farms); limit our voting to local elections, forgo national elections with their "choices" of the two wings of the ruling class (even if it's only to remind ourselves how corrupt our fraudulent government is); remodel the Fourth of July into a celebration of women, people of color, Indigenous people, children and other marginalized people in our culture; cancelling our credit cards and buying items only when we have cash; getting out of debt; making friends with Mother and the nonhuman beings of the world; not joining the police/military complex; and reducing/eliminating our consumption of products from Big Oil, Big Pharma, Big Chemicals, Big Corporation, in general, and increasingly go local. We do this while at the same time actively seeking out and cultivating cooperative living arrangements, and friendships with people who value honesty and integrity, and who share our desire to make our lives happier.

Most importantly, we maximize our opportunities for responsible, moral, loving arrangements with all living beings with behavior that invites commensurate behavior in return. Perhaps nothing is as significant in the withdrawal/creation dialectic as our relationships with other people. As one of the parties involved in these interactions, we are a significant factor in how these transpire. Though there are no guarantees that matters will work out the way we would like them to in each and every encounter, there is also the possibility that they will, a prospect not likely without our proactive contribution.

The dialectic of withdrawal and creation is an opportunity to deal with the power relationships in our lives, to clean them up so they reflect the values we are committed to, especially ones involving gender, race, class, and age, as well as other power arrangements that have blighted our social landscape over the years. This is huge. The dialectic is something we no longer leave to good intentions alone, but purposely embed in the fabric of the world we are building through our present relationships with one another. This can only be done in face to face exchanges and contacts of everyday life. It is a matter we must attend to personally, not through virtual space, if we want to live in a more liberated, truly transformed world. There is no other way.

What is especially interesting about this dialectic is that all the examples cited above have one thing in common: the withdrawal of our participation and creation of the alternative are both grounded in the present moment. They shape the "future" we are working for because the "future" we're creating is alive and well right now.

We must keep in mind that there are many nuances in this dialectic. While seemingly insignificant when viewed in isolation, they are the building blocks of the new world we are creating. We're not dependent on some authority outside of ourselves, a government policy or a corporate product to do any of this for us; what needs to be accomplished can only be done by ourselves in collaboration with others. We have all we need if we only consult our heart values, connect with those same values in others, and do the best we can. Despite difficulties and setbacks, acting with moral integrity is good enough. With each and every act of withdrawal and creation, we further reduce another of the life-diminishing hooks we've attached ourselves to over the years, supplanting them with the empty space of liberating possibilities.

We will choose, at times, sometimes out of necessity, to operate within the existing institutions and structures of our current society. We cannot help but do so as they are part of our world and we are connected to the political world.

But we must keep in mind that these institutions are incapable of transforming our lives and transitioning us to the world we aim to live in. Thus, transformative activists avoid the mistake of trying to realize change by petitioning the authorities to redress our grievances or contesting them for political power. Rather, we recognize this approach only further legitimizes their power arrangements, ensnaring us in their coils and precluding the changes we seek. Most of all, it robs us of the time and energy we require to attend to the transformation which we must dedicate our lives to.

What often discourages people from striking out on the path of withdrawing our participation and creating the alternative is a failure of imagination. We limit our vision to the overwhelming context of our capitalist, industrial world. Of course, in that closed room, there doesn't appear to be either the space or viable opening for initiatives on our part, because in that context there is no alternative space. All the oxygen has been sucked out in the service of the Empire. We are overpowered—disempowered—by this world, which is precisely how we're intended to feel in a political society. There are no choices, there are no options, only those chimeras that reinforce the present system.

While the omnipresent creature of our culture does penetrate all areas of our lives, we mistakenly conclude that to experience real change our only alternative is to completely withdraw from or to destroy the System. This can only result in failure, since, as history has demonstrated time and again, this path does not produce the liberating consequences we seek. We can neither withdraw from the world, for where would we go that isn't colonized by capitalist culture? Certainly not a desert island that's about to be inundated by the rising oceans of climate change? To withdraw in this absolute manner would certainly meet the approval of the powers who would like all discontents to quietly, ineffectually disappear. Nor can we destroy the System, for that would only entail adopting variations of the same force and violence we're trying to move beyond. The challenge of revolution can appear to be insurmountable.

It appears this way at least until we consider withdrawal and creation as a whole host of little, insignificant behaviors that are intimate to, and performed daily, within our present existence. In the details of our moment-to-moment lives, these two essential steps for transformative change can be effectively taken. They are not necessarily dramatic, grand statements of our purpose, and are best performed quietly, hidden in plain sight. It is in our best interests not to bring ourselves to the attention of the forces we oppose. We have no need to advertise ourselves in order to be successful, especially when what we're doing is in opposition to the existing order. Rather than unnecessarily confronting or opposing, we step aside, go over and around. Quiet success will bring us to the attention of other similarly disposed people. Growing large is not our purpose; to the contrary, being small is a much better way to go.

LIVING A MORE MODEST WAY OF LIFE

Bringing the revolutionary alternative we seek to life, while at the same time withdrawing our participation from our oppressive existence is best realized by adopting a simpler way of living that increasingly removes us from the pervasive consumer culture that renders us unfree and contributes to societal collapse. This is proactive resistance.

Breaking our addiction to compulsive consumerism is basic to living the simpler existence that activists need to exemplify. Significant to transformative activists is our willingness to pare down our material possessions to what is essential. We find that the more elementary and uncomplicated we become, the closer we approximate the sparks of life that we are. We become less dependent on "things" to fill our lives with, to define who we are, and we stop commodifying others into objects to dominate or be dominated by.

Additionally, removing ourselves as much as we can from consumerist culture eases the material burden we have taken on over lifetimes of acquisition. It is true that this reduction and elimination will be increasingly imposed on us by Mother without any say from us as we move further into collapse, but in the world of the "long emergency," to use James Kunstler's felicitous expression in his book of the same name, we don't have to wait until the water is up to the roof to make life-saving changes in our way of life.

I have already discussed the advantages of purposely divesting ourselves of our surprisingly unessential belongings. The corollary to lessening our material load is learning to make do with what we already have. This reduces our habit of having to buy one more of what we already have and necessitates the employment of skills that many people in the not too distant past routinely performed for themselves, skills that, for the most part, people couldn't afford to hire others to do for them as we do today. Fixing, repairing, growing, building, knitting, sewing, cooking, cleaning, making: These are some of the abilities that perhaps our parents—and our grandparents, for sure— knew and regularly practiced before the Age of Convenience became the apotheosis of where the ego-corrupted American Dream was going all along: not having to take responsibility for ourselves, creating a world where others (especially people of color) do that for us.

Another dimension of consumer culture that we remove ourselves from as we simplify our lives is the degrading and humiliating image of ourselves that is constantly being sold to us through its incessant advertising. This is a message that tells us we lack something essential to our existence that can only be cured through the purchase of whatever is being sold. We are portrayed as passive consumers of products and services that are guaranteed to solve the problems in life that we never knew we had before being told we did, a message which preys upon the inherent insecurities we have as "I" living in a political society. This is the allure of consumer transformation: the promise of a new and better "I" than the person we presently are. Invariably comes the hangover after the intoxication of the purchase when we wake up to the inescapable realization that we have allowed ourselves to be fooled once again and are still the same old one-down us, dressed in the threads of freedom.

When we withdraw our participation in compulsive consumption, we are that much freer to open ourselves to the values of a liberated human. No longer do we have all this stuff and all these things to worry about, take care of, earn money to pay for, that distracts us from the real concerns of life. By simplifying, we reduce being a consumer of life and become more an agent of heart instead. It goes without saying that this is what a transformative activist is all about.

Despite the unavoidable discomfort that such a transition might entail for many of us, numerous studies have shown that the sense of well-being and satisfaction with our lives does not increase with greater material wealth. The proverbial rat race and suffocating indebtedness that are entry requirements for players in the consumer game—along with related social issues such as the growing class disparity, disappearing middle class and growing underclass, decline in community cohesion, greater environmental degradation, and increasing mental health problems—don't result in a commensurate feeling of happiness. They only produce the grim smile button that so many of us pose behind these days in our effort to convince others (and especially ourselves) that life is okay. Simple living results in a marked uptick in the quality of our lives. True contentment can only be found within a more modest existence, arising from the intrinsic rewards we derive from a life that while at times challenging, disappointing and painful, is basically satisfying, even joyous when lived with heart values.

This is a life that is not predicated upon the amassing of material goods, but rather on experiencing those areas that make people genuinely happy during our brief moment on this planet. Beyond having sufficient water, food, shelter, clothing, and any other basic necessities we require to sustain life with, our basic needs are comprised of loving relationships, meaningful activity, a sustaining spiritual life, and a deep connection with the rest of the natural world.

Currently, we spend the best years of our lives living from paycheck to paycheck, trapped in a nine-to-five dollar chase to buy all the things we don't need. An existence that is reduced to our essential needs is one spent engaged in values-centered existence, doing the right thing for ourselves and others as a regular feature of our daily lives. A simpler way of life provides the necessary material basis for a values-based life.

As transformative activists know, a revolutionary dialectic can also operate between a modest way of life and a values-based society, each serving as both the cause and effect of the other. Together, the two are the necessary halves of a sustainable whole.

Taken one step further, living a simple lifestyle is supported by being a part of a values-based community whose members consist of other similarly inclined folks. Through sharing, collaboration, and mutual aid, the challenge of a simpler existence becomes a joint enterprise with community members who have made a similar commitment. We cannot move away from the death spiral of industrial consumerism by being islands alone in an adversative sea. A supportive, embracing, albeit smaller community, or community-within-a-community—like an affinity group or intentional communal living arrangement whose members are moving toward a more basic lifestyle—is necessary if we are to succeed.

Our resistance to making the changes necessary to breaking a consumerist way of life is understandable. After all, it is life as we've known it to be in political society. "I" is attached to our material possessions. In fact, the one cannot be separated from the other. Along with the act of shopping itself, our goods are very basic to our Self-identity, to how we know who we are, and especially our value. In the political world, where appearances count for so much, possessions are often the way we judge the worth of ourselves and each other. Compulsive consumption is deeply connected to (stuck) ego that attaches us to such a drive; thus, letting go of the unnecessary things in our lives is meaningful to becoming unstuck. Breaking this addiction represents a major opportunity to move beyond ego's power and influence, to become more fully realized adults.

Simplicity does not mean, as some may fear, that we will be forced to return to the privations of our Stone Age ancestors. Time has moved on, and in so many ways, so have we. In so living, we have learned a thing or two that will be helpful in the new world we're entering. Although all too often used in the past for selfish and destructive purposes, we can retain the best of our industrial and technological civilization for socially-responsible, earth-friendly use in a post-petroleum age. However, this will only be accomplished by a people committed to simple living within a world that we are intimately a part of.

Joining the rest of the natural world as a member of an interdependent whole has potentially enormous benefits. When we are no longer locked into an incessant effort to feed the voracious appetites of the gods of perpetual growth, compulsive consumerism, and unrestrained human greed, we are able to shed so much that, while vital to "I," is only a hindrance to living an interconnected, impermanent existence. This is an opportunity to move away from the death values and violence of industrial civilization, where the so-called "good life" is obtained, or so it is thought, through control and domination. When we cast off the superfluous and unnecessary things that we carry around, we evolve away from this Civilization and more toward a way of life that is not at the expense of living beings.

A paradigmatic shift of this magnitude will only be possible when we begin living a more spiritually motivated existence that allows us to get in touch and practice with regularity the values we prize. We'll have fewer things in our lives, for sure, but this will mean fewer things to fight over, guard, and protect, less to work harder and go deeper into debt for, and to be ultimately dissatisfied with when the momentary rush of our latest purchase passes and we crave yet another hit. We come to see that a sustainable, socially just existence—one whose expression is informed by kindness, generosity, and compassion—is more than a fair trade off for what we are losing. Excluding the glittering false promises of consumerism's fool's gold, simplicity does what materialism can never match, providing us with a sense of purpose and a life worth living.

A PRACTICE OF SERVICE

As contradictory as this may at first appear to be, transformative activists are not concerned with trying to change others to our version of the *correct* path. Rather, we are more interested with being a helpful, useful participant of the larger community we are part of, whether as a member of an affinity group, an activist collective, or as an individual person. In this time of rapidly escalating societal collapse, driven by climate catastrophe, racial crisis, continuing pandemic, an unjust economy, and an oligarchic/authoritarian government, there is much that we can do to assist others. This is what activism is all about in this day, where our values are on the line, challenged to be enacted through practical acts of compassion, courage, and selflessness —this in the service of unconditionally standing up for life in a world where the extinction of ourselves and other living species is threatened.

A dramatic example of how this might unfold was evident in the noble efforts of the Occupy Wall Street activists who rendered well-organized aid and relief to the beleaguered residents of Rockaway, Queens in New York City during the 2012 Superstorm Sandy. This was absolutely necessary because traditional public services were overwhelmed and unable to provide emergency aid. Given the fact that the climate crisis is proceeding much more rapidly and violently than had been predicted by scientists just a short time ago (see, e.g., the 2021/2022 reports of the United Nations' International Panel on Climate Change), along with all the other signs of our deteriorating societal, economic, and political situation, being of service to people in our communities may well be the most important activity that we can engage in during the time ahead. This is both an opportunity for our values practice to be displayed and put to the test, as well as demonstrating its pricelessness for living a worthwhile way of life. How we respond to our present situations is what a transformative practice is all about: do we go about matters in the same irrelevant ways of trying to exact control over our circumstances? Or do we forge innovative approaches that model a culture of mutual aid through the practice of cooperation, generosity and compassion, from which people are inspired to take care of themselves and each other? With societal collapse now an imminent possibility, we can be of enormous help in aiding our fellow citizens, during an emergency situation as well as the preparatory period beforehand when it is important not to wait until the catastrophe is fully upon us.

Emergency preparedness is a clear and present need in light of the unprecedented fires and weather events we have experienced in recent years. Think of the horrific wildfires in Australia in January 2020, and then in America's western states. Or the continuing worldwide COVID-19 pandemic that, as Roger Cohen stated in the *New York Times* (December 13, 2021), people are beginning to fear *"will go on for years, like plagues of old."* Because these kinds of events will be experienced in the present tense, and will be especially noteworthy by how *suddenly* they are upon us, emergency preparedness will be an increasingly felt need. People will likely be responsive to the efforts of activists to organize meetings and trainings to help them become better equipped and organized in the face of catastrophic events. Just coming together as a neighborhood or community to acknowledge the reality of the present moment is a beneficial first step toward preparedness.

Community-engaged activists who recognize the importance of being relevant in this age must see that the nature of our circumstances requires people to become *adaptable and resilient.* We can neither avoid what is coming nor what is already here. Instead, we must learn how to live with our situation as best we can, despite that at this moment we may not have a clue as to what this involves beyond the pursuit of collective efforts at building relocalized, resilient, and sustainable communities.

It is unrealistic at this point to entertain any illusions that we are going to prevent the unfolding of climate disaster. As environmentalist Bill McKibben has stated,

> It's too late to stop global warming, that's no longer on the menu...even if we do everything right at this point, the temperature will go up. The main question is whether we'll be able to hold the rise in temperature to a point where we can, at great expense and suffering, deal with those crises coherently, or whether they will overwhelm the coping abilities of our civilization. The latter is a distinct possibility.

We must accept that we may no longer be able to change our circumstances sufficiently to avoid collapse, learning at best to live with the catastrophic change that is inexorably bearing down on us. Specifically, we must recognize that as wonderful as it would be to mitigate the worst consequences of our situation, we need to focus our attention on what is known as "deep adaptation," an approach that, in acknowledging our pending collapse, seeks to moderate its impact through accommodation and adjustment, while engaging in practices that transform our failing capitalist industrial world.

It is essential to build a network of relatively self-sufficient communities in neighborhoods and towns that can take care of themselves in an emergency. This would include the ability to immediately pick up and leave with a previously prepared bag or two of necessities, as people in states prone to the effects of natural disaster have already learned, sometimes the hard way.

Emergency community preparedness includes creating resiliency and adaptability around such essentials as food, water, health requirements, and community self-defense. A major assumption we should operate under is that, as the society breaks down and the services we presently take for granted are overwhelmed or no longer there for us at all, we need to begin planning now how we're going to live without them and become as self- and community-resilient as we can be.

Importantly, being service-oriented and focusing our efforts on building adaptable communities are the essential ingredients for creating a culture of mutual aid. The latter is basic for a values-oriented society. Ironically, our dire circumstances are almost—*almost!*—a blessing in disguise. It is when we are caught up in a life and death situation that human beings become suddenly aware of and act upon our state of interdependence. Our need for each other is experienced as a *felt need,* a good idea that moves from the head to a heart-inspired action that we respond to instinctively. Unfortunately, it seems to be the make-up of Civilized human beings that we only move toward a transformative way of life when our backs are up against the wall and our lives are on the line.

But as proposed before, activists cannot wait until the crisis is full-blown. We must be of service now, engaging in a variety of actions. Some of these include organizing community conversations where neighbors explore with each other the credible threats they face and how they might deal with them collectively; informal neighborhood preparedness get-togethers of food, video watching, and planning; encouraging individual households to take what early steps they can now to become more self-sufficient; and organizing ourselves with the necessary training to act as emergency responders.

In making service the centerpiece of our practice, we also act as informal and unannounced spiritual guides whose efforts with others reflect our values. In this manner, we not only support others in their own spiritual growth, we also provide a modest example of what it can mean to be living in a time of calamitous circumstances.

RIGHTEOUS LIVELIHOOD

Perhaps the most important, yet no less challenging way to reduce our participation in the culture of death is to make values-based decisions around the manner in which we "earn a living." Is it possible to find work that meets our material needs while being morally reputable and personally rewarding in a society where work is performed under capitalism?

The aforementioned is a system within which the vast majority of us spend a major part of our waking hours during our adult years working at a paying job. It is also one which privileges profit over life and only functions through the exploitation of sentient beings.

For blue and white collar alike, being gainfully employed involves selling our labor, for which we are paid wages or a salary. A minority of us are fortunate to find work that is satisfying beyond financial compensation, in which we enjoy the physical, emotional, or intellectual demands involved in doing our jobs while not being morally compromised in so doing, or are otherwise able to support ourselves outside the capitalist system. For most of us, however, these options don't exist. Rather than being a source of enjoyment and spiritual fulfillment, work is just soul crushing drudgery, however subtle and invisible, a necessity we return to day after day in order to survive to the next.

Since profit is its dominant concern, capitalism is inherently exploitive of workers who produce the capital which accumulates in the hands of the wealthy. Not only is the labor of workers absolutely necessary to creating the wealth of the ruling class and their business enterprises, they do not receive fair compensation with a truly living wage that is remotely commensurate to the value of the products produced or the services rendered, upon which the whole system rests. Wages are kept low so as much net income as possible can be squeezed out of the business operation for the profits that are enjoyed by investors and owners of a company. There are many jobs in which workers cannot earn enough to meet their basic needs and have to depend on the income of their spouse or government programs such as food stamps just to get by while chief executives take home hundreds, even thousands of times more than the average worker in salaries, bonuses, and stock option packages and other compensation.

The immoral nature of work under capitalism is also evidenced by the unhealthy and dangerous conditions that workers are often exposed to. These arise from cost-saving measures implemented by management, but they are often profitable only at the expense of the workers' well-being.

Another side of this coin is that the work often involves the manufacture of products or the carrying out of tasks that are harmful, even lethal, to other living beings.

In such an unwholesome context, where the worker as a whole human being is generally ignored, the capitalist workplace seldom, if ever, reflects concern with such matters as worker self-actualization, autonomy, and decision-making. That is why workers are more accurately known as "wage slaves." By the same token, the logic of work is dominated by the rhythm of the machine, which dictates how a job is done and a worker's performance evaluated. Such a development over the years has evolved into workers having to merge into machine-like behavior. No wonder the universal mantra amongst workers is "TGIF": Thank God It's Friday!

The drive for profits places workers in jobs that involve the extraction of "resources" from the earth and the resulting destruction of the environment. The oil industry is a classic instance of this practice: its own scientists have known since the 1980s that the burning of fossil fuels had a deleterious effect on the climate that would lead to catastrophic consequences. But this knowledge has been suppressed through corporate campaigns to confuse and misrepresent to the public the connection between human-induced carbon emissions and climate change.

Other instances of this wanton criminality include corporations who know a commodity they manufacture is dangerous to their customers, even, lethal, yet decide that it is less expensive for them to pay for the lawsuits of people who are injured or killed than pay for the cost of pulling the product off the market and re-engineering it into safe and healthy merchandise. The tire industry scandals, which involved reputable companies who continued to sell tires that they knew were defective and causing fatal accidents, are prime examples of this nefarious practice. We can also look at several pharmaceutical companies who, although they knew that the opioids they were manufacturing were highly addictive, causing thousands of overdose deaths, continued to sell them to the public without including warnings of their lethality.

Perhaps there is no more dramatic instance of the unconscionable nature of capitalism's obsession with profits and the dependency it creates amongst all of us for its survival and continuation than the military-industrial complex and its $738 billion taxpayer-funded budget. Without its presence, our economy would plunge into a serious depression, causing unemployment amongst thousands of workers. After all, it was only the advent of World War II and the weapons production that went into its fighting that finally pulled us out of the Great Depression. The unsurpassed military expenditures of the Cold War which immediately followed have continued right up to the present time, allowing us to keep our economy afloat over the past 75 years. In this way, entire communities—in fact, the nation in general—have become addicted to the manufacture of the instruments of killing, and perhaps of war itself, because the creation of newer and more heinous weapons creates the demand that they eventually be used to see how effective they are. (Since 1945, the United States has been in involved in more than 40 armed conflicts and wars.) Many workers are so dependent upon military-related jobs that to consider slashing the military budget and closing down the many facilities that help to make the advent of war almost a necessity would be political suicide for any politician who even hinted at doing so.

The purpose of this outline of the most salient, outrageous but representative features of the American capitalist economy is to illustrate the hurtles involved in locating righteous employment. With notable exceptions, especially if we are fortunate to have the skills to be self-employed, or have the right paper credentials to land one of the few decent jobs within the system, it is difficult to find employment that allows for personal satisfaction, moral integrity, and reasonable pay. In order to work in the mainstream economy, most of us have to resign ourselves to accept what is offered to us, believing we have no choice but to do a job that is boring and monotonous, doesn't draw on the best of us, involves cutting moral and ethical corners and harms other living beings. A job, in other words, that we know in our hearts is a piece of shit. This is the dependable breeding ground for a defeated, cynical body politic, the ideal populace for an authoritarian regime to rule.

In this reality, we can easily become pessimistic about work in particular, and life in general as we compromise ourselves five days a week, eight hours a day, so that we can pay the monthly bills at the company store. The damaging consequences encompass entire lifetimes consisting of dreams about finally living our deferred existence when we reach a romanticized retirement that, for all too many of us, never turns out quite the way we imagined it to be. This is our fate when we remain stuck in a life that has been postponed to sometime other than now.

The legitimate necessity of moral conciliation in finding employment is something that transformative activists must come to appreciate, especially those of us who see compromise as the sin of sins. We must both accept and respect this fact about living in this world, and see that it is not fair just to dismiss it as "selling out." To the contrary, compromise can be as much related to liberation as any other choice we make. There are times when there just aren't any other realistic choices in the living moment (especially the kind we would like to choose), but the one we have to make at this moment.

Compromise is not necessarily an obstruction to being a free human being, depending on how we respond to it. Much as ego is momentarily essential to our growth and development as free beings when we don't become stuck in it, so too can compromise be part of the pathway to liberation—as long as we don't resign ourselves to the notion that this is the way life is and will always be for us, making it part of our Self-identity. When we accept the *moment* of compromise as just that, while remaining open to the moments that follow, alive and responsive to opportunity as it arises, prepared to seize it, we are able to live with compromise in a way that avoids having it congeal into a lifetime.

So what are we to do?

Our first step must be to make contact with and (re)commit to our heart values. This is a pre-requisite to living successfully with any passing moment, but especially when that moment is painful and challenging. Though seemingly unrelated to the matter of securing righteous work, making intentional efforts to be true to our values—to make a point of a practice of the practice, of right speech and right conduct in all aspects of our life, including the employment we have had to accept to meet life's basic needs for ourselves and others, and to do so especially at times when we least feel like sucking it up—has an inestimable salutary effect on our lives, period.

What is imperative to understand is that as important as it is, our quest is not simply one of finding a job more compatible with our values. At least equally crucial is the question of how we go about living our lives right now. Consciously being a person of moral values, especially in our everyday relationships with our partners, children, friends, and neighbors, but with living beings in general, is the context within which our efforts take place. This includes living our lives in a righteous manner while doing the work we don't want to do but have to show up for anyway to earn a living. Though this will have a positive effect, it will additionally take us in directions we hadn't anticipated originally.

Whenever we approach life with an attitude of doing the best we can, we are always moving in the proactive direction we must in order to be available for whatever salutary change comes along. We are better prepared to both recognize and take advantage of opportunity when it arises. Being that person right now is the precondition of realizing liberating change. While no guarantee of finding the job we want, living our lives in this way is the only way of realizing the liberated existence we want, even if it turns out to not include the work we would prefer.

RIGHTEOUS AND SELF-RIGHTEOUS BEHAVIOR

It is challenging for a transformative activist to be righteous without being Self-righteous. The latter is the death of the former, befouling our virtue with the stench of an "our shit don't stink" attitude.

In order to be an exemplar of moral behavior, the attitude of our approach must be clean of our usual Self-certainty of what is Right and what is Wrong, devoid of the need to have the world see things our way. What we do is virtuous not only by what we do, but also because it is done *invisibly,* an act that doesn't call attention to itself. While it is important for transformative activists to exemplify moral conduct, this can only be accomplished through the way we go about doing so. For it is *how* we do *what* we do that determines whether we're simply righteous, or if we are so with all the baggage of Self.

Nothing is deadlier to morality than when we suffuse its expression with a *moralistic* and *moralizing* whiff of judgment. This is all too common for those who place a high value on morality, the risk being especially high with activists who believe we know better. After all, isn't virtuous behavior grounded in doing what we know is right and opposing what we know is wrong? This is the distinctive quality that calls us to activism in the first place.

But Self-righteousness is not simply a matter of acting as if we know better. Unfortunately, when we combine this stance with an attitude that exudes a moral superiority over others who believe differently, we then judge others as being the problem.

By personalizing our position, we indict the other, overwhelming the liberating potential of our righteous position and rendering it impossible for the other to hear.

Be aware that conviction of one's moral superiority is the attitude behind authoritarian conduct. It legitimizes not only efforts to dominate and control, but justifies as well all kinds of reprehensible behaviors to enforce compliance under the banner of righteous preeminence. Free from heart-conscience, such a mindset allows us to claim an assumption of power over other beings deemed less worthy.

It is most tempting for "I" to expropriate morality and use it for its own purposes of control and domination. One might say that such an outlook is basic to the personal identity of a Civilized human being. After all, possessing superior morality is what being Civilized is all about: being superior to the rest of natural existence. Regrettably, it also infects activists, found most egregiously in the Revolutionary State and its enforcement of political compliance through practices that range from creating laws that mandate conformity to our version of morality, to imprisoning and executing those who defy our edicts.

This usurpation of moral authority from the province of individual human beings also appears with certain religions and so-called "spiritual" practices, couched in the presumed mandates of a higher authority (God, "holy" guru, sanctified doctrine, etc.) that rationalizes efforts to force others to live their lives in a prescribed manner.

Truly righteous behavior is such because morality is rooted in a reverence for life and respect for all living beings. It is expressed in a nonviolent, noncontrolling, and nonauthoritarian manner, regardless of how we might take exception to the other's beliefs and behavior.

This is no guarantee that in standing up for the sacredness of life we will not find ourselves conflicted, perhaps even tempted to respond violently—an especially strong possibility when confronted with such contentious matters as male supremacy, white privilege, and the industrial exploitation of nature. These seriously impact the deeply invested Self-interests of those benefiting from such power arrangements, on the one hand, while going to the heart of values that we hold dearly as sacred to life, on the other. Because they touch us deeply with moral concerns, they are also ripe for a Self-righteous practice, one in which ego can license behavior contrary to our principles and readily excuse our acts as morally justifiable. In a world as violent as ours, exhibiting selfless morality is critical if we are to avoid degenerating into its moralistic opposite.

This is one of the great challenges for a transformative activist given that morality is so central to our practice. It can only be dealt with successfully if the latter is grounded in an acceptance of life, including those whose oppressive way of life we find abhorrent. Only then can we listen with an open heart to others with whom we disagree and resist any life-negating behaviors they may attempt while at the same time not rejecting the person. Though perhaps not perfect, this is nevertheless how a transformative activist can engage in a moral practice that has the potential of touching the hearts of others.

ANGER, SKILLFUL AND UNSKILLFUL

Perhaps no single emotion better characterizes human beings in a political society than anger and its "I" expression, ego-rage. How could it be otherwise? Anger is the inevitable response to living in an inherently unjust world of power relationships, where indecencies—petty and horrific alike, common and exceptional—occur daily because of the prevailing social arrangements that privilege one-up at the expense of one-down. It is a rare one amongst us who emerges unscathed.

Not surprisingly, one of the most serious challenges we have to face as activists committed to living a life of transformative change is how to be skillful and wholesome with our anger.

This reaction to our circumstances begins at birth with the authoritarian arrangements imposed on children by adults along with the force, violence and abuse that often accompanies such a presumption. These are reinforced by similar relationships found in schools, later in workplaces, and at all times by the corporate security state. They manifest especially in relationships between genders, races, and classes.

Anger is living proof that domination and subjugation, along with the suffering they cause, are not natural to the species. Quite the contrary, it is the visceral response of the violated heart, the instinctive reaction to a world that denies and suppresses us from being true to who we are. At its best, anger is the canary in our existential coal mine, signaling that something is very wrong. It is the warning bell of a healthy organism to a pathological situation.

What makes anger problematic is that "I" invariably identifies with and expropriates this emotion as its own. Anger becomes something we attach to. Ego personalizes injustice, interpreting it as a slight at the expense of its inflated sense of Self, or worse, a threat to its existence. The resulting anger, which is otherwise a legitimate response, becomes both exacerbated and distorted. When it becomes exaggerated as ego-rage, it loses its specificity and assumes a global presence being used to hold the world off from us, defending its insecure existence. Often we do not let go of it easily; it becomes a significant part of our identity, especially but certainly not exclusively for men. As such, it is a major player in how we respond to the world, characteristically resulting in behaviors that are not constructive and healing, but which make matters worse with the development of a reactive personality that seeks to get even, to retaliate, to hurt whoever "I" perceives as having offended its sense of Self. This is unfortunately true for many activists whose anger becomes a central feature of the activist identity.

Anger is expressed in a variety of ways, including the familiar behaviors of loud, aggressive, threatening voices, as well as physical violence that intends to push back and assert our power over another. Frequently, however, it is sublimated into more socially acceptable behaviors, couched in less direct ways. Passive-aggressive methods are no less harmful, as their dishonest expressions and failure to get to the heart of the matter allow us to remain unable to recognize much less resolve the issue at hand. Additionally, the other party on the receiving end of this behavior is aware of the anger, but often doesn't have a clue as to why it's being directed at them.

Obvious examples are the general lack of sensitivity, graciousness, or kindness—even basic civility—in our dealings with each other. The so-called "jokes," unflattering nicknames, mean-spirited gossip, put-downs, sarcasm, and cynicism that constitute much of the discourse in political society are all manifestations of the rage we carry around with us.

All too often, it is a mindless outburst where we take our anger out on an innocent party, directed at someone who is not deserving of our behavior. The intensity of this free-floating anger is indicative of unresolved issues from some other time in our lives, perhaps from an earlier violation or abuse we're still clinging to. In any case, its present expression is disproportionate to whatever is actually taking place. The force of this anger, the power of its expression, reveals just how painfully bound we are to whatever insults and injuries we have suffered.

This is fatal for relationships in general, but especially so for those of us trying to work toward a more peaceful, equitable world. An angry personality typically does not exhibit the virtues that help build a wholesome cooperative community, nor inspire by its example a positive response from others.

The question arises, especially for a transformative activist:

what do we do with this anger while also effectively attending to the injustice that provoked it in the first place? How do we deal with both matters in ways that successfully advance our liberating purpose in a constructive manner?

Understand: in spite of the legitimate reaction to violation and abuse, unmediated anger is invariably a corrosive response. We must avoid becoming so consumed by it that we are swept away by behaviors that are neither adept nor healthy. By their very nature, these acts are contrary to the values we stand for. They only add to the enmity of the situation and make us part of the problem.

The special irony of anger is that through its mindless expression we hurt ourselves. What we do to others, we always do to ourselves (a feature that is invaluable when it comes to expressions of love). By plunging a knife into the heart of the other, either by word or deed, we also thrust one into our own heart.

However, when skillfully employed, anger is potentially an important ally. Though raw and undisciplined, it is nevertheless a statement of the heart, an unfiltered, inchoate cry for justice. As such, our anger is an expression of those values that make life worth living. If it is recognized as such and dealt with mindfully and skillfully, it can open the door to these values so we empower them with the heartfelt energy that makes all the difference in everyday behavior.

In order to do this, we must effectively deal with its tendency to hurt and destroy. The same brilliant light of righteousness that can inform our behavior is at least as likely to inflame and blind us as well, causing us to act against our best interests. Meditation can be helpful in advancing the more mindful response.

To sit with rage without acting out on it is challenging, to say the very least. Allowing the injustice we have experienced to come to the surface of our awareness, and seeing it for what it is while remaining unattached to and letting it pass as it will, as the saying goes, *takes practice*. But when we can let go of the strangle-grip that ego has on our anger, we are able to make notable progress with living our lives beyond ego-rage.

This process begins with our acceptance of anger as an authentic response to defend our integrity as living beings against that which tries to deny our claim to life. Following this, we can work with our anger to make it an ally of peace and justice, to make it our friend. As problematic as it can be, anger is also an invaluable comrade once we learn to ride with it, giving in neither to the impulse to act out or the pressure to be politically deferential by denying its presence. When we arrive at a state of equanimity, we begin to release a major source of ego's energy.

As this unfolds in our practice, we might also become aware of whatever pain and suffering we have inflicted on others (and ourselves) when our anger has been expressed in undesirable ways. This awareness can be extremely painful as we come to see not only how we have been counter-productive to our liberating intentions, but most importantly, how we have hurt others and ourselves in the process. Performing a conscientious exercise of asking for forgiveness from the other, as well as extending it to ourselves for our misdeeds, can be helpful. Practicing this exercise in our meditation is obviously more powerful when such an act is actually done with the person of whom we need to be asking forgiveness.

Acceptance of our anger is crucial. Because of our agonizing recognition of its consequences, many of us want to banish its presence from our lives, to deny its existence. As serious activists working for peace and freedom, we are susceptible to believing anger has no place in our practice and must be totally expunged.

The penalty for not coming to a larger view of anger only renders an ugly appearance of this very behavior more likely.

Rather than heal and regenerate, denying our anger only makes it probable that its suppressed expression will, like a Whack-a-Mole, eventually pop out of another hole. We must appreciate both its positive and destructive contribution to our conduct and begin to achieve the balance required to choose a wise course of action.

By accepting our anger, no longer will it be allowed to remain in the shadows of our existence only to leap out to sabotage what, in a more reflective state, we would do differently. Hence, we are less afraid of our anger and become more adept with its expression.

Another part of accepting our anger includes the recognition that it lends necessary balance to our practice. For as much as we must say "yes" to the more complete, values-informed expression of the emerging person we have long repressed, so too must we say "no" to that which denies life. "No" is just as essential to liberation as "yes." They each lend credibility to the other and are equally legitimate expressions of the open heart; in fact, one is largely meaningless without the potential expression for the other.

The question is not one of whether, but of *how* "no" is expressed. When done with consideration for the other as a fellow being, without blame or judgment, it serves a most necessary function.

Anger can be expressed with both conviction and compassion, and in fact, it is most effective when each is expressed at the same time. When saying "no," we address the other with the respect they deserve; even more, we communicate that we care for the other and in no way wish them harm in our effort to stop the damage and injury they are doing. However, we make clear that we mean what we say, without suggesting our position is indecisive or weak of purpose. To accomplish this, we must detach from the typically personal response we have with anger.

We avoid being consumed by this emotion and do not allow it to curdle into Self-righteous acting-out.

We can begin to do this within the relatively safe milieu of our meditation space. Because of its ubiquitous presence in our lives, anger will invariably come to the surface for most of us while meditating at one time or another, perhaps in surprising ways. This is particularly so when we are at a retreat for several days. It is in these moments of uninterrupted solitude when matters that are otherwise deeply buried within us may surface, including repressed anger. We must stay with our anger as best we can when it appears, and not push it away as unwanted.

Instead, we are curious about anger, acknowledging and examining its presence, even befriending it by expressing our gratitude for the message it has for us, while allowing it to pass on as it will. Our anger may take a variety of forms, some of which I suggested in earlier remarks. We can see and acknowledge its manifestations in our irritability, annoyance, impatience, resentment, envy, hatred, murderous fantasies, competitiveness, temper outbursts, and everyday grouchiness.

What we might discover is that these expressions are rooted in earlier, more personal moments of injustice, when our identification with a nascent "I" was all we had to deal with abuse or violation of our being. Given the painful history it has, the passion we have for making things right at present—for being an activist, in the first place—is very personal. Beyond an injured ego is an injured us. The two are very much part of who we are. This may be what makes justice such a burning issue for us now and gives it intensity out of proportion to what is actually happening in the present moment.

When displaced, anger that is not honestly dealt with in the past can also reflect a denial of the present moment. Take for example how difficult it is for many of us to face a significant other and speak frankly about behavior we experience as unkind, unjust, and unacceptable. Or how easy it is to push aside the legitimate outrage we experience when we bear witness to the wrongs we see committed in society because we fear disapproval, ostracism, retaliation, or because we don't have the time to get involved. We are intimidated into denying what must be said or done because of its explosive potential from that which was not dealt with at an earlier time, and the resulting fear that we will be out of control, vulnerable, and defenseless if we truly express ourselves.

Meditation practice empowers us to begin to come to terms with all of this. The empty space of meditation permits us to be dispassionate with our passionate heart. It allows us to see more clearly what our anger is all about, and in so doing begin to acquire the equanimity we need to choose how we will use this anger in a proactive manner. It allows us the choice of acting wholesomely, and not acting out.

Given its challenge, a solitary meditation practice around anger is only the first step. Anger is best dealt with in a collaborative context, with compassionate, forgiving people whose interest in helping us is selfless. For that reason, a well-functioning, mature affinity group can be very helpful. It has the emotional and spiritual solidity that might better guarantee a successful intervention.

Compassion, generosity, forgiveness, reconciliation and the other attributes of a loving kind practice may be in short supply when we begin an intentional practice of dealing with our anger. These challenging behaviors can't be left to chance, however, if we wish them to increasingly become a part of the everyday. Buried as they are beneath layers of ego defenses, we must work with them gently, kindly, lovingly, and most of all, consistently, to make challenging behaviors more habitual. Though soft in their expression, without the force and violence commonly associated with anger, a practice of this kind nevertheless provides the compassionate conviction we require to say "no" to the other and mean it.

As I want to be free of anger and hatred, so may everyone be free of anger and hatred.

As I forgive myself for having hurt others in my expression of anger, so do I forgive others for hurting me.

As noted earlier, this kind of exercise is especially powerful when we direct these sentiments to specific individuals with whom we are angry—a parent or spouse, a boss or teacher, the President of the United States or the CEO of Exxon/Mobil. As *impossible,* even totally unreasonable, as this may initially appear to be, as artificial and hollow as it sounds to us right now, directing lovingkindness toward others with whom we are angry will begin to melt our hearts to make that anger less of a weapon and more of a useful ally. *Bless Donald Trump, may he be free of pain and suffering, may he know peace and happiness.* No, this gesture on our part will not likely have the desired influence we would like to have on our former President, but, yes, it is a positive act in the process of helping us to increasingly realize our virtuous potential. Modest as this behavior is, being able to forgive someone in the privacy of our meditation sanctuary allows for such sentiments to become possible for us in the larger world. It is a necessary step to acting more effectively with our anger.

The challenge comes when we're off our cushion and dealing with people in the real world. Situations arise where we can be instantaneously flooded with anger. Without discipline and practice, the blossoming meditative mind can be suddenly blown away.

When we've come to accept our capability for impulsive expressions of unmediated anger, we must commit to going into the world with the mindfulness and skill required when anger appears, as well as a willingness to be compassionate with ourselves when we fall short of our intentions. This may simply be a matter of focusing on a word—*kindness,* for example, or *forgiveness*—or some associative word to prompt the desired behavior, reminding us of what we want to be as we open the door to the day. It's also helpful to be aware of our breath —inhale, exhale, inhale, exhale—for the space it provides in each moment, a necessary ingredient when dealing with anger.

I have found recognizing and naming anger as it arises to be particularly helpful. Even in this briefest moment when we are not personally identifying with our anger, space is created. Within that space, possibility arises. We have the room to make the right choice.

Above all, anger is best dealt with through a practice of lovingkindness. This is a most relevant companion for anger that speaks in a way that, even if we can't initially embrace it, our heart wants to hold in order to extinguish the suffering of our anger.

LOVINGKINDNESS

May the road rise up to meet you.
May the wind be always at your back.
May the sun shine upon your face,
The rains fall soft upon your fields.
And until we meet again,
May God hold you in the palm of His hand.
—Traditional Irish Blessing

Lovingkindness is, above all, most basic to the revolution we seek. Though not offered wholeheartedly in a political society as a regular feature of our behavioral repertoire, lovingkindness nevertheless suggests the transformative possibilities that exist when it is in full bloom as friendliness, generosity, compassion, and caring.

Lovingkindness is the quintessential expression of the moral conduct that allows peace, freedom, and social justice to be well-grounded and operative. Cultivated by a consistent display of moral behavior, it is the critical mass of heart values that bring to life our revolutionary ideals. When lovingkindness is present, the acme of a values-based activism—being of service to the well-being of others—naturally arises, present in all that we do.

It is acceptance, extended without limitation or boundaries to all living beings. Every sentient being qualifies for its blessing, including ourselves.

Lovingkindness can only fully manifest with recognition of our interconnection with all beings and the universal condition of impermanence we share with all instances of life. It is in this moment of *knowing* that each of us is part of each other, and that we will all die momentarily, that our hearts melt; we stop trying to protect ourselves from the vulnerability of being real. Aware that we have only the living moment to be who we are and to do what we need to do, we are not likely to waste it with any behavior less than what is heartfelt. In that moment, we are free to love ourselves and others.

Obviously, when we are in a loving kind state, we no longer require ego to get us through the day. A heartfelt existence provides us with all the power we need. It allows us to champion solidarity, to extend compassion to all beings without reservation, and to exhibit the equanimity that maintains our constancy of composure.

Because lovingkindness is ultimately not "I"-conditional, it is able to avoid the pain and suffering we typically experience in romantic love when sentiments are not reciprocated. Extending love for its own sake, we do not expect something in return.

From a political perspective, the practice of lovingkindness is scorned as the position of a naïve person. The "realist" warns, "I" do not give love to another without expecting to receive something in return; otherwise "I" withhold my love. The person of lovingkindness, however, replies with sadness, "What a pity!", knowing how much the realist is missing through their practice of a love economy.

But despite being dismissed as impractical, lovingkindness is actually the realistic basis of a transformative practice. It literally goes to the heart of matters, poignantly addressing the void that Civilized human beings have suffered for millennia because of the domination and control that we have substituted for being real about living life as it is. Lovingkindness touches us where we count the most, and in so doing, exposes power relationships for the charlatans they are, with the paucity of joy they provide in return for their false promise of the good life.

Lovingkindness is the living expression of the world we have sought all along. It translates the intrinsic values at our core into commensurate acts in our everyday lives that we want for ourselves. When we grasp this state, we are able to both love and be loved. In so doing, we return to our original state of moral clarity and boundless space.

CHAPTER NINE

ORGANIZING VALUES-BASED COMMUNITIES

Forming the new society within the shell of the old.
—Industrial Workers of the World slogan

PREFIGURING THE TRANSFORMED COMMUNITY

E ssential to being an effective activist for transformative change is to fully accept the paradox that while we are inextricably part of an interconnected/interdependent universe, we are also on our own. That is to say, we are the people of the Long Emergency, the collateral damage of having bought into the false consciousness of the American Dream. We cannot depend upon the Government, the Corporation, the Ruling Class to save our sorry butts; our myths of Rugged Individualism and American Exceptionalism, not to mention our selfie-centered culture will not be of any use to help us survive the brave new world we have entered. There is no silver bullet out there; no technological fix for what is essentially a spiritual crisis, no cavalry riding to our rescue at the end of the third reel. There is only momentary us, which, when we strip away the

Civilization of "I," is all there has ever been. We have only ourselves and each other.

As stunning as this assessment may be, catastrophic events can serve to disappear the illusions which we have allowed to blind and deceive us about living in this world, leaving us with little choice but to face the reality of now. In this moment when everything is on the line, we cannot afford to be anything other than real.

There is an important difference, however, between our particular situation today and those of past crises. The issue for us now is not simply a matter of survival flavored with the not unreasonable belief that this too will pass. But ours is not our garden variety, temporary crisis where the effects of the disaster may last for weeks, months, perhaps even a year or more, but eventually we return to a reasonable facsimile of the world we knew before the crisis.

Rather, because of its existential character, the pending collapse of our Civilization is a threat not only to our individual lives, but to our entire way of life: this is finished. Gathering like ominous dark clouds on the immediate horizon, this crisis distinguishes itself as apocalyptic, requiring us to spiritually transform ourselves into a people who must consistently be our moral best, not only for a brief time, but as a way of life: for all the moments of now. Nothing less will do if we are to success-fully live with the new normal of the "long emergency" that everyday life is rapidly becoming.

We have reached the tipping point of our spiritual evolution. Stuckness is no longer an option. We cannot postpone any longer what we are here to do. We have to fully realize ourselves, right now!

Communities where people are able to come together as a community of interbeing around a consensus of core values and civic virtue are basic to both surviving a collapsing social order, as well as living the adaptable, resilient, creative, accommodating, imaginative new paradigm required by the emerging reality.

A central task for transformative activists, therefore, is to help cultivate and encourage these communities into being. We do so through the affinity groups and intentional living arrangements we organize and become a part of. Through these relationships that hopefully we exhibit with one another, as well as the larger community we are part of, we prefigure the transformative community.

RELOCALIZATION AND COMMUNITY

Community is the social expression of everyday relationships. Through our moment-to-moment social intercourse, we play out with each other the people we are, creating and re-creating ourselves as we do so. This, in turn, defines us as a community.

It is also why community is so important to human liberation. Potentially anyway, it is the heart of our collective liberation, the communal expression of a values-based practice. We have had glimpses of this possibility in the past, when our essential goodness rose to the occasion in a time of hardship, misfortune, and life-threatening emergency and together as a people we did the right thing for and with each other.

Community has a certain cachet. Much like mom's apple pie, it's seen in an approving light by most people, and properly so when it approximates its ideal of being an association of people who care for each other, enjoy each other's company, pitch in and help out when one of us needs help, and most importantly, who basically *get along* with one another.

To whatever extent we are blessed to live in community in the best sense of wholesome interactions and relationships, we have a leg up in our efforts to nurture a community of civic virtue and core values we now require in the age of social collapse.

But as many of us know, communities can also exhibit a dark side. Though they can represent the best of human beings coming together in good will and common cause, they can also be places that are hateful, unkind, and violent—basically, unneighborly as we usually understand the term. This is particularly evident for people of color who can experience in mixed communities the varied expressions of white supremacy. In contrast to one of positive energy, this kind of anti-community is united around some of the worst sentiments and behaviors humankind is capable of exhibiting.

In general, and despite the virtues that some have, our contemporary versions of communities are generally a mixed bag of attributes. More accurately, they consist of episodic expressions of good will, but typically don't exhibit a more enduring, day-to-day care and concern for the well-being of all members. In contrast to some indigenous and peasant communities, where what happens to one person is viewed as happening to everyone, there is a general absence of communal closeness in contemporary Civilization. Rather, privacy, a close cousin of radical individualism, is prized instead, as seen in the ideal middle class family home where each member has a room of their own, and each home is viewed as an island, a sanctuary from the rest of the world.

Our lives within our communities are therefore insulated from others, our involvement minimal and superficial. We generally don't spend face time with one another or engage in ways that allow for time to share ourselves and who we are, an essential interaction for these relationships to grow and be central, rather than peripheral, to our lives.

As a consequence, we find ourselves isolated and alienated, absorbed in our own lives. We are usually polite with our neighbors, wishing each other a "Good morning!" and a "How are you?", but outside of the atypical emergency moments, we are not engaged with their daily lives. Many of us would consider it intrusive and improper—an invasion of our privacy—for community relationships to extend beyond arm's length, where neighbors would spontaneously "drop in" unannounced and unprepared for. Their importance to us is situational, intermittent, and shallow.

Over the past 150 years, this lifestyle has been exacerbated by the decline in directly meeting our basic needs through our own labor. From growing, hunting and raising our food and making our clothes, to home building and barn raising, we took care of ourselves within the context of and often with the help of the community we were part of.

As life has become more industrial and technical, however, we usually provide for our material needs not by performing the work itself, but by earning the money to pay someone else—the plumber, the bureaucrat, the industrial "farmer"—to do this for us. We continue to meet our needs, but are now one step removed from doing so. We don't do the actual labor of taking care of ourselves. This has significantly loosened the bonds of community.

Significant to this trend, as well as greatly contributing to the fragmentation of community through the automobile and its itinerant lifestyle, has been the appearance of abundant cheap oil. This has also been instrumental to our falling prey to the siren of consumerism and the false consciousness of convenience, two other developments that have weakened community. Together, all of these have conspired to devalue the importance of community. Behind the surface of the shallow sociability of our "social" media, we're still a lonely crowd made up of Self-isolated individuals who privilege private interests over the common good. No wonder that loneliness has become such an urgent mental health issue in our society today.

We have become powerless consumers of our lives, not active decision-makers and participatory agents, which are significant in a community of self-sufficient souls. Throw it away when it no longer works, vote in someone else with a new promise of the Good Life, but increasingly leave it to the others to take care of us.

———

All of this could change with the foreseeable end of the petroleum age. These circumstances could force us to change, to do more for ourselves. The highly technological and industrial world we've created over the past two centuries, while not vanishing, will become a less monolithic, constant presence in our lives because of the absence of the energy source that brought it into existence. A collapsing society will necessitate a more local and modest existence, as we learn to live with less oil in our lives, hence less *stuff*. We will depend more on our own industry, initiative, and creativity, but most of all, we will need wholesome relationships with the people next door, down the street, around the block.

As we experience the need to greatly reduce the burning of carbon emitting fuels, we will have to become more directly involved in meeting our needs—food, energy, transportation, the production of basic goods, healthcare, education, recreation, and so on—and to do so in ways we haven't done as a people for many generations. Important skills that have been forgotten or marginalized will be learned and re-learned. Physical labor will once again be valued. Taking care of our basic needs will gravitate away from eating dinner at McDonalds to eating out of our community gardens. Grandparents who know how to put food by, work with tools, knit a sweater or darn a hole in a sock will be valued beyond their willingness to babysit for the weekend getaway. Life will slow down because there will be less oil in our lives to speed us up, or to bemuse and distract us. Rather than sitting in isolation in front of a blue screen, an evening's enjoyment will consist of communal pleasures, where we come to know more about our neighbors and ourselves then we do about the characters on some TV "reality" show. In short, we will become relocalized.

As this evolves, we will discover that meeting our needs in the isolated ways of the fossil fuel community is just not practical anymore. What will arise is a felt need to do things collaboratively, to develop a communal approach through mutual aid to matters that we previously hired out as individual households or expected funding-starved public services to take care of for us. Founded upon a practice of personal and collective responsibility, this is what an empowered community begins to look like.

This can only occur over time, with people coming to trust and value one another through contact and experience with each other. Unless this happens, the kind of community I'm discussing here will die in stillbirth. An essential trust and integrity must develop between people, one in which the values of peace, freedom, and social justice come to prevail: the linchpin of any viable, post-collapse community.

As I've argued throughout this book, to realize a values-based community while living with the contrary messages of our political world necessitates intentionally pursuing it. This is the task of transformative activists. We need to penetrate the fog that separates us from each other, to bring people together around our common need to be loved and respected, to give expression to our frustrated capacity for acceptance. Operating from the conviction that people are essentially good people who want to do the right thing and understanding that this can only achieve full expression through a communal practice of values-based conduct, our task as activists becomes one of community organizing: of encouraging, promoting, and helping to facilitate the conditions favorable to such a transformative arrangement. This is our job, our service, our practice. We are community organizers.

We must take the first steps now to purposely come together, creating and personifying through our practice this community before the crisis is fully upon us. Otherwise, we could easily be overwhelmed by the circumstances of our situation, unable to respond in ways that are both appropriate and effective. By organizing ourselves into resilient, adaptable communities while we can, we won't be totally unprepared as matters continue to unravel.

Facilitating the acknowledgment of the world we live in and the extraordinary situation we face, we will be helping people to live their lives from a point beyond square one when hundred-year storms hit us with increasing regularity, a drought or flood ruins this year's harvest, new kinds of climate-related diseases threaten our wellbeing, or climate refugees from coastal cities wash up in our towns seeking shelter from the storm. Communities that have already thought about these possibilities and have taken whatever steps we can to prepare ourselves for these scenarios will be just that much further along when catastrophe hits. We're not traumatized into immobility by what happens; we're at least as prepared as we can be, practically as well as psychologically and spiritually, as we accept our situation for what it is. Being so, we are better able to respond more mindfully and skillfully, with heartfelt solidarity, than we would have if we remained totally inactive, in denial about our world as it is.

It may only be a couple of degrees that separates us from where we are at present, but becoming increasingly conscious of and intentional about how we operate in the world provides an exponential step towards this state of preparedness. A community that acts from an enlightened, accepting perspective can make all the difference in our ability to be real about the world we are presently in, the one collapsing around us with each passing day.

GOING LOCAL

A values-based community is local. It is important that we share geographic proximity to allow physical access and face-to-face contact with each other. In such an arrangement, people can be more naturally involved with one another daily and express our heart values through personal contact. Depending on the quality of the relationships of the community, people who share a common space—a town, an apartment, a block, a campus, a neighborhood—have a greater potential to be organized into a transformative community. From family and friends, the neighbors next door and down the street, to people we work and go to school with and folks who we have a nodding acquaintance with, we are typically familiar with many people when we live within a local setting. We potentially at least have relationships that provide the fertile, grassroots soil upon which to grow a values-cohesive communal whole.

As this suggests, community is significantly a matter of size. There isn't a specific number of people that defines such an entity, but generally we think of community as the people we live with, that we know at least by name or face. Community is therefore of a size that enables people—at least potentially—to take time and care for each other, to have a voice in civic affairs, to create an environment where one feels prompted to say "hello," neighbor and stranger alike, when our paths cross.

When community grows beyond a certain size, and we feel as if we live with strangers, these kinds of local relationships begin to wane; a community doesn't seem to feel like *community* anymore. We lose a vital connection, becoming faceless with one another when we walk by, avoiding eye contact. As a consequence, whatever accountability we may have had to the civic whole gradually erodes. Community is no longer a place where people feel at home with one another. In short, we are without the necessary ingredients from which we can cultivate a values-based community. We lack square one.

Thus, we must remain local in order to create a community that is of viable size to care for, where one is recognized and feels valued, as a consequence. We should avoid trying to work where the numbers are beyond a point that invites participation and inclusion, though these are flexible and arbitrary standards, and, depending on the collective spiritual strength of the community, subject to change. Not coincidentally, these are also qualities that are as necessary for a functioning democracy as they are for a values community—which are really one and the same.

A vibrant local community is characteristically made up of many smaller communities composed of people with a common background or interest. These smaller communities-within-communities can consist of religious or civic organization members, officials of town government or small business owners in a chamber of commerce or Lions Club, children's scout troops, sports teams and book clubs, a chapter of the VFW or an Elk's Lodge, women's centers and youth centers, and so on. Depending on our situation, we organize a values community wherever we can, in the communities where we live, work or go to school, and with people we associate with in our religious, fraternal, civic, and other organizations.

REGULAR JANES AND JOES

Relationship building is a complex process, involving nuanced and subtle, seemingly unimportant, immediately forgotten moments, like a brief encounter on the street that is little more than an exchange of pleasantries, or a phone call we answer in a friendly manner. Little moments. But everything counts. Even the smallest act leaves an impression.

It also includes more obvious and deliberate efforts like

getting together over a cup of coffee, quaffing a beer or two, watching a Netflix, or enjoying a barbecue. During the first weeks and months of becoming a presence in the community, we spend an appreciable amount of time engaged in a variety of low key, informal, but essential socializing with our neighbors, where we talk about our children, our jobs, the local sports teams, and other matters we have in common.

Over time, and within the context of our growing relationships, we increasingly share ourselves and what we're up to in our move into the community, talking openly about our motives for doing such a seemingly drastic and odd thing as collective living with a variety of people because we believe that this might be a way to live a more sustainable, adaptive, simple life in the face of the growing climate crisis. It is important, however, that we talk about this global purpose within the context of how we go about our daily lives—earning a living to provide money for the group's expenses, mutually taking care of our children, collaboratively attending to the many chores of managing a household, and so on. Hopefully, this will help reduce our unavoidably exotic and mysterious (not to mention suspicious) appearance, and lower barriers so that our relationships with our neighbors become more relaxed and comfortable.

It is also in these moments that we come to know more about our neighbors. Through active listening and judicious questioning, we invite greater transparency from them. Most people welcome the opportunity to share themselves—including matters that at first blush might be considered private—especially when in the company of someone who demonstrates genuine interest in what they have to say. Within the isolated lives that so many of us dwell, there is a palpable hunger for this level of contact and involvement. When given the opportunity, we're not quite the private people we appear to be.

Needless to say, this offers a great advantage to nurturing values communities.

COMMUNITY ORGANIZING

There is no greater service that activists can perform for their fellow citizens in the age of social collapse than as community organizers (CO), people who encourage, support, and facilitate the empowerment of others to realizing the power of their inborn interconnection.

This is particularly so if the work we do is for its own sake, without an ulterior motive of trying to convert people to our vision of the way things ought to be, or promoting any other Self-serving agenda . The community organizing we do as transformative activists is a service we perform for people, helping them to live successfully as free human beings in the world as it is. We do this through a practice of heart that is values-based, allowing our example to be our "message" of liberation.

A community of core values is the heart of a revolution we require to live in a collapsing world, the transformative alternative to political society created through relationships of compassion, courage, acceptance, and integrity. Building community is the alternative to the conventional way of approaching revolutionary change in the sense that it does not go about advancing peace and social justice by opposing the political power structure. Rather, it creates the alternative by being a liberated entity that exists within the world as it is right now.

For activists to be effective with this task, we must understand that the role of the CO is not quite what it was back in the day when we were organizing rent strikes, welfare rights protests, community control of schools, sit-ins at local draft boards, boycotts of corporate malefactors, and other kinds of confrontational and adversarial activity intended to help a community force an oppressive institution to change. While this type of practice is not a thing of the past, and may very well be necessary when circumstances call for such as a legitimate expression of a community's felt need and solidarity with one another, it nevertheless is no longer the centerpiece of what we, as activists, need to be concerning ourselves with in order to cultivate transformative change.

There are basically two kinds of community organizing we need to be involved with when shaping a values-based community, both of which should complement each other. As suggested above, the one revolves around a single project or concern. But activists who are trying to establish a community that is a viable social organization in a collapsing world are engaged in a long-term effort to promote and support the general well-being of all the inhabitants. Their activism, in short, is the community, and not just some aspect or dimension of it.

What is particularly distinctive about this effort is that it is directed not only during a moment of crisis, but as a matter of everyday course. In fact, the two are the same: the greater our awareness and acceptance of the unprecedented existential crisis we are in, the greater our acceptance of its daily routine.

This is a "long emergency" that we have entered. We can only realize the mindfulness and focus required for transformative change by unleashing both our imagination and courage in the face of the unknown, and by responding to the community by consistently living our values with the consciousness and care that what affects one affects us all.

Community, therefore, becomes a way of life central to our individual everyday lives. It is not just a place where we live, noted for its friendly but otherwise superficial interactions. Rather, in response to the simpatico needs of surviving the great threat of collapse and extinction, and the equally compelling desire for relationships of love and integrity, it is a social space built upon a morality of the acceptance of each other. Through the display of those values that accompany such a practice, we can more and more evolve into a community that encourages and reinforces the well-being of each other.

We know that given our shared social context, this won't be

easy. Since relationships are the key to a community's transformation, what we must figure out are the ways that we can deal with that which we have frequently dismissed as "only human nature"—the inevitable interpersonal fallouts over differences, the ego-embedded needs to dominate and control, and the hostilities and conflicts that will arise in the course of relationship building. We will have to discover how people of varied levels of commitment and purpose, contrary beliefs and interests, and disparate emotional temperament and spiritual development can hang in there with one another so that the community continues to grow as a collective entity, retaining its legitimacy and credibility with all concerned on the process. As always, this journey is two steps forward, one step backwards, and several steps to the side.

We will have to learn how to police ourselves without being policing; to be responsible to ourselves and accountable to others in a way that is also just and fair, forgiving and restorative; and to figure out what it means to be accepting of each other when one or more of the preceding behaviors is absent from our practice. We have to develop an appreciation for our differences and transmute them into communal strength and respect, avoiding as best we can division and discord. Basically, we need to love one another as the fellow instances of life we all are. This has always been the challenge for human beings when we come together, and will be no less so for those of us who are trying to fashion a values-directed community in the midst of the Civilization breakdown.

Perhaps we fail, or perhaps we only succeed with some in the community and not with others; these are likely possibilities. The question for transformative activists, however, remains as it always has been—figuring out how we live as liberated human beings in a world populated with others who are walking different paths.

This is a tall order. There will be the temptation to resort to the conduct of our upbringing and social conditioning. But a community with Self-centered values is not the kind of community we're nurturing. It is not one that is amenable to the imposition of rules and regulations, the use of force and subjugation. Rather, it's founded in the living example of people doing the right thing that resonates with the values of peace, freedom and social justice. As activists, we can only lead by example, as imperfect as it undoubtedly will be.

We play a crucial role in forging communities that encourage and reinforce our well-being, especially when they act together as a group, and not just as individuals. Serving as a behavioral example is greatly enhanced when we're a group interacting with each other. That is a much more powerful example. Our collectivity adds resonance and volume; virtuous behaviors are better displayed and more convincing when done in the context of ongoing relationships.

In any case, this is where being an activist who consistently displays heart-affirmative values is most helpful. Through a practice that includes active listening, skillful facilitation (especially when matters get testy), timely, compassionate interventions, succinct and wise observations when the timing is right, and being a selfless, calm presence who has no agenda but to be present, we can help move this process along. We need to do so not only in the moments when situations arise that are relationship ripe, but beyond the here and now to the here and now that follows next. Whether this leads to a satisfactory conclusion we will not know until we get there.

One of the key values in this process of community organizing is the gut realization that we're all in this together. While we may intellectually comprehend the oneness of humanity with all sentient beings, most of us don't live this knowledge in our daily lives until we are able to experience this wisdom for ourselves. Up to then, any understanding we have in our minds that we're all part of one another is short-circuited by the demands of "I" in its incessant efforts to accommodate us to the radical individualism of the political world.

Community organizing can help people realize the latent power in their inherent state of interbeing. By organizing people around their instinctive tendency to engage in collaborative efforts and mutual aid, people demonstrate to themselves the power of a community that is grounded in moral principles.

Becoming aware of our actual social reality, a sense of responsibility for the well-being of each other naturally blooms. An understanding that was always there in our hearts is activated. When this occurs, we also become aware, usually after the fact, that what we do for another we also do for ourselves. Not only is virtue its own reward; we also come to see, perhaps for the first time, the essentially good person we are. The defensive, protective split between us and the other cannot help but melt in this circumstance. It no longer makes any *sense*.

This translates into behaviors of compassion, the foundation for a community of people who are concerned with the welfare of one another. This in turn inspires related tendencies for cooperation, solidarity, and mutual aid. Accepting our state of interbeing as synonymous with life itself, the true meaning of community emerges. We are able to engage with others in a values practice that allows for the possibility of human liberation.

Though recognized instinctively by most of us when we *see* it in action, unconditional acceptance resists definition. Beyond preordained edict, it is a practice that is best "defined" by the circumstances of the moment and how we play with what we have been dealt, swimming in the flow of what is with patience and equanimity. In this way, we might elicit the inherent goodness of others.

Being one with the law of interbeing is fundamental to realizing a state of acceptance. When this occurs, we cease believing that we can go it alone, that we don't need anyone else to get by in life. Rather, we embrace our interconnection for the blessing it is. With acceptance, our hearts are truly *free*, open to what is, no longer bound by judgment's walls. They become major players in our lives. The realization of our inherent capacity for a togetherness that liberates, while not suffocating our autonomy as unique expressions of life, eclipses the binary relationships we have been tied down by through the years. The polarization between Us and Them dissipates; the possibility of communities of people that genuinely care for one another begins to ascend as a viable alternative. We are growing toward an understanding of what is necessary for us to live as a moral people in an immoral world.

As we have discussed, though CO can also be done in a community we have recently moved to, it is decidedly advantageous for activists to already be part of one which we have lived in most or all of our lives, or now return to after years away. Doing this work in communities we are already familiar with, and in which we know many of the cast of characters would seem to offer important advantages in our efforts to organize into a collaborative, resilient body. We'll be a significant step up from being a stranger organizing strangers.

In this context, it's important to underscore that COs who are building communities of the transformative kind are not itinerants. Community is not a place we parachute into as "professional" organizers and move on from when the job is finished, to organize somewhere else. It is critical for organizing a community around the long emergency that this be our community, our people, our life. As least as much as anyone else, we have skin in the game—our own survival and well-being are also on the line. This invariably raises our game and lends us credibility.

While we are committed to the community and involved with its people at a very personal level, we nevertheless avoid becoming ego- invested in the community and its residents or in the fate of our efforts. This is "best practice" for a transformative activist. We experience success and failure, joy and disappointment, and strong friendships, but we don't personalize these and other feelings we have or become attached to them. While not allowing ourselves to become enmeshed in the sound and fury of our various relationships, we are nevertheless engaged and mindfully involved with the community and its citizens.

We are therefore able to more selflessly relate to the people in the community and their varied personalities, without "taking things personally." Even though some people we may find irritating or offensive, and some we may like better than others, as best we can, we will relate to everyone with equal respect, care, and concern. In this way, we are able to maintain a practice that is both skillful and wholesome, characterized by relationships that are free of either craving or aversion and are therefore heartfelt without entanglements.

Of course, because we are human beings and because it is the game of life that we are playing, there are always the possibilities of wild cards making their appearance—e.g., romantic relationships that blossom with their own logic, or just the heartbeat of change that beats all the time, rendering yesterday's commitment into today's doubts and questions—that can easily throw a monkey wrench into our nicely scripted scenarios. They will require creative and imaginative approaches, hopefully within the scope of valuing life above all, and accepting it for what it is…at least at that moment!

At this point it is also worthwhile to recall the importance I have attributed to the affinity group and intentional community for the support they can lend the individual activist. This is especially significant in doing the face-to-face work of relation-

ship building that is central to community organizing. Specifically, COs are much more effective when we do this together,
and are well advised to do this in pairs, most especially as a
woman and a man. Because of the example and relative balance
it provides, this arrangement is the ideal when doing such
fundamental work as hanging out with people in the community
over a cup of tea or coffee while having a conversation. This is
more effective when what we do is more like a duet than a solo
act. Working with another affords us the opportunity to model
values-informed relationships, something that is central to our
efforts, and when this is done with someone of a different
gender, it provides the opportunity to display wholesome gender
dynamics. The dyad is more comfortable for all concerned,
including those we are conversing with who aren't overwhelmed
by the sheer numbers of a larger group, but also by those of us
who find this arrangement to be an improvement over a more
challenging, less effective solo act. As a pair, we have someone
to pick up the ball so that we're not always on the spot to carry
the conversation, to add to or correct, cover something we have
neglected, contribute their additional perspective, and just to be
another presence.

Doing CO as a collective group of activists provides
constructive accountability, compassionate reality checks, and
the moral support we all require when doing this challenging
work. But it also can serve as the germ seed for the kind of
values-intentional community we are trying to encourage
through our individual and collective example in the larger
community.

This is only possible to the extent we avoid isolating
ourselves from the larger community, a potential problem for an
affinity group whose behaviors can be perceived as an exclusive
club if we are not mindful of them. This is the consequence of
not being sufficiently integrated within the larger community.

To avoid this, members of the affinity group must be actively involved in the life of the community in a variety of ways. We participate in its civic, educational, and municipal functions, not in a know-it-all fashion where we lecture others about how they should be doing things, but in a manner that communicates a desire to learn how things run. We involve ourselves when something needs to change or improve, without judgment, from the standpoint of supporting and building upon its already existing strengths and virtues. In that vein, we volunteer to be foot soldiers, doing grunt work, participating with some of the heavy lifting that helps the town, school, or community function well. It is through activity of this kind that whatever leadership or knowledge we have is offered.

A bottom line for activism in building relationships is that people have to trust us. This is second to none for the effective practice we hope to exemplify, especially with a consistent embodiment of the values we want to represent. We do this by how we handle ourselves on a daily basis, moment to moment. This certainly does not suggest any kind of perfection. But we do need to maintain a behavioral congruency, where in whatever situation we find ourselves we maintain a basic decency and equanimity in our interactions with others. Whether handling a fractious moment at a meeting we're facilitating, offering a point of view at the monthly Select Board meeting, dealing with someone who personally doesn't like us, or being at a social gathering where someone makes a racist or sexist comment, we should not sacrifice our commitment to a values practice in the face of these and other provocations. Rather, we must rise to the occasion. It is during these times that we may experience strong feelings of injustice, even outrage, where ignoring an incident is not an option, but must be done in a righteous, selfless manner.

We may not always succeed. Most likely there will be

moments when we react in ways we regret. However, trust is built not only through a constant practice of values, but also by the way we handle ourselves at those times when we fall off the wagon, when we are not the decent human beings we intend to be.

When this occurs, how do we conduct ourselves? Do we become stuck in all the ways that Civilized beings so easily do by muddying the waters of what just happened, blaming the other for our behavior, acting as if we didn't act the way we did, or just outright lying? Or are we able to accept this lapse in behavior as who we were in this moment, to own and acknowledge it to ourselves as well as to others, to clean up the consequences of such an act, and to move on? Our honesty becomes just that much more credible when we can hold ourselves accountable for our letdowns and inconsistent moments, allowing ourselves to be seen as someone who takes responsibility even when (especially when) we behaved irresponsibility.

Only when we are true to the people of heart we inherently are do we have something of value to offer others as they walk their own paths of spiritual actualization. This is the quintessential expression of honesty. As community organizers, this is all we can ever be, all we can ever give to another. But it is a most precious gift nonetheless, and especially so because it gives twice. Being real with others means being true to ourselves as well. Together, they are the interdependent source of revolutionary power.

Of necessity, as the truth of interbeing tells us, our own liberation is intimately bound with the liberation of others. At the end of the day, not only is our purpose to live life in the heartfelt manner we were intended to live, but to do so by being of service to others. The one, in fact, cannot be accomplished without the other. To be heartfelt in the world is to come out of the privatized, individualized shells of our protective Selves, and extend ourselves to others for their happiness and wellbeing.

When we act in this way we are true to ourselves and are there-fore of genuine service to one another.

If there is to be a revolution of everyday life, social transfor-mation cannot take place without personal transformation. The first will not happen without the second, but neither will the second take place without the first. This is the dance an activist performs who is engaged in organizing communities of civic virtue and core values.

WHO IS THE COMMUNITY?

Our initial efforts as a transformative community organizer might center around bringing together a core group of comrades who are willing to commit themselves to this effort. These are people who share the importance of ethical, adaptive, resilient communities. We would be something like an affinity group or an intentional living collective, who commit ourselves to helping create a transformative community.

Our purpose, however, is to always be open to the larger community we are living and organizing in, to expand formally or informally, to increasingly eliminate an "us" and "them" separation. This is one of the ways to integrate the original group with the general community.

We are open to anyone in the community who is prepared to commit to a values practice and purpose, or simply to attend and participate in our meetings and other activities as they choose. By conducting itself in an egalitarian, inclusive manner, the original group of activists behaves as a living model of a values-community without ever advertising itself as such. As a matter of group practice, we "proselytize" with behavior that walks the talk.

In order to organize a values-oriented community, we must be open to everyone. Inclusivity is essential to helping lower the walls of political relationships that so often result in the ignorance, suspicion, paranoia, and hostilities plaguing human society.

Being open to others is also important for our own security and well-being. Values communities are not private clubs with privileged membership, though they could evolve in this direction if we are not mindful of how an elitist, separatist attitude and behavior can surface, however unintentional. From the very beginning, we must be sensitive to being perceived as a select group—a "values clique"—which is both counterproductive to our purpose, as well as dangerous.

Contrary to the notion common in political society, walling ourselves off with our "own kind" does not provide us with refuge from the so-called "outside world." Conversely, exclusion is more likely to breed envy, suspicion, resentment, hostility, and especially ignorance on either side of the wall. Not surprisingly, this defended way of living only exacerbates the insecurities we're trying to protect ourselves from with our internal and external walls. A community of people cannot fulfil and act upon a sense of interconnectedness and mutual dependence without contact and connection with all members of the world, as difficult as this may be at times.

In order to advance inclusion, it's not enough to pin a notice on the bulletin board of the town laundromat, for example, or have an announcement in the local paper when we want to hold a community meeting or other gathering. While useful, these methods are no substitute for more intentional, face-to-face efforts, where people are welcomed to attend as members of the community.

This is complemented in the first moments of any social affair, where we ask people to introduce themselves and welcome them. It is vital that folks feel included right from the start of anything we initiate.

Obviously, not everyone will attend community gatherings we organize, especially in the beginning. This doesn't mean the business of the group is suspended until an arbitrary number is achieved, because the community *lives* with whoever shows up.

But it does mean that we, as organizers, treat the general population of the community as if they are part of the transformative community in progress, regardless of their attendance or participation. We don't divide the population into "members" and "nonmembers." Participation is always voluntary, all citizens valued equally, regardless of their involvement with us and what we're doing. By keeping people in the loop through a website, group e-mail, widely distributed newsletter, or in passing conversations with people we meet for the first time, we always include a message as to what the group is up to along with the invitation for people to join and participate whenever they wish. The attitude emphasizes there is always an open door.

This kind of approach to people is something we make a point of at the very beginning, at our first meeting. Welcoming people is the way we underscore our life-affirming culture and the importance of values interactions and relationships. We do so without any undue fuss and bother, just being who we are, respecting and valuing the existence of others. This all helps make for a more open and trusting community.

ORGANIZING A VALUES-BASED COMMUNITY: EXAMPLES

Not surprisingly, the most challenging dimension of transformative community organizing requires the very best from us. And that is organizing people around the values that people need to practice in everyday life in order be liberated, living a life of peace, freedom and social justice in a collapsing world.

Organizing a community around life-respecting values is about a way of life, bringing to consciousness how people order our communal moral existence. Doing this practice involves a deep dive into people's hearts, both of those who we're organizing, but especially ours if we're to do this work with the open heart that is required.

Centering largely around everyday relationships, the great variety of situations we find ourselves in, and the ways we choose to react or respond to them, we're operating in an environment that is frustratingly grey, less subject to definitive markers and guidelines, more disposed to risk-taking consultations with our gut sense of what's right.

Though we never talk about it in this rather clinical fashion, the community serves as a living laboratory—not only of the values themselves, but of how they can be introduced, promoted, and rendered intentional. We do not cultivate this growth by formally demonstrating them through lectures or workshops, or by having community members attend classes or read about what life might look like if we actually lived an existence of peace, freedom, and social justice in our everyday lives. These activities have their place and may be useful at appropriate times when there is genuine interest that voluntarily arises amongst people to increase their effort through a practice of the practice. But as I have addressed earlier, values are demonstrated largely through interactions—people talking with one another about matters in our lives that are important to us, for example, and being engaged in activities together that address our felt needs—that bring those values to center stage.

The question is, how do we as community organizers, in the most practical sense, promote and help advance these conditions?

THE COMMUNITY CONVERSATION: CREATING PARTICIPATORY DEMOCRACY

People talking with one another about their vital concerns and making decisions as to how they want to deal with them is basic to a transformative community. It is the heartbeat of a truly functioning democracy.

When it comes to life and death issues like the climate crisis, it takes on a special importance for a community to figure out ways to both address and go about tackling them together. This is why activists focus their initial efforts at organizing their community around the establishment of a Community Conversation.

This forum has potential opportunities for people to seriously discuss matters that are barely mentioned during everyday conversations where topics that are uncomfortable are typically avoided, especially if they have the potential of instigating interpersonal conflict. Equally pivotal, the Conversation also allows openings to arise that are values-laden, especially when it comes to how we interact with one another. From having a facilitation that allows for all voices to be heard and is sensitive to male domination without making a big deal about it, to arriving at consensus-based decisions that everyone can live with even if they don't totally agree with the outcome, and dealing with discussions that become highly charged with strongly-held opinions, life-affirming values are constantly challenged to be present and active.

If these and other matters are not handled skillfully, with love and respect for all concerned, the Conversation could easily descend into chaos that would likely signal its demise. This is only accomplished with the presence of skilled facilitators. Until members of the larger community are prepared to run such gatherings, or are revealed to have the necessary skills, activists who are well-versed in facilitating a values-run meeting are required. Only then will the Community Conversation serve as a means to work through their differences, and become something by which people discover their common ground and come closer together around matters they agree about.

From the start of the project, the community organizers

should come to terms with the fact that while we are committed to a process that emphasizes community leadership, this is most likely not possible in the beginning, when taking the first steps like creating the Community Conversation and doing what is necessary to get if off the ground. This is especially so because we will have devoted a lot of thought and discussion in our group meetings not only about this particular project, which is likely the first one we undertake because of its strategic importance to everything that follows, but to the business of leadership in general. Significant factors include our experience and our values development through immersion in the practice of the practice.

Given our strong preference for the best practice of incubating and cultivating community leadership, we still enlist likely candidates from the general community to join us as part of an ad hoc leadership group whose purpose is to help plan and facilitate the early Community Meetings. These are people who, during our first months of integrating ourselves into the larger community, have shown interest in what the collective is all about and who recognize the importance of building a more resilient, sustainable presence throughout the community. They may be of various levels of experience in the skill set required for the challenging job of being a facilitator, but by making them part of the ad hoc group, and through their active participation, they will have the opportunity to hone the talents they bring to such a position.

In addition to their interest and capacity, these potential community leaders are also generally respected by others in the larger community, and in some instances may already be seen as leaders. Their presence as meeting leaders is key in establishing the credibility and legitimacy of the Community Conversation, not to mention the decent turnout we hope to generate in the early stages. Sooner than later, these community leaders will gradually replace their activist counterparts.

The first meeting should establish the vision and tone of how the following gatherings should proceed. For example, while formal in the sense of the seriousness of its content, the meetings are also informal social affairs with time set aside at the beginning and end for neighbors to chat with each other over coffee or tea and other light refreshments that are provided. The meeting should start and end on time, though a gathering that elicits passion and interest might easily stretch beyond if the gathering so agrees. Space and time should always be planned on for those who want to continue informal conversations with each other, while others are leaving.

The first order of business has facilitators introducing themselves and stating their function in the Conversation, followed by everyone else introducing themselves and being welcomed by the facilitators. While this is happening, a sign-up sheet for joining the Community Conversation mailing list is circulated.

The meeting should be moderated by two people. Ideally this pair consists of one person from the larger community and the other from the activist collective, preferably of mixed genders. It is especially inadvisable for two men to lead the meeting. In addition to facilitating a democratically-run meeting, the significance of gender pairing is to demonstrate how the two sexes can work together as an effective dyad.

After presenting the agenda (which has already been publicized with notices about the Conversation throughout the community), the facilitators request any additions from the larger body. Again, as time goes on, there will likely be requests for other topics, which will raise the issue of whether or not they can be accommodated that evening (depending on the urgency of a particular issue) or if they should be added to a future meeting's agenda. This problem can be bypassed by establishing a policy that requests that any additional item be

communicated to the facilitators several days before the Conversation, with the latter then making final decisions, with the
understanding that an urgent issue that demands immediate
attention can always be presented at the Conversation.

At the first meeting, the foremost order of business is to
establish the democratic behavior protocols for community
meetings (e.g., not interrupting or dominating the conversation,
avoiding judgments, not making personal attacks, etc.), which
are written down in large letters on a poster board that will then
be prominently displayed and referred to at all future meetings.
Because they are generally understood as common sense by
most people, this is best done by having the gathering establish
the norms. This recitation of what for most people are obvious
values-based behaviors is not only another way to reinforce the
control people have of their Community Conversation, it also
serves to *remind* them in an unobtrusive way of their essential
decency, an opportunity that should always be taken advantage
of.

With the introductions and protocols completed, the facilitators introduce a prepared statement of the purpose of the
community meetings. It makes clear that this is an initiative of
the activist collective, the success of which will be determined
by the participation of larger community. This is a brief statement which is prominently displayed and referred to at the
beginning of every meeting, serving to remind regular attendees
as well as inform new participants. It is little more than a slight
extension of what has already been broadcast throughout the
community, stating that the conversation is an opportunity for
people to come together to discuss community issues and how
they might respond to them through collective action.

The facilitators might then open this statement for general
discussion. This would provide the opportunity for members of
the collective to mention the garden, root cellar and greenhouse
they plan to start to help feed themselves, and how they would

be open to a limited number of others in the community to participate if they so desire. Another member could briefly talk about the growing danger of the climate crisis and how forming the collective is an attempt by its participants to take care of each other and engage in emergency preparedness. In this way, the Conversation serves as a way we can raise the potential of other community projects, which can be returned to by having them placed on future Conversation agendas.

This isn't accidental. While envisioned as having value in its own right by serving as a germ seed for the development of participatory democracy, the Conversation is also seen as introducing matters relevant to people taking care of themselves and each other as a community in a time of societal collapse.

In this vein the first agenda could conclude with a screening of the powerful 56-minute video *The Wisdom of Survival,* followed by a freewheeling but facilitated discussion of people's responses that is aided and abetted by the available refreshments.

At the close of the meeting, the facilitators make a point of collecting whatever names haven't been added to the e-mail list. The group sets the time, date, and place for the next meeting (which it is best to always hold on the same day(s) of the month, time, and place) with the idea that one agenda item could be be devoted to talking about what people are already doing individually, and what they could do as a community to deal with the growing crisis. Linking this meeting to the next one imparts a sense that what was just done in the previous couple of hours was not an isolated event, with little if any value, but rather something that leads into future Conversations where members of the community might translate their discussions into plans of action around specific projects. Concluding a meeting with an agenda for the one to follow is essential to not only convey to people that what is happening might actually lead to getting something done, but also to create a sense that what they just participated in wasn't a waste of time.

———

The Community Conversation is both the harbinger and genesis of participatory democracy in a community. It serves as a living example of how people can govern themselves around everyday issues that affect the quality of their lives.

Decisions are made but not imposed on people. Consensus is the practice that is understood by all, which means that a third way is sought when there is disagreement about how we manage and resolve a community issue. The situation is further discussed until a resolution is arrived at that at a minimum everyone can live with.

As the Community Conversation progresses and people learn to accommodate each other and the various issues that arise over the course of time, it can become an exercise in a functioning democracy, where the citizens of the community experience genuine civic power. This is challenging, and will take all the skill and spiritual development of the activists involved to help the community navigate the growing steps along the way. Never will it be so necessary for us to rise above the turmoil and yet be so present with it. Needless to say, the heartfelt values that speak to people's essential goodness will be called upon time and again; we will otherwise not be able to successfully negotiate the inevitable potholes (not to mention occasional craters!) we will encounter along the way.

But nothing in the repertoire of communal activity that we can introduce has greater potential to creating a transformative community than its regularly held Community Conversation. It is precisely the turmoil, challenges, differences and conflict that arise which allow for the emergence and expression of the values that will hopefully carry us to our goal as activists. In organizing Community Conversations, we create the very situation in which this can happen. As long as it remains real, dealing both with issues that matter to people, as well as with the community values that it makes possible, the Conversation is second to none in advancing a transformative people.

The Conversation is a constant reminder of the kind of people we are and can be, from the very beginning of the first meeting when the participants establish the common sense behavioral norms they want to govern their conversations with each other, and onward as an exercise in participatory democracy and self-governance where people can make decisions about matters that impact their lives, and then act on them.

THE COMMUNITY GARDEN: AN EXPERIMENT IN SHARING

As with the Conversation, working together on projects that speak to the felt needs of a community is an accelerant for the transformative communal solidarity. When residents address something larger than their own individual selves, they provide a social basis for a consistent practice of moral values, which then allows a nascent transformative community to become a resilient and sustainable body.

But given the absence of a sense of community amongst so much of the citizenry in our society, this motivation may be something that activists will have to awaken by introducing projects that have a reasonable chance of resonating with some people. Food is typically a good choice.

While not necessarily something that many give mindful thought to because of our supermarket, convenience mentality, food nevertheless is something that increasing numbers of us are aware of because of health concerns. In addition, gardening is an activity that many of us enjoy. Thus, the attempt to start a community garden has a realistic chance of succeeding.

A good way to approach a project of this kind is for the activists to begin with a garden of their own, one that helps to meet the collective's food requirements and increase our self-sufficiency, but which is also large enough to accommodate others from the general community who would like to join us. Not only does such an endeavor present us with an additional opportunity to work with and get to know some of our neighbors, it should also be undertaken with a couple of wrinkles that advance our concern with values by making it a truly community garden.

For one, we operate with the understanding that the harvest of the entire garden is available to all participants, provided that each person is willing to share their produce as well. If they are not, and want their crop for themselves, then it is understood that they don't help themselves to the results of anyone else's efforts. Since the original garden was intended to feed the household of the activists, the latter may need to place some limitations as well.

Sharing is a value, not a law; though modeled by the activists who initiate the garden, it isn't imposed on others as a matter of correctness. Rather, it is something that is negotiated amongst all concerned, and may require revisiting over the course of the growing season.

Nothing here is perfect as people learn to work together in a neighborly fashion, either in the garden or at the gardeners' informal gatherings over beer to talk about matters that arise and need to be addressed. It's an ongoing process that involves the give and take of accommodation and generosity, a behavior that is acquired or strengthened, not with a rule book, but through situational experiences where a consensus is found that the various parties can live with.

As interest grows, the original garden will need to be expanded to include other plots around the community. These may consist of gardens of two next door neighbors, where people essentially grow their own, or a larger plot where each participant has their own space. We encourage all efforts, but in the garden we're a part of, we emphasize the idea of the several gardeners sharing with each other.

A second kind that promotes sharing is even more challenging than the first because it is based on the idea that it is OK for non-garden participants to help themselves to that which they had no part in growing. We introduce this practice when a community garden is initiated with the intention of being worked on by all who care to, in order to create food for anyone in the community who needs it. Despite the worries of some that it will be taken advantage of, or the age-old idea that the harvest should be reserved exclusively to these who did the work, we generally find that this arrangement goes surprisingly well, and is used by people who really do need but can't afford what the community garden offers. People can generally be trusted and this is even more so when trust is extended to them. This is further evidenced by the positive response to the sign we post in the garden, which not only welcomes people to take what they need, but thanks them as well for any weeding, watering, or other chore they might contribute.

From community gardens of one kind or another, we can extend cooperative efforts to building cold frames, greenhouses, root cellars, and the purchase of tools, where people share not only in the labor involved in their creation, but also the expenses of the materials involved. This practice can also include organizing community canning projects, where participants bring the product to be canned and the jars and other materials required, and leave not only with a product, but knowledge of a skill they didn't have before.

All of this happens over time as people grow into an awareness of the benefits of gardening cooperatively and strengthening community ties. In addition to the sheer joy and satisfaction they realize from growing their own food, the reduction in food bills also educates folks in the benefits of becoming a little more self-sufficient.

By initiating the community garden process, including the issue of sharing, we are likely to stimulate controversy and conflict. Our efforts touch upon a variety of values like fairness, justice, generosity, and gratitude that people usually don't give much conscious thought to, though they often go to the very core of our being in terms of how we respond to the world.

This is something that we need to keep in mind, recognizing that these values are lightning rods for feelings held strongly by members of the community. While generally given lip-service, sharing, for example, can cause people to have a strong, negative ego-reaction, especially given the culture of what's-mine-is-mine we have grown up in.

When handled skillfully, however, this can be a gateway to spiritual growth. This includes not only the evolution of a culture of sharing, but also one that respects those who don't want to share, avoids making them into bad guys, and is accepting of their way instead. Allowing for what may be a minority viewpoint contributes as much to the building of a values-based community as promoting the practice of sharing. More likely than not, there will not be an ideal resolution to thorny situations in most instances that will satisfy everyone in a community. That is why beyond any particular value, the value of love—of accepting what is—is the bedrock of what we're trying to create.

What is most important is that all members are and feel accepted as long as what they do is not at the expense of someone else. Accepting and learning to live with differences is a necessity to a transformative community. And who knows what may arise from such an attitude? Some may continue to feel that one should work for what they get, but because they are accepted as a member of the interconnected whole, they have the space where they might come to understand why that's not always possible, given another person's circumstances. By facilitating a process that enables people to grow and expand their view of why someone would take something without having contributed their fair share of labor, it softens their viewpoint and makes them less rigid, unforgiving, ungiving. The emergence of this kind of embryonic culture—generous, compassionate, kind—is what allows a community to become a body that is embracing all of its members—not necessarily best friends, but at least ones who allow each other to live in an atmosphere of peace and acceptance. If, along with the other bonuses we receive from doing community gardens, the ongoing debate around sharing veggies, or not, helps to grow people's acceptance of each other, then it is totally worthwhile.

EMERGENCY PREPAREDNESS: BUILDING A CULTURE OF MUTUAL AID

Increasingly, the climate crisis is hitting us at home. For many of our fellow Americans who have experienced wildfires, catastrophic storms, drought, flooding and heat waves, the calamitous effects of a climate increasingly out of control are no longer a brief news item that we watch from the comfort of our living rooms. It has become all too real.

Whatever silver lining there is in this dire situation exists in the fact that it has awakened many former deniers and skeptics who had defended their absence of concern with the insistence that it won't happen here. Increasingly, the climate, or more accurately, the human emergency that has developed because of our failure to care for Mother with the love She deserves, has made the idea of emergency preparation a need that is progressively felt by more citizens. The fact is that we need to come together, talk with each other, and act as a community.

For those of us who are already deeply involved with our town or neighborhood, the best way to go about this is to organize a meeting or request a time of the ongoing Community Conversation we've already organized that can be devoted exclusively to emergency preparedness. We then do a lot of publicity, especially through face-to-face conversations that stress the importance of this meeting, targeting in particular those folks who we have found really *get it.*

We begin by facilitating a conversation about the likely scenarios we can expect to encounter, based on our own experiences as well as what we've seen in other parts of the country. Next, we pose important questions such as, "Are we prepared to meet these potential emergencies today, as individual households and as a community? What did we do the last time we experienced a severe weather event, like Hurricane Irene? What did we not do that we wish we had? And what did we learn that would be useful today?"

What is interesting is how easily people can get into talking about this subject, especially when they're reminded of their own experiences with prompting questions. People open up and have much to offer, which is one of the brilliant things that can happen when we are brought together to focus on a mutual concern. Common sense and group wisdom kick in. A lot of good ideas surface once the conversation gets rolling. It is as if people gain confidence in themselves and their abilities once they center their attention on the issue at hand, when they are in the supportive, compatible audience of others like themselves. Emergency preparedness isn't rocket science; it's simply a matter of putting our heads together and collectively brainstorming.

We end the evening with making a list of things that each one of us needs to do in order to prepare our own families and households for a calamitous weather event, like when electrical power is down, perhaps for a considerable time, when roads are washed out, grocery store shelves are increasingly bare, gas stations are only operating if they have generators, and ATMs are not functioning. To help stimulate the discussion, we might pass out information that (hopefully) our appropriate state agency can provide to help families become emergency prepared.

———

One of the key aspects of emergency preparedness is to develop a plan for how we might take care of ourselves during and after a serious weather event, at least as best we can, when everything is so volatile and uncertain. There are at least three dimensions to this: preparing to take care of our needs as individual households; preparing to take care of each other as a community; and being forced to evacuate from the community when the severity of the destruction is life-threatening.

Therefore, we should leave the meeting having started the first draft of a work-in-progress action plan that begins to focus on some of the great ideas we came up with. Now the issue is to act on them. This is what we agree to do between now and the next meeting, by outfitting our homes with all the essential needs, equipment and supplies we have agreed that we require in a weather disaster. Finally, a date, time, and place for the next meeting must be established before anyone is allowed out the door, at which time we'll update each other on our progress, along with a reminder to bring along a friend next time.

This business-like approach may seem to run contrary to our usual way of doing community organizing, though one would only conclude this who had not been observant of the systematic and purposeful way we go about CO work in general. These characteristics are especially apparent with emergency preparedness, when being well-organized may very well be a life-and-death matter. It is necessary for us to push people (gently and respectfully, of course, but push nevertheless), though we will find that most appreciate this approach. It is best practice for getting things done in the imperfect, too often mindless world we all live in, encouraging us to move off of dead center and helping to activate people.

Additionally, attending to the emergency needs of individual households might at first glance appear to be contradictory to our purpose of helping build collaborative communities. Yet the group would be well advised to agree that the first step toward emergency preparedness is for each household to take responsibility for its own readiness. A community that is developing a culture of mutual aid is one that not only works together and helps each other out, but is also composed of resilient individuals and families who will be more available to help others when they have taken charge of their own matters. Focusing on individual household preparedness is the way to build community preparedness. Mutual aid can only become a community practice when its members are also taking responsibility for themselves.

When the group reconvenes, each member describes the progress they have made in building greater preparedness in their home. The group helps out by suggesting where one can find a particular item that has eluded the search efforts of others, or with recommendations of ideas they have come up with. It is generally agreed by the end of this second meeting that everyone will complete the task of household preparedness by a certain date.

The conversation then moves on to community preparedness, where people talk about endeavors they could mutually engage in that would benefit all. If one has not already been started, a community garden could be created to include plots in a variety of locations, done with intentional plans around what to grow, especially with regard to those vegetables that can be canned and stored with sustaining infrastructure of root cellars and canning bees, and vegetables that can be grown year-round in greenhouses.

We could also initiate regular community suppers at different homes or community locations like schools, fire houses, VFW lodges, etc., that can accommodate large gatherings, or some other collective activity that brings people together for fun and celebration of the latest achievement.

Community preparedness is an exercise of neighbors sharing with each other. This can include such disparate things as childcare to a community solar energy project. Again, with the activist collective serving as an example of how to communally deal with the demands of daily living, once the idea of both the necessity and benefits of doing things together begins to take hold, the possibilities begin to open up.

This is best approached in a relaxed, volunteer manner, where individuals make decisions amongst themselves and not as part of some larger collectivist plan. We need to keep in mind before we get too carried away that living this interdependent, interconnected lifestyle is a radical departure from the individualistic way of life we have been conditioned to. It won't happen automatically or without resistance to what may appear to some as an attempt to "Sovietize" the community. As we see with sharing the harvest, there will be a number of folks who will be opposed to this departure from what they're used to.

This will be another of the challenges that we, as transformative activists, will need to address if we are to prevent the community tearing apart over differences such as this one. One of the ways we do so is to not be overly sensitive to the presence of difference, but also to give it its due, to appreciate the balance a community needs to achieve between being a cooperative interbeing and allowing adequate space for individual difference and preference to both thrive and be respected. It is in the realization of such a dance that the best in people is likely to surface.

Basically, we take the position of not excluding anyone because of their differences, unless the latter's expression of opposition includes violence against others; at the same time, we encourage those who want to pursue a practice of sharing to do so. We always want to keep in mind and to exhibit behaviors which reflect that a community is not a uniform entity where everyone conforms to the same beliefs and conduct, but rather is one where the residents learn to live with one another in a wholesome manner, accepting their differences without trying to change them.

One of the matters we must discuss and plan for is what we do if the members of the community must suddenly move ourselves to ensure our safety and well-being. We will not necessarily be able to live in a geographically stable area which we can take for granted for the foreseeable future because of the depredations of climate change and societal collapse in general.

Of immediate concern, and the one that is most likely to grab the attention of others, is the growing incidence of disastrous weather events that have become more extreme. Immoderate rain has become more destructive, along with strong winds that have caused major property damage, injury, and loss of life.

I must underscore that we are not just referring to storms when we discuss emergency preparedness. The all-encompassing nature of the climate crisis includes the contributing role or total responsibility for other threats to our survival, such as repetitive killer heat waves, uncontrollable forest fire holocausts, galloping species extinction, glacier melt which constantly outstrips computer predictions and is accompanied by oceans rising sooner and faster than expected, increasing drought conditions throughout the world with resulting crop failure and famine, the appearance of new diseases and the revival of old ones, ocean acidification and its approaching death, climate refugees, and the inevitable armed conflict that people will resort to out of desperation and fear in life-threatening circumstances like these.

Encompassing all of these potential catastrophes and yet a distinct consideration of its own is that community, in the sense of being a physical entity—a given piece of land, a mailing address, the actual place where we live—can be summarily wiped out literally in the blink of any eye. In this circumstance, community ceases to be homes and property, but consists of people banded together on the road.

We know that this is not a far-fetched possibility; our TV screens these days are filled with images of climate refugees who are fleeing drought, wildfires, and storms. There is no reason to believe that we couldn't be next.

According to the UN High Commission on Refugees, at the end of 2020 at least 82.4 million people around the world have been forced to flee their homes (1 in every 95 people) as a result of conflict or persecution. One quarter of these, or 26.4 million people, were refugees who were displaced by weather. They bear heartbreaking witness to the volatile, disintegrating world we are increasingly living in.

As collapse becomes more pronounced, our seemingly stable situation may suddenly change (as those in the west, particularly in California, can testify to). Circumstances may dictate the need to immediately relocate. Whether due to horrific weather events, extreme wildfires, rising oceans, famine, or violence borne of desperation, we can abruptly and unexpectedly become refugees on the road with a few personal belongings, seeking at least momentary safety and security from the devastation we are fleeing. We need only view the news footage of people walking out of Central America to what they hope will be a better future in America, or the thousands pouring across the Mediterranean from Africa and the Middle East to Europe, to get at least a remote idea of what the life of a climate refugee is all about.

In the era of a collapsing civilization, people must plan for a disastrous contingency so we can act quickly, should the need arise. Naturally, this is best done as part of a community, sharing the burden of what is required, helping one another to survive. Given our history of rising to the occasion when faced with a calamity, there is good reason to believe many people will respond in appropriate ways.

As community organizers, however, we don't want to leave to chance people's response to disaster. In the world we live in today, the spontaneous righteous behavior demonstrated by many people during such catastrophic but short-term events as the San Francisco Earthquake, 9/11, and Hurricane Irene, while splendid, is no substitute for preparation for the Long Emergency of social collapse.

Given what we presently know and can reasonably anticipate, we must be a community light on our feet. We must be able to respond to the unexpected without being burdened by excess baggage, either physical or psychological. Success hinges on people being prepared to let go of anything that is not essential, and to have ready whatever is vital to our existence for life on the road. Such is the overwhelming nature of the threatening situation; we may need to abandon without notice our present environment: our home.

We must also be able to do so with sufficient equanimity and solidarity, so we don't create additional problems for ourselves and others. This is the way of letting go, where we prepare for what we can see coming by being especially mindful of our present situation. Preparedness becomes something we need to be doing right now in our daily lives before we are hit with a catastrophic event. Hence, when and if the decisive moment arrives, and we must move on quickly, we are more likely to be able to do so.

CHAPTER TEN

BEING PEACE IN A VIOLENT WORLD

"Violence is American as cherry pie."
—H. Rap Brown

While I have argued throughout that in order to effect the transformative change we seek we must engage in a consistent practice of life-valuing behaviors, I have not, at the same time, given our political world its proper due in the sense of better appreciating what we're up against in trying to effect a values revolution. Though apparent, it is crucial nonetheless to acknowledge that the heart, too, is subject to the larger universe it is inextricably part of. Its values, as innate as they may be, are not independent agents operating autonomously from outside influences, malevolent and benign alike.

To that point, how might a moral practice be effective, or even survive, in a social environment hostile to its presence? As much as anything else, this question is critical to our purpose; for the answer, though tentative, aids us in determining whether transformative revolution is credible or not.

As we know, activists have responded to this quandary in the past by adopting a political approach with the purpose of eliminating the present power arrangement and replacing it with one of our own. This has been viewed as our top priority, the one that must be accomplished before all other considerations. We yield, therefore, to the apparent necessity of contention and conflict because we believe that the only way to resolve political problems is with political solutions.

But as history demonstrates, however "democratically" this is done (e.g., the American revolution), employing a power-over approach only postpones our liberating goal beyond a forever vanishing horizon.

———

Violence is the signature behavior of Civilization.

As appalling as power relationships are, what makes them especially odious is that they unvaryingly rely upon violence in one form or another—physical, sexual, psychological, social, economic, legal—to enforce their arrangements of domination and subjugation. As lovingkindness and compassion define the behavior of a liberated people, violence is the nature of a dominator/dominated relationship. In all the ways it is expressed, violence is the red line we cross whenever we try to control life.

The primacy of violence in our lives is located in the iron logic of political power. As long as the control of one being by another is considered legitimate, violence is sanctioned, whether implicitly or explicitly, to enforce the relationship. As evidenced throughout Civilization's history, political power is sustained with the threat or act of violence.

It is an inevitable outcome when we consider that power relationships are unnatural to the values-based heart. The latter will instinctively resist efforts that seek to suppress it, or to countenance life constrained. That is why we must in one way or another be *forced* to submit to domination and control; it is seldom, if ever, a voluntary act on our part. And while efforts are made in a democracy to modify its expression, ultimately there is no shared understanding that states unequivocally, "Violence is not okay," as long as it is performed in a Civilized manner and for Civilized reasons.

As much as the behavior itself, the mere suggestion of violence is often sufficient to force us to submit. The persuasive power of violence rests not only in the pain and harm we wish to avoid, but also in the fear of death, the potential for which is always lurking in the background of any violent act. For those reasons, while most of us do not willingly submit to power arrangements, we acquiesce nevertheless due to our fear of violence and its consequences.

Beyond the enactment of laws and the use of violence deemed legally acceptable as punishment for crimes, we have not developmentally matured to the point where we are able and willing to forgo violence as a way of life. Part of the difficulty here is that violence is self-perpetuating, an act that reproduces itself with each instance. Violence maintains our need with the seemingly reasonable justification that we require it to defend ourselves from violence. Or the belief that objectionable behavior can only be cured through spanking, beatings, incarcerating, or killing. This is all Self-deluding. As the resort to violence has historically demonstrated, its use only encourages and inflames people to respond in kind, to get even, to pay back for the pain and harm we have suffered at the hands of the violent other. Violence does not end violence. It only begets more violence.

The ego-driven urge to be in control, the engine force of power relationships, also prevents our revolutionary aspirations from attaining fruition. Affected as we are by its many private and public expressions, the omnipresent violence in our interconnected society traumatizes dominator and dominated alike into being so much less than the peaceful beings we could be. Violence terrorizes us into abandoning our best intentions, hindering our evolution to becoming liberated human beings. Revolutionary activists are no more immune to this consequence than the oppressor they are trying to overthrow.

As even the most casual reading of our official history tells us, violence is the means by which civilizations have established themselves over millennia through war, slavery, imperialism, colonialism, genocide, exploitation, rape, torture, murder, lynching, execution, and the brutal rule, in general, of a dominant class over a subjugated people. Despite what some of us might want to believe to the contrary, nowhere is this history more graphically revealed than in the American Civilization. As Hari Kunzru noted, *"If we look at the American story as one of violent struggle and contestation, formed to some large measure through the Atlantic slave trade, we arrive at a very different picture from the one that starts with a formal claim of rights and expands in the direction of an 'ever more perfect union.'"*

To put the matter unequivocally, Civilization is largely the history of violence, of the rule of white men over women and people of color. This is not the whole story, of course; the practice of domination and violence is not the exclusive domain of a particular gender or race. But when one looks at the history of Civilization with a dispassionate eye, it is hard to deny the great responsibility white men bear.

Despite its official rendition as a Self-congratulatory narrative about the "progress of mankind" (sic), couched in the celebratory language of conquest and overthrow, history cannot disguise the fact that Western Civilization could not have been realized without violence. Though our official history textbooks acknowledge it, violence is often represented as "glorious achievements," or explained away by some variation on the themes of "necessary evil," "self-defense," "collateral damage," or the dozens of other rationalizations we use to excuse our crimes against humanity and other living beings.

The ubiquitous violence of power arrangements has served as the overseer of our Civilization. This is the context within which the peaceful, just world we seek to create must emerge and evolve from. From everyday abuse within the intimacy of our homes and the ubiquity of white supremacy, to the stockpiles of nuclear weapons and the Sixth Extinction of the planet, its universal presence in our interconnected society affects all of us alike, limiting us to being so much less than we could be otherwise. As activists for transformative change, we must understand and appreciate the phenomenon of violence itself, particularly its endemic nature in our Civilized world and the devastating influence it has on sentient life. Doing so, we can forge a values practice relevant to our world, one that speaks to this violence in such a way that it allows morality to evolve as a central presence in a revolution of everyday life.

THE DARK BEFORE THE DAWN

As transformative activists, peace is at the heart of our activism. It is the commitment in practice to not harm another living being. Along with freedom and social justice, peace is one of the three legs supporting the project of human liberation.

Unpromising as the circumstances may appear to be and with no guarantee that we will never encounter violence, being a person of peace at least assures that we won't be the cause of violence. Non-adversarial, non-confrontational, being true to our values is ultimately all we can do to contribute toward a peaceful world. Not being a self-righteous moralistic presence is being peaceful.

Perhaps most challenging in being a person of peace is attempting to be so with (stuck) ego, a presence which becomes particularly inflamed in violent situations. Being true to our values when faced with the incendiary speech or physically violent acts of another is difficult. We more than likely will want to strike back in defense of ourselves. Many of us will be tempted to suddenly abandon our non-violent intentions, and to do so believing, not unreasonably, that we're being realistic in the face of our circumstances.

But there are many times we can avoid such encounters by anticipating their possibility beforehand, being awake to and mindful of their potential in the circumstances of the preceding moments, and therefore taking measures to either not risk such encounters or better prepare to deal with them peacefully. Granted, such may suddenly come upon us in unexpected ways, and there's not much we can do but defend ourselves by not retaliating beyond the need to take care of ourselves. In this way, our conduct remains as peaceful as the circumstances will allow.

Another potential trap in trying to be a peaceful presence is when we are motivated by changing the other with our "peaceful" behavior. Certainly, it's wonderful when our adversary responds to our overtures in a commensurate fashion, but it is a serious mistake to enter a potentially violent situation with expectations of this kind. More often than not, they will not be reciprocated in a commensurate fashion. With our expectations unrealized, it is quite possible that we will then act out our disappointment and engage in behaviors that sabotage our peaceful intentions.

We can easily fall into the trap of mistaking appearance for reality in our sincere desire to act on our values. This is almost always because our expectations of how the interaction should go change when ego takes charge of our intentions. It hardly satisfies "I" to know that being a person of peace is a lifetime process, during which we may not always see much in the way of the desired change. When "I'" experiences a need for Self-validation, it is easy to be tempted to resort to unskillful and unwholesome behavior in a misbegotten attempt to make our adversaries conform to our expectations for them.

The only cure for this is the awareness that we corrupt our best intentions whenever we don't act on them for their own sake. It reminds us that ego is alive and well, that it needs to be accepted as an active presence in our lives. We come to further appreciate the distinction of acting on our values unconditionally, of doing the right thing simply because it's the right thing to do, without hopes of personal gain. Regardless of ego's continuing presence, this is something we can learn to do.

By mindfully noting ego's presence and the effect it has on our behavior, as well as forgiving ourselves for being less than perfect, we can rescue ourselves from further damage. Even more, by snatching insight from the jaws of mindless error, we actually transmute a momentary act of ignorance into one of awareness.

Acting without expectations underscores the importance of continuing to behave peacefully, from one moment to the next, regardless of our success. Despite consistency, as Ralph Waldo Emerson noted, being "the hobgoblin of little minds," it is also true that, short of divine intervention, a *consistently* peaceful practice is the only way we can begin to introduce peaceful behavior as a way of life to ourselves, since we have long been habituated to political relationships.

The project of human liberation is a process, one that may take lifetimes, and whose outcome is uncertain. A values practice rolls with the rhythm of change, with no final destination. Such a practice functions from a continually flowering state of mindfulness, one that not only sees the living moment, but also what we have "learned" along the way during previous moments of being consistently aware.

We must keep in mind that while human beings have exhibited a capacity for unfathomable cruelty, we have also demonstrated an equally impressive potential for lovingkindness. This is seen at the present by the fact that there are many of us who are rising to the occasion in the face of the emerging existential crisis, and doing so in the name of love and other heart values. We are witnessing instances of this especially among the millions of young people who recognize it may be up to them to prevent the species from global catastrophe. In his book, *Blessed Unrest: How the Largest Movement in the World Came into Being and Why No one Saw It Coming*, Paul Hawken writes about what he terms a "movement of movements" consisting of at least some two million socially engaged organizations who are willing to risk something different in order to build a peaceful, nonviolent world through peaceful, nonviolent means.

We are the people who are capable of the unconditional expression of love required by this moment. We are ready for the new deal a values-based practice offers. Not only do we know we cannot continue to do business as usual, we welcome the opportunity to try something that resonates with our sense of what is right. We are those souls who are no longer willing to settle for the political hand we've been dealt. Who have wised up to the old order of oppression, injustice, and violence. Who are tired of warfare, whether in the home, on our streets and highways, or in the world. Who are yearning for a fair and just society. Who want to return to the Mother we abandoned but never left. Who want to live a life of heart. Who recognize we all have but one life, momentary as it is, and this life is really not worth much unless we finally live it right. We are arriving at the stage of our millennia-long development where we are coming unstuck and moving toward transformation.

Although a cacophony of violence dominates the culture and often drowns out so much of what is decent, a new order is nevertheless being birthed at the very same moment the old order is collapsing. This emergence is a variation on the old saying that "it's always darkest before the dawn."

Unfortunately, we are all too often invisible to each other. More than anything else, we must become aware of each other, and in so doing, come together in acts of solidarity and community.

To do this, we must trust each other and be increasingly transparent and open. We must risk peace in all of its various expressions. This is why a values-based practice is so crucial to our purpose. To be able to come together and work together, we must behave with one another in the wholesome ways that allow us to trust one another. We must be people of peace.

By offering ourselves to each other in this manner, even if it's nothing more than a smile from the heart reflected in our eyes as we look into the eyes of another, or an attitude that acknowledges to the other their legitimate presence in the world, we are advancing, in our own modest yet essential ways, the social basis of a new world order. This love and respect for all living beings is the bedrock upon which a credible practice of peace emerges.

ENGAGING OUR ADVERSARIES BEYOND EGO

"A nonviolent revolution is not a program of seizure of power.
It is a program of the transformation of relationships."
—Gandhi

Being at home with our heart values when we are true to who we inherently are empowers us to be at peace with ourselves and our world. These same righteous values are the antidote to violence, the peace which resides in our hearts and, when we allow it to be, the actions and words that inform a virtuous practice.

We must keep this in mind as we engage with our adversaries with a practice dedicated to being nonviolent. Though this may go against the grain of the moralistic stance we traditionally assume toward people we judge as "bad," we cannot realize the peaceful relationships we want by selectively conducting them with those people we judge as "good." Out of necessity, a transformative revolution calls for a practice of peace that includes our enemies and our adversaries as well. This only strikes us as impossible because of the polarized world we have created, where matters are either right or wrong, good or bad, and the infinite strands of grey have been eliminated.

But when we commit to nonviolence and no-harm, we go in a different direction, one congruent with our values. Declaring a commitment to peace is the first step to making it more likely that such a practice will be peaceful.

Our adversaries don't become our new best friends or converts to our point of view. Acting on our values is not done with the intention of conversion. We are peace activists, being and doing peace ourselves, not missionaries with the task of changing others to what we define as "peace." All we can enact is how we move on from being angry, hateful, violent adversaries toward our designated enemies, to engaging with them in a more skillful way.

Ego thrives in response to our distressed, naked heart because the behaviors of our adversaries exploit and violate its exposed state. The undefended heart is particularly vulnerable in such a situation, and is susceptible to the intervention of ego. It can be tempted to act out defensively. With "I" in charge, we take the situation personally, and our reaction is to strike back.

While our defensiveness may be perfectly understandable, this position leaves unanswered how we forge a practice that addresses the issues we judge as intolerable in peaceful, nonviolent ways. For spiritual activists, we must actively resist the use of power-over, where we end up enmeshed in our own variation of life-diminishing actions.

One of the important first steps we take is to remove ourselves from the oppositional equation, which always requires two parties in order to operate. By absenting ourselves from this dialectic, and no longer playing the power role to the other's counterpart, we change the dynamic of our relationship in a very profound way. Both figuratively and literally, we must return to the passing breath as best we can. Within the turmoil of the rising conflict, we ground ourselves in the transient moment, being mindful of what is present, including the roiling "I" which insists upon having a dominant, outraged voice in our interaction with the offensive other.

If we are successful, we defuse the personal nature of our response to the other so ego is no longer a participant. We oppose the offending behavior without attacking the personhood of its author at the same time. In this way, we avoid making our necessary contribution to a power relationship.

This is easier stated, of course, in a few short sentences than it is to actually execute in the living moment. In significant part, this skill can only be accomplished through our involvement with a dedicated, everyday effort to make it so. Through such efforts we acquire critical space between the specific circumstance that prompts our response and what we actually do: the same pause between the intake and outtake of our breath. This is the nanosecond where spontaneous choice lives. Expanding ourselves through the practice of mindfulness, however slightly, we see beyond being ego-reactive to where we can risk—we can choose!—a more wholesome act. This response is only likely to be available to us, however, if the practice of peace has become habitual through a regular practice of the practice as previously described.

In the end, our effort at a practice of peace with adversaries cannot achieve its desired results if it doesn't come full circle by offering the possibility of reconciliation centered upon an attitude of the common humanity we share. We can never realize peace with the enemy as long as we exclude them from the human community.

One of the barriers to peaceful resolution is an activist practice that, however unintentional, communicates that the other party is no longer part of *us:* they are forever condemned to being *them.* This is often at the heart of conflicts and is what makes their resolution so intractable. Nothing makes peace more unlikely than this exclusion and the power relationship that accompanies it. From the beginning, we must abandon any sense of a Self-proclaimed right to judge and punish the other for what "I" interprets as *unforgivable* behavior. We must forsake any sense of a power relationship, of wanting our efforts to ultimately result in the domination of the other by having the conflict conclude in a victory of *Right over Wrong.*

As we increasingly see the interconnectedness of life and cease to view the real world in a mutually antagonistic way, it becomes possible to break the habit of attaching moralistic judgements to otherwise neutral phenomena. It is possible, that is, to see those we previously viewed as polar opposites as the human beings they are, before all else. When this takes place, it's a game changer. It significantly alters how we pursue a practice of peace, as well as our relationship with our adversaries.

We come to recognize that labeling our adversaries as "evil" and "wrong" is a subjective consideration. Their behaviors are tools of "I," which politicize our awareness of what is real. These concepts pollute the waters we both swim in, adding a further personal dimension to what is at heart a non-political matter. Our vision is clouded; we demonize the other, and are not generous, receptive and forgiving as we need to be.

Despite the challenge of seeing adversaries in this more generous fashion, a proactive practice is much better served when we begin to act toward them not only as human beings, but even (gulp!) as people much like ourselves. Peeling away all the layers of misrepresentation dividing us from one another, we see they are only acting out their capacity for evil, the potential for which resides in us all because of the universality of the Civilized ego. We humanize them, and by so doing, soften ourselves as well. We avoid addressing the other—including their ego—with our own ego. That is an act of peace.

Basically, we come to recognize how important it is not to challenge the enemy's power, which is what ego struggles are all about, and has so often been the basis of our activism. Rather than pick a fight with the other, or try to one-up them, we see our purpose is learning how to live with them in more creative, peaceful ways. This can only be done without "I."

Granted, we cannot count on the other to share this interest, especially at the beginning of our relationship. All we can ever do is to choose this selfless way for ourselves, knowing that we do so without expectations of reciprocity, and that behavior of this kind leaves us vulnerable and undefended. Conduct guided by the values of the relationships we seek to have in the world is not risk-free, and requires moral courage to undertake and sustain.

In this vein, we must also understand that behavior we practice as peaceful and nonviolent can even be interpreted as threatening by those to whom it is directed. It takes little imagination to understand why an adversary might construe an act of civil disobedience as hostile and harmful to their vested interests, even though we intend it as peaceful. Despite how nonviolent they may be, acts of this kind are always challenging to both political authority as well as the right of the adversary to continue doing what we oppose. By its very nature, civil disobedience is power-confrontational. The mere interference with, or resistance to, business as usual—which of course is the purpose of direct action—is reasonably felt by the other as unreasonable.

This apparent contradiction is not necessarily fatal to our

liberating purposes, though it must be seen and accepted for what it is. Nor does it deny the importance of nonviolent resistance as part of an activist's repertoire, especially when life and death issues are at stake, as with our present situation.

But this apparent contradiction suggests nonviolent behavior does not necessarily promote peace, per se, and can just as easily fan the flames of the same old *Us vs. Them* dynamic. This liability is inherent to our simple opposition to the behavior of the other. No matter how nonviolently we may express it, opposition is opposition, necessary when life is threatened, but by itself creating a challenging barrier between us which requires more imagination and creativity when we stand up for our moral principles.

While in a best case scenario we may touch the hearts of our enemies with our values-informed practice, a liberated people is nevertheless the antithesis of political society, where we are expected to conform to our designated roles and live the twilight existence of being one-down. The emergence of free human beings who take responsibility for ourselves, live in self- and community-sufficient ways, and who are therefore less dependent upon those in power to run our lives for us, is a threat to political control. Inherently at odds with an authoritarian, hierarchical society, we are correctly viewed as unlikely candidates to continue to live the mindless, heartless way of life necessary for a national security state, its corporate sponsors, and a ruling class to prevail in.

To the contrary, we are seen as unacceptable. Rather than embraced in kind, we should not be surprised if we're responded to by the guardians of authoritarian correctness in the repressive ways they typically employ against those who threaten their rule.

So what are we to do?

As best we can, our practice is informed by forgiveness and reconciliation; we seek accommodation in whatever principled ways are available to us. The values we live by are flexible and accommodating, expressed through the prism of what is appropriate at any given moment that is congruent with peace, freedom, and social justice. This approach allows potential for a dynamic that short circuits the political paradigm from operating smoothly and automatically. When we are successful in following such a path, we find this new *modus operandi* better enables us to live with the presence of the adversarial other in ways that allow peace for all.

By cultivating and nurturing these values, we introduce liberating possibilities which didn't exist before when we were still active participants in the political dyad. Eschewing either abject surrender or violent response, adapting alternative strategies instead, we place the other in unknown and disorienting territory. Their typical ways of dealing with us lose some of their effectiveness. They no longer work the way they might have in the past, especially as it becomes less clear we are the rival they thought we were. We're suddenly not doing what the oppressive other needs in order for them to comfortably react to us in ways they are familiar with.

In pursuing a more imaginative, nonviolent course, we empower ourselves through our behaviors to be the people we must be as free human beings. In so doing, we provide the opportunity for a new relationship paradigm with the oppressive other. While apolitical in nature, this nevertheless has the possibility of empowering the other with a sense of sufficiency, of being good enough. Ultimately, this is what our relationship with the adversarial other as a transformative activist is all about—to be the liberating supportive people we are with all human beings. This is a gift that political power, by its very bottomless nature, has never been able to satisfy, resulting in eternal frustration and dissatisfaction. Whether they're able to join with us and accept this opportunity is, of course, uncertain. Some will take advantage, while others will not. As always, it's more or less a half-filled glass we are dealing with. All we've done—and all we can ever do when advancing our values—is to provide space and opportunity for such a choice.

SELF-DEFENSE

"The supreme art of war is to subdue the enemy without fighting."
—Sun Tzu

In a world as disposed to violence as ours, we would be remiss to not discuss how to best prepare for its possibility in the time ahead as we work to help create peaceful lives and transformative communities. Having argued that a peaceful world can only be accomplished with nonviolent conduct, I am left to address the question of whether or not this behavior is sufficient to deal with the inevitable prospect of violence. Does non-violence stop violence? Certainly in our interactions with others we can enhance the opportunity for peaceful encounters with our opponents, as we saw in the last section.

But is there any guarantee that they will respond in kind? Of course not! In fact, we have good reason to believe that an adversary who has demonstrated that they will use force and violence to impose their will upon us is very likely to continue to do so, interpreting our non-violent behavior as weakness. Though there are undoubtedly exceptions, generally speaking, someone who resorts to violence, however that may be expressed, will continue to do so until it no longer works in their efforts to dominate and control. That is why I emphasized the importance of non-violent resistance in the earlier chapter on acceptance.

But will this be enough, not only in a political world characterized by greed, hatred and delusion, but one that is collapsing, where people could be driven mad with raw desperation to simply survive? The innate moral values of the human species must not blind us to the capacity for human depravity and evil that, while we choose to see them as aberrant, appear just as natural and "heartfelt." Being kind and compassionate does not render us immune to violence. While our values have often emerged at times of emergency, there is no guarantee they are sufficient by themselves to prevail against violence that is driven by ego-crazed individuals or the chaos of societal collapse. In order to walk the transformative path with any degree of confidence, we must live and act effectively with this more complete picture of our dangerous situation.

The prospect of barbaric violence could challenge this approach. We will have to come to terms with what it means to defend ourselves and others in this situation, and whether this can be done peacefully, without resorting to force and violence. Having to make a decision of this kind, a real possibility, cuts to the heart of our values when we try to live in the twilight moments of industrial civilization while the terrorism and mayhem we are already witnessing continues to unfold. Many of us could easily be pushed beyond our limits by the unraveling of the apocalyptic climate and breakdown of societal norms. We could be tempted to secure our basic needs by any means necessary. Degeneration to a dog-eat-dog scenario must be seriously considered and prepared for if we arrive at the point where humankind is faced with the extremes inherent to collapse.

Must we sacrifice our commitment to nonviolence? If so, isn't this pretty much where revolution and the struggle for a peaceful, just existence has always ended up?

Or rather than resort to violence, is it best to just die off, to become extinct as a species? Given our history as a Civilization, with all the pain and suffering we have inflicted on ourselves and other living beings, we could argue that it might be best for all concerned if human beings ceased to exist, confident that life on earth would continue quite nicely without us. I return to this question in the last section of this chapter, "A Survival Worth Surviving."

Or could we just disappear somehow, make ourselves invisible, maintain our commitment to peace—not only by making ourselves unavailable to violence but through being peaceful in the full sense of the word, accepting life for what it is in all we say and do, think and feel? Is that even possible? If it is, this may allow us to transcend the very condition that allows violence to remain in our collection of behavioral reactions: we may be able to cease trying to control life.

If we believe this option is possible, we must begin preparing now to face violence as peaceful living beings. As with most behaviors contrary to those of political society, we must be clear on what a practice of peace in a hyper-violent society would look like, and commit to a practice of that practice now so we are as prepared as we can be. These behaviors need to be increasingly adopted and practiced throughout our daily lives in order to have a reasonable chance of behaving in this manner when confronted with violence. Though sudden and unexpected as the event of violence could be, practicing now provides us with the opportunity to strengthen the inherent good that exists in us, scraping off the rust from its disuse.

———

A practice of peace is first and foremost a communal activity. The practice is not one that can be performed successfully as individuals; there is greater strength in a group of people who are committed to working together peacefully for the benefit of all.

Though not exclusively, it is also a practice that is best initiated locally, done with people we know in our neighborhoods and communities, affinity groups and communes we have organized with self-defense in mind. At least in the beginning, our best companions for these efforts are family, friends, neighbors, and comrades, the people we interact with in our everyday lives. Organizing a collective for peaceful self-defense with people we have a relationship of sufficient trust and comfort with is the basis of any attempt to create a community of mutual values. It is especially important that these relationships are ones we have confidence in to have each other's back when violent situations arise, to be on the same page with the values we live by.

Although advisable for activists to initially limit our organizing of a peace collective to those like-minded folks who are on the spiritual path as well, this should not preclude involving other fellow citizens over time who demonstrate similar values and interest. We might be surprised to find that there are many who abhor violence, but are real about its presence and are receptive to being a part of an effort to developing a collective peaceful alternative for self-defense. The vast majority of people want to be peaceful whenever possible.

A truly peaceful community is one where a reigning priority is the inclusion of a diverse variety of folks. We cannot be truly peaceful without living the values of peace, which at its heart means acceptance in all its expressions. Living the values of peace also means accepting those whose behaviors have been violent in the past, but who now demonstrate through their practice a commitment to nonviolence.

The best thing activists can do here is create an active example of a peaceful presence through our daily interactions and our consistent expression of right speech and right conduct. What this means is that we must intentionally work on being peace amongst ourselves, and in all the ways in which violence of one kind or another arises. In this way, we may serve a socially useful function, a living example that may touch the hearts of others. As when ice skim first appears on a New England winter pond, and then suddenly one day has hardened into thick, substantial ice, capable of supporting us all, so too can a modest, seemingly invisible practice of peace help nurture an atmosphere of heartfelt expression of peace to come together.

The practice of peace must be out in the world. While it has a significant inner function, we cannot confine it to our private world alone. It must also be an active, visible presence, one that is exhibited in all kinds of situations in the political world. Depending on the situation, it may be humility, or kindness, or silence, or forgiveness, or courage—but only when it is real as spontaneous, consistent acts, suitable for a particular person, condition, and time, does peace demonstrate its practicability. We do this not because it's the law, or a politically compliant expectation, but simply because being a moral presence is the way of peace. It feels right.

The question of when violence is in the service of life, and hence a necessity, is raised in stark relief by the prospect of societal collapse. Specifically, how do we respond to this situation, especially toward those who heedlessly continue to extract fossil fuels in the service of their bottom lines, with no apparent concern for the welfare of humanity, and other sentient beings? This is a dilemma we face as nonviolent people. The fossil fuel industry is the most powerful corporate entity in the world; it's worth nearly $5 *trillion*, much of this based on the known reserves still in the ground (80% of which must remain there if we are to have any chance of avoiding an irremediable cataclysm and possible human extinction). The wealth and power of this industry rests upon the continued extraction and burning of fossil fuels. Having yet to demonstrate any interest or willingness, it is not likely the oil barons will graciously step aside and join others at the community table of reasonable and productive conversation. This would involve walking away from the trillions of potential Petro profits that we know must stay in the ground. From the vast sums the industry and its allies spend on denial, disinformation, and the discrediting of climate scientists and activists, to the purchase of our elected representatives to protect and advance their interests, as well as their frenzied exploration for and drilling of unconventional fossil fuels, we cannot expect the fossil fuel industry will put people, as well as the rest of the living planet, before their profits.

Compounding this problem, we are saddled with a corrupt and polarized political system seemingly bereft of enlightened, nonpartisan leadership. The system is captive to Big Oil and the rest of the petroleum-dependent corporatocracy, rendering them unresponsive to the needs of other living beings. The recent administration of Donald Trump, and his denial of climate change, have left us with little reason to be hopeful of any improvement on this score. Additionally, as I have argued, it is best to be extremely skeptical of a political solution to this or any political problem. By burrowing in the deep pockets of the fossil fuel industry and the corporate oligarchy in general, our official policy allows for the continued and indefinite burning of fossil fuels and the extraction of tar sands, hydro fracked gas, heavy oil, and deep-sea petroleum. Such actions caused us to set record-setting carbon pollution (as of this writing, we have reached 416 parts per million of carbon, leading towards a record-breaking warming of the planet). Despite the solar panels and wind turbines we erect, the coal plants we shut down, and the politicians who congratulate themselves about the nonbinding, nonverifiable, nonfunctioning climate treaty they signed in Paris in December 2015, our situation is truly precarious.

Time is rapidly running out for us to do anything remedial—the conservative report of the United Nations' Intergovernmental Panel on Climate Change (IPCC) in October 2018 gave us 12 years to avert disaster. Bill McKibben stated in early 2020 that we had to turn matters around this year (which we didn't come close to doing) or it would be too late, and subsequent reports, such as the IPCC report of August 2021 and February 2022, have only echoed this alarm.

In addition to an unresponsive government that pathologically refuses to accept certifiable reality, we as a people continue to live our consumerist, industrial way of life as if it will go on forever (at least until a pandemic like the COVID-19 temporarily shuts it down). We must acknowledge its terminal state, and allow ourselves to at least begin to consider and talk about what this unprecedented situation means for us, what the alternative might entail, and how we might live otherwise.

What do we do when the largest global enterprise is privileging its profits before life itself, threatening not only our very existence, but that of our children and grandchildren? Within these circumstances, the question naturally arises of how we the people can stop this murder-in-progress, this crime against humanity and against life itself. With the precious time we have left, how are we to disarm this knife at our throats? Does the nature of this life and death threat warrant the use of force? Is this a necessary, life-saving situation, one that, while contrary to peace and nonviolence, nevertheless justifies their employment on life-affirming grounds?

Or are we just kidding ourselves when we raise questions like these, playing the kind of mind game Civilized human beings are all too capable of, where we twist words to excuse and rationalize otherwise reprehensible behaviors?

There is no definitive answer to these questions. As life-affirming souls living in increasingly violent times, I would argue that resorting to physical force and the violence it entails —no matter how righteous such action may be—is a serious mistake. It can only add to the chaos of our existence, further contributing to the barbarism already characterizing life on everyday earth, without creating the sane alternative we both need and seek.

The case for people committed to a nonviolent practice to make room for a violence-of-necessity exception is an extremely slippery slope. On the one hand, there is no virtue in a practice that does not defend the value of life. There may be moments when nothing other than force is necessary to protect ourselves or others. Sometimes physical force becomes what philosopher Kathleen Dean Moore has called "a moral obligation." At these times, we must put our bodies on the line. Much as when a predator invades our home, stalks our neighborhood, or assaults us on our streets, we must intervene to effectively render them harmless. This may necessitate the most dangerous options of all—the use of force and violence.

How we go about doing this can only be answered by each of us in the actual moment we find ourselves in. Hopefully, in that moment, we are spacious enough in mind and heart to act with the necessary mindful skill we're capable of. We don't engage in gratuitous force which extends beyond the minimal requirements of self-defense. The physical force we use is relative to that which renders the other harmless. Reconciliation and a return to a peaceful situation is always the ultimate purpose of our actions.

To defend (or to put it more accurately, affirm) life is the very nature of a liberated existence, the antithesis of the death culture we have submitted to for so long. If we are to be real about life's value, we must disarm, restrain, neutralize, and otherwise pacify the other when the dignity and preservation of life is violently threatened.

Having confirmed this rationale for physical force and violence, I also must stress that this approach requires enormous skill and presence of mind. It cannot be undertaken lightly. By employing force at whatever level we do, we enter into our more problematic regions. Violent behavior can spin out of control lightning-quick, tapping into the dark potential that resides within each one of us, becoming a four alarm emergency for "I." At this point, we are beyond the intervention of appropriate values.

However, wholesome behavior is proportional to a minimal but adequate response, one preventing the other from threatening our lives while remaining as harmless as can be. We are strengthened in behavior of this kind when we engage in a discipline of nonviolent self-defense, where we learn to use the aggressor's own energy against them to disarm and pacify. Such is the approach of certain martial arts. Again, this requires a practice of the practice which will help us develop the skill to use our bodies in wholesome yet effective ways. When our basic motivation is not to harm, practicing nonviolent self-defense will help us develop the necessary humility to ask forgiveness of anyone we injure or take the life of in the process of defending life.

As it becomes increasingly apparent that time is running out, that what needs to be done is not happening, and that social collapse is imminent, people will be increasingly desperate to avoid their fate. For many, this bleak situation will lead to the conclusion that only through the exercise of violence-of-necessity can anything be done at this point to save the species.

Would this involve acts of violence against the fossil fuel industry and the government? It has been suggested by some, for example, that taking out the power grid by a committed cadre of activists would at least slow down, if not stop, the fossil fuel industry altogether. This assumption is highly questionable; furthermore, there is no doubt such an act would produce a great shock and cause much suffering to many people. Such an act, most likely carried out in secrecy, would amp up the level of mistrust in all sectors of society. It would precipitate long-term deprivation amongst the general population, intensifying confusion, fear, and rage, only adding to the growing sense of desperation people would have already. Within the context of the violent world we live in, this would exacerbate a tendency toward the violence we want to mitigate, and likely push the state in the authoritarian direction it has been traveling for some time now, discrediting the actions of legitimate, nonviolent activists, and justifying, legalizing, and resorting to acts of random violence amongst the rest of us.

Engaging in actions of individual violence, performed by small, secret cells, only isolates activists from the people we're trying to work with. At the least, we would justifiably be equated with "terrorists" who jeopardize the lives of the same people with whom we're trying to build community, solidarity, and a culture of mutual trust and aid. These efforts would be undermined. Despite its romantic associations of some "revolutionaries," a values-based practice is not successfully performed as an outlaw. Committing violence as lone rangers fosters the kind of mistrust, alienation, and paranoia that already distress so many of us. Violence of this kind only compounds people's sense of being powerless, reinforcing the fear that their lives are out of control.

The evidence that the climate has deteriorated beyond human intervention and remediation is increasingly persuasive with each passing day and the latest peer-reviewed scientific reports. The first and most important thing we can do about our situation is, ironically, to accept it for what it is. We must accept the unacceptable, to acknowledge, as the moderate Bill McKibben has said:

> It's too late to stop global warming, that's no longer on the menu...even if we do everything right at this point, the temperature will go up. The main question is whether we'll be able to hold the rise in temperature to a point

*where we can, at great expense and suffering, deal with those crises coher-
ently, or whether they will overwhelm the coping abilities of our civilization. The latter is a distinct possibility.*

Not surprisingly, this is from a man who, if nothing else, is
always clear-eyed real.

What would this look like? In addition to doing whatever we
can to curb the most extreme consequences of an over-heated
planet, the best approach to dealing with the violence of our
situation is to learn to adapt to what is and increasingly will be.
Deep adaptation becomes our mode of learning to live with the
violence of climate change, learning to live with the world as it
is becoming, by doing our best to create a resilient, sustainable,
adaptable post-apocalyptic alternative.

There is no denying our prospects right now appear to be
poor, no matter what we do. They will still involve enormous
pain and suffering, as McKibben states; we have entered the
long emergency. We can't avoid this pain and suffering. Climate
change has been allowed to grow beyond the point it was 30
years ago, when we could have taken proactive steps to escape
the worst consequences of what some scientists have labeled
"Hothouse Earth." But matters have gone beyond that now; only
if we act with the comprehensive urgency that is called for
might some of the species at least survive.

But if we are going to do so, not only do we have to
somehow stop the burning of fossil fuels, but we will also have
to learn to live with an unavoidably challenging world, one that
will continue to be increasingly very different from the one we
are used to. This is where a values-based practice becomes a
necessity. We will have to fully embrace our oneness with the
rest of humanity and other living beings. Accepting that we're
all in this predicament together, we therefore might recognize
the value of acting collaboratively and cooperatively, which is
certainly our only and best hope.

Essential to a values-based way of life, women would play a very active and significant role in creating a successful adaptation and transition. As the traditional champions of the life-affirming values required of us right now, women would provide the kind of leadership we need. The Buddhist nun and teacher Thanissara expresses the matter well in her "Engaged Buddhist Manifesto for Our Earth," *Time to Stand Up: "For survival as a species, there has to be a deep revaluating of the innate qualities of the feminine, which are to do with interconnection, unconditional love, inclusion, cooperation, receptivity, relatedness, intuition, compassion, heart, and nurturing."* These are the very qualities that activists—of any gender—must exhibit and nurture in others.

Not only is this so in general, it is also true when dealing successfully with violence in the world. Women are the people we must increasingly turn to in order to adapt to the violent world in peaceful ways. They will provide the leadership that recognizes the foolishness of individual action and will promote creative and imaginative collective preparation and response instead, approaches that step outside the political paradigm of dominance and control. Women will see the value in this being a community issue, one in which we all have a voice in shaping what is to be done, as well as a responsibility to carrying out the consensus of the group. And if in the end violence is deemed necessary, it will be done so with feminine leadership and wisdom informing the considered actions we take.

A SURVIVAL WORTH SURVIVING

When considering a practice of this kind, we must recognize the real issue before us is not simply one of our survival as a species. As important as this is, survival per se is not necessarily our bottom line. This is particularly so when it means continuing to live the way we have for thousands of years, engaging in the latest iteration of the life-destroying, soul-numbing, and spirit-deadening way of life that has brought us to our present state. In that instance, what are we surviving for? More of the same-old same-old? Is just being technically alive good enough?

Leave aside for the moment that survival through the domination and control of life is not an option anymore. Unless we can get our act together very quickly, it's going to be game-over for the human species. The ancient power dynamic which has brought us to this point in time only guarantees our inevitable end as a species, as we are reminded by the current climate chaos of wild fires, horrific storms, the extinction of so many species, growing famine, the increasing disappearance of water, the hundreds of thousands of climate refugees, and so on.

As I stated previously, there are those of us who are perfectly serious when we ask, might not the planet be better off without a human presence if we cannot live more mindfully and peacefully with ourselves, as well as with the rest of life? Short of that, wouldn't it be best for all concerned if human beings just exited the planet as gracefully as we can?

Our only real choice for any survival worth living is to finally opt for the life-affirming existence we really want and require. This is the case even if we were to ultimately fail to avoid social collapse. We could be true to our values, and not have sold them out, once again, as the price for living one more day of an unfree, unjust, unlivable existence.

And who knows what a liberation that lives right now might actually produce tomorrow, and the next day, and the months and years beyond that? As Thich Nhat Hanh put so well, *"The future is being made out of the present, so the best way to take care of the future is to take care of the present moment."* After all, and above all else, it is this commitment to living a values-based existence, right now, that is required if we are to survive to a life worth living. Beyond green technology, we can only avoid catastrophe and evolve to a liberating order through a practice that is truly transformative, both in fact as well as in name. Only in this way will we avoid the paradox of our revolutionary forebearers: of losing even when we "win."

The key to any success in creating a sustainable way of life is to step into the unknown, trusting ourselves to a practice of heart. This requires moral courage, as well as personal integrity. There is no substitute for anything less. We must accept there is no silver bullet in this scenario, no easy on/easy off ride down the liberation highway, no technological breakthrough that will ride to our rescue in the end. It's only us, doing what we're capable of doing as best we can with as many comrades as possible. Only in this way are we finally the people we've potentially been all along. If we have the courage to be these people now, this may be good enough.

EPILOGUE
CRISIS AS OPPORTUNITY: THE CHOICE
OF NO-CHOICE

"The nature of the current crisis demands extreme action.
It may seem impossible at present, but as the situation unfolds
there will be opportunities to make fundamental changes
to how we think, to how we live and govern ourselves."
—Norton Smith

T hough the two characters in the Chinese ideogram for "crisis" are commonly misunderstood by Western motivation speakers as signifying both "opportunity" and "danger," what is ironically most promising about our situation today is that the same circumstances that confront us with social collapse and possible extinction also conspire to present us with an unprecedented opportunity to finally get it right: to live the values-informed existence we have been searching for all along, and that we now require more than ever. This is because there really is no other choice: the near certainty of societal collapse leaves us with the option to either allow our present way of life to simply proceed as it will, or to take advantage of this opening, actively colluding with the collapse by engaging the ever-widening empty space it provides with efforts at creating transformative change. This is the choice of no-choice.

The origin of "crisis" is Greek, designating a decisive moment when life is on the edge of imminent and profound change, when matters could go one way or another. While there is no question that our situation today is fraught with peril that points to the near-certain demise of our Civilization in the not too distant future, it is because of this very condition—our lives on the line, social collapse pending, time running out—that it is also pregnant with transformative possibilities.

But—and this is critical—the latter must be recognized for what they are, and their revolutionizing potential seized through behaviors that act on such an awareness as if our lives depended upon it. Because, of course, they do.

Everything is in flux. We have entered what Joanna Macy calls "the great unraveling." That which we thought was certain is now in doubt. The old normal is coming apart; it is no longer dependable and predictable—not that it ever was. Quite simply, we can't count on that which, just the day before, we took for granted, and assumed would last forever.

With the collapse, we are discovering that what we presumed was factual has turned out to be illusory, and that lies are more often than not the currency for what is routinely consumed as truth. "Common decency" has joined the endangered species list. We elect gangsters to be our leaders and then are outraged when they behave as gangsters. Though The Man's rules are completely discredited, so many of us continue to play by them, as though, if we just try harder they will eventually work for us.

The empire is collapsing. Always a charade for the vast majority of citizens, the American Dream is increasingly exposed to the rest of us for the fraud it is. The rich continue to profit big time at the expense of the poor, who suffer more than ever. The same Civilization whose alleged triumph over nature we've been so thoroughly schooled in is unraveling in a variety of ways; its warp and woof are coming apart, throwing into serious question our increasingly discredited belief that we're in control. We are discovering that Mother does indeed bat last.

Despite how frightening the demise of old faiths and certitudes are, it is nevertheless this chaos at the heart of life which they were supposed to protect us from that turns out to be the creative ground from which transformative possibilities emerge. This absence of uniformity and order creates possibility simply because the resulting vacuum shock-awakens us to our situation and the moral values that have been slumbering in our hearts.

As present circumstances vividly demonstrate—accelerating climate crisis, serial COVID-type pandemics, the intransigence of white supremacy, the supplanting of democracy by fascism and the national security state, the acceleration of a class society into greater polar extremes at either end, the nuclear holocaust that is always hovering over us, and so forth—we cannot hope (or want!) to return to some white man's wet dream of a golden past because it is precisely this horror from which the present state of affairs originated. The latter didn't just drop out of the sky one day: today is the consequence of *back in the day*.

Recognizing this situation for what it is, we are left with the choice of *no-choice*. We finally come home to what is truly important in life, and thus potentially we are able to respond to our circumstances appropriately, to do the right thing. Most of all, being truly cognizant of our circumstances for what they are, we can fully appreciate life for the momentary affair that it is, and live it in heartfelt ways, understanding that we don't have forever.

Our intrinsic moral center emerges. The good news is that we're not starting from square one. We are by birth the good people we need to be. We are values-centered people who can be true to ourselves and our values in our everyday lives if we so choose. As stated by David Graeber, the highly regarded anthropologist and anarchist activist that I transcribed at the beginning of this book, *"The ultimate hidden truth of the world is that it is something we make and could just as easily make differently."* This is the choice of *no-choice* that we can choose.

Otherwise, we are left with only the "choice" of the barbarism that our Civilization was founded and built upon as it completes its life-negating descent into absolute nihilism.

We will only realize the possibility of transformation if we seize this opportunity to live a moral existence that is based upon a reverence for life in the midst of the unavoidable chaos that has always been with us, and at the same time is now becoming increasingly apparent. We can only succeed, that is, by being our best at a time when we are facing our greatest challenge.

The additional good news is that people have demonstrated a tendency to exhibit this exemplary behavior at catastrophic times when our lives were on the line, when we, as a people, were on our own. This is when, spontaneously, *instinctively,* transformative moments emerge. This is when imagination and creativity, integrity and courage, and lovingkindness and compassion have surfaced in our everyday lives.

Unfortunately, without the stimulus of crisis, we have typically reverted to our ordinary selves. We became the spiritually lazy folks we had been before the crisis. Routine matters that could have used our moral courage as a common, everyday behavior were not responded to with the mindfulness, compassion, and generosity of spirit they required because, spiritually, we were asleep.

And while it has been these everyday unacted-upon moments that have created the world we live in today, it is precisely these same everyday moments that, right now, provide us with the opportunity to respond to our present unprecedented crises with the moral excellence they require.

The questions that arise at this point are twofold: one, given the fact that human beings notoriously don't respond to approaching danger until it is a felt need, can we respond now to what is truly an unprecedented crisis before it is too late, rendering our efforts futile?

And two: if we do respond now, and finally live in the life-valuing ways that make life worth living, can we then sustain this kind of moral and spiritual conduct on an everyday basis, creating as we do the transformed existence that we require?

While there is no guarantee about the outcome, it is nevertheless possible that choosing to be the good people we are could bring forth the life we have wanted all along, at least in the present moment, which is the only time that really counts.

Our issue, therefore, becomes not one of returning to some illusory past or saving ourselves for some kind of fantasized future, but of living our lives now, in the present moment, as wholehearted, righteous beings. Even if it's too late and we do eventually flame out over the precipice of no return, at least we do so on our own terms, being true to ourselves, and not selling out as the price for living one more day of an uncivilized Civilization.

The times we are living in call on us to exhibit both moral courage and personal integrity, to be true to our heart's loving essence. We are potentially the people we need to be: we only need to act as these people now.

With that in mind, I close with one final piece of good news: this potential is increasingly being evinced even as I write and you read these words. There are countless examples of people around the globe, as well as right next door—undoubtedly, you are one of them!—who are engaged in efforts to build transformative communities, promote social justice, and work for peace and freedom, while giving their best with whatever they do, loving their children for who they are, and accepting life with compassion and generosity. There is a growing movement of citizens who *get it*. Who are working for the decent world that most of us want. Who are practicing the values-informed behaviors that are at the heart of the transformative change we seek. We are not alone!

In essence, we recognize that we can no longer afford the luxury of putting off our lives to sometime other than now. We are privileged to be living at a time when our situation is one that commands personal and collective excellence. Every moment of life counts.

As the man said back in the day, this is the worst of times and the best of times. Most of all, it's a very special time to be alive.

> *Since death is certain, but the time of death is uncertain,*
> *What is the most important thing?*
> —Pema Chodron

www.ingramcontent.com/pod-product-compliance
Lightning Source LLC
Chambersburg PA
CBHW020822270326
41928CB00006B/413